An Incentives Approach to Improving the Unemployment Compensation System

Paul L. Burgess
and
Jerry. L. Kingston

Arizona State University

A National Chamber Foundation Report

1987

W. E. Upjohn Institute for Employment Research

This report reflects the views of the authors on this subject. It does not necessarily represent the views of the W. E. Upjohn Institute for Employment Research, the National Chamber Foundation, the U.S. Chamber of Commerce, the Private Sector Task Force members or the companies that financially supported this study.

36.44
B95i

Library of Congress Cataloging in Publication Data

Burgess, Paul L.
An incentives approach to improving the
unemployment compensation system.

(A National Chamber Foundation report)
Includes bibliographies.
1. Insurance, Unemployment—United States.
I. Kingston, Jerry L. II. W.E. Upjohn Institute
for Employment Research. III. Title. IV. Series.
HD7096.U5B87 1987   368.4'4'00973   87-23128
ISBN 0-88099-049-X
ISBN 0-88099-048-1 (pbk.)

The National Chamber Foundation (NCF) is an independent, nonprofit, public policy research organization affiliated with the Chamber of Commerce of the United States. Since its inception in 1967, the National Chamber Foundation has studied emerging issues vital to the economy and the business community, and has served as a catalyst for the discussion and debate of new public and private sector policy initiatives.

THIS PROJECT HAS BEEN MADE POSSIBLE BY GRANTS FROM

m.R.   Burlington Industries
             Ford Motor Company
          General Motors Corporation
             Marriott Corporation
             Pillsbury Company

ii

Authors

Paul L. Burgess and Jerry L. Kingston are professors of economics at Arizona State University. Both specialize in teaching graduate and undergraduate courses in labor economics and in researching a variety of issues related to the unemployment compensation (UC) system. Together they have designed and implemented several evaluations of the UC program, starting with a 1970 evaluation of a special reemployment assistance project for UC recipients. They have conducted extensive contract research on the UC system for numerous state agencies, for the U.S. Department of Labor and for the National Commission on Unemployment Compensation. This research has resulted in more than 50 academic articles and technical research reports on the UC system. This extensive background on the UC system provides the basis for this book.

Paul L. Burgess holds a B.A. and Ph.D. in economics from the University of Colorado at Boulder. Jerry L. Kingston received a B.A.E. from Wayne State College, a master's degree in economics from Colorado State University and a Ph.D. in economics from The Pennsylvania State University.

For their love and support, we dedicate this book
to our wives, Marie and Gayle.

Acknowledgements

The ideas and conclusions in this volume have resulted from nearly two decades of study of the unemployment compensation (UC) program. Neither memory nor space permit us to identify all those who have aided us so effectiely and influenced our thinking so importantly during this period. Hence, we acknowledge here some, but not all, of those who have helped us along the way.

The book itself was made possible by the generous support provided by the National Chamber Foundation (NCF) of the U.S. Chamber of Commerce. This support made it possible to devote more than a year exclusively to research for this book and other papers related to it. We particularly want to thank John Volpe and Gale Thompson of NCF for their support and encouragement. In addition, we thank the firms that so generously supported the work for this book with both financial contributions and outstanding UC system experts who served on our NCF advisory panel. In fact, these firms and individuals are elsewhere separately acknowledged because of the importance of their support. To their credit, this employer community advisory group never attempted to narrowly focus our attention on just issues of interest to employers, although they effectively presented employer views on issues we raised. Unfortunately, we were unsuccessful in our attempts to also obtain representatives from organized labor to serve on this NCF advisory panel.

The support of our university also was essential in completing this study. Arizona State University granted us sabbatical leaves for the 1984-85 academic year to devote our full time to research on this book and on related articles. The strong support and encouragement provided by the chair of the Department of Economics (William Boyes), the College of Business and the University created the environment necessary for productive work on this manuscript. In addition, Burgess thanks the Dean's Council of 100 of the College of Business for a 1986 grant to support substantial revisions in portions of the manuscript.

We have a large debt to numerous experts who served as our UC mentors through the years, but we directly acknowledge here only some of those who most directly impacted on our work for this book. The largest of these debts is to the numerous state UC agency personnel who showed dedication and integrity in participating in the first efforts to accurately identify and analyze payment errors in the UC system. Arizona, New York, Oklahoma, Pennsylvania and Utah volunteered for participation in the original overpayment study we conducted under the sponsorship of the National Commission on Unemployment Compensation (NCUC), despite the fact that finding overpayments is not likely to make life any easier for UC administrators. These efforts were strongly supported by NCUC research director Ray Munts, whose encouragement and integrity in tackling a difficult issue has always been greatly appreciated. Wilbur Cohen (former NCUC chairman, now deceased), Robert Goodwin (former Unemployment Insurance Service director) and Robert Edwards (former Unemployment Insurance Service director) also provided invaluable assistance and encouragement.

Five additional states—Illinois, Kansas, Louisiana, New Jersey and Washington—volunteered to assist in pilot testing the Random Audit (RA) program methodology for the U.S. Department of Labor even before the NCUC study had been completed. Among these 10 states that were central in developing and refining an operational methodology for detecting UC payment errors, we especially wish to acknowledge the cooperation of state UC directors David Murrie (Oklahoma), Duane Price (Utah) and James Ware (New Jersey), together with project supervisors Mary Pat Frederick (Washington), Natalie Londensky (New Jersey) and Evan Mattinson (Utah). Florence Bade, NCUC project supervisor in Arizona, deserves special recognition for her tireless efforts in teaching us about the UC system. Her contributions to our UC education went far beyond anything that reasonably could have been expected and we are indeed grateful.

A total of 11 states recently have been assisting us through the Quality Unemployment Insurance Project in the analysis and use of data from the RA and Quality Control (QC) programs. These states are Alaska, Arizona, Illinois, Louisiana, Missouri, North Dakota, New Jersey, New York, Oklahoma, Pennsylvania and Utah. We express our gratitude to the UC directors and QC supervisors in these states—too numerous to mention individually—for their foresight and enthusiasm in productively using the data produced by these special programs.

We also thank the field investigators in the NCUC, RA and QC projects for carrying out their eligibility verification responsibilities with such integrity. We know that any analysis of the data from these special projects is of potential benefit only because the field investigators who produced these data were so diligent and professional in their work.

Numerous individuals in the national and regional offices of the U.S. Department of Labor also have supported our research efforts over the years. Because our debts in this regard are extensive, we identify here only three of these individuals: Robert Schaerfl (current director of the Employment Service and former director of program management for the Unemployment Insurance Service), Carolyn Golding (current director of the Unemployment Insurance Service), and Robert Johnson (associate regional administrator for Unemployment Insurance in Region X). We thank each of you and many others on your staffs for encouragement, advice and support on matters too numerous to enumerate.

The employer community has offered consistent and substantial support for both background research and for the preparation of this volume. In particular, J. Eldred Hill, Jr. (Unemployment Benefits Advisors, Inc.) always has been willing to share his wealth of UC knowledge with us. Thank you again, Eldred, for the support and encouragement that turned the idea for this book into reality.

Many individuals, in addition to several identified above, reviewed all or parts of several versions of the manuscript. Saul Blaustein, recently retired from the W. E. Upjohn Institute for Employment Research, provided an in-depth review of the entire manuscript. We thank you, Saul, for your generous contributions of time and expertise. Tom Vaughn, Arizona's UI director, reviewed the entire manuscript and was particularly helpful in aiding our understanding of constantly changing administrative financing procedures. Gerald Dunn, recently retired as New York's UI director, and Raymond Thorne, Oregon's Employment Division administrator also were particularly helpful to us, both as manuscript reviewers and for insightful evaluations of numerous UC-related problems and reform proposals. other reviewers of the manuscript to whom we are indebted include Sally Ward, the Employment Security administrator of Illinois, and Cheryl Templeman of the Interstate Conference of Employment Security Agencies.

We express our appreciation to the W. E. Upjohn Institute for Employment Research for its continuing interest in the UC program, as evidenced by their publication of this and many other studies. Robert Spiegelman of the Institute read the entire manuscript and offered numerous helpful suggestions. Valuable editorial assistance was provided by Judy Gentry. We also gratefully acknowledge our continuing debt to Lynnette Winkelman who patiently and skillfully typed several versions of this manuscript.

Finally, we must thank our colleague, Robert St. Louis, for his invaluable contributions through the years. His influence is reflected in numerous places throughout the manuscript since he participated with us in developing and testing the methodologies used in both the NCUC and RA studies mentioned above. His influence also is reflected by the fact that he is a coauthor of many of the articles and reports cited in this book. Beyond these contributions, Bob always has given willingly of his time and expertise. In addition, he provided valuable comments on several versions of the ideas contained in this book. It is difficult to adequately acknowledge such a large debt, but we do absolve him of any responsibility for ideas and conclusions with which he does not agree.

Preface

This book addresses the issue of overpayments and other quality problems in the unemployment compensation (UC) program. In contrast with previous treatments of these topics, overpayments are seen as symptomatic of other and potentially more serious problems that the UC system must confront as it begins its second half-century. As the title of the book suggests, the major issue addressed is improving adverse incentives for all UC system participants (claimants, employers and state UC agencies).

Although many of the ideas expressed in this volume have evolved over nearly two decades of involvement in the UC system, this manuscript has been in preparation since 1984. In 1985 and 1986, a complete rough draft was widely circulated among state employment security agencies, the U.S. Department of Labor, the employer community, academic experts and elsewhere. This distribution not only produced useful comments but, together with other factors, may have set in motion some changes in how the federal-state UC system actually operates. No matter what the causal forces at work may have been, the result has been that our description and commentary on current UC system operations has been in nearly constant need of change since the manuscript was first drafted.

These circumstances have been particularly evident in the procedures and policies used by the U.S. Department of Labor to provide administrative funding for state UC program operations. The chapter on administrative financing has been completely rewritten on at least four separate occasions to accommodate either proposed or actual changes. We believe that the description and analysis of these and other features of the federal-state UC system are reasonably accurate as of June 1987. Given the pace of change in a number of UC program areas over the past year, however, some parts of our commentary may become dated in the near future.

Our intention in writing this book has been to strengthen the unemployment compensation program by highlighting its principal problems and suggesting reasonable and effective responses. While we believe this effort was an important first step, we fully recognize that the cooperation and support of all UC system participants, including federal and state policymakers and administrators, will be required if fundamental improvements in the UC system are to be achieved. It is hoped that some of the ideas in this book will encourage improvements in this 50 year old system of support for unemployed workers.

PRIVATE SECTOR TASK FORCE MEMBERS

The following individuals, representing expertise in business and unemployment compensation, constitute the National Chamber Foundation's project advisory panel for *An Incentives Approach to Improving the Unemployment Compensation System.* The presence of their names on this report is testimony to their participation in the project and the invaluable aid they provided in the course of the study. It must be noted that this listing does not signify or imply endorsement of the views presented in this study, either by the advisory panel members or by the companies or organizations which they represent.

Stewart Bailenson
Senior Vice President
James E. Frick, Inc.

Don Beusse
Manager of Insured
  Compensation Benefits
Burlington Industries, Inc.

Warren G. Blue
Senior Vice President & General Counsel
R.E. Harrington, Inc.

Frank Brechling
Professor of Economics
University of Maryland

Christopher Costello
Director, Industrial Relations
Maryland Chamber of Commerce

Eugene Dassonville
Administrator, Social Security Taxes
Aluminum Company of America

John P. Davidson
Unemployment Benefit Planning
Chrysler Corporation

Samuel E. Dyer
Vice President, Tax Department
Federated Department Stores, Inc.

Karen Glass
Staff Associate for Employment
  and Vocational Training
National Governors Association

Michael Hatcher
Director, Technical and Legislative Affairs
Unemployment Compensation Operations
Gates, McDonald and Company

William L. Heartwell, Jr.
Executive Vice President
Interstate Conference of
  Employment Security Agencies, Inc.

J. Eldred Hill, Jr.
President, UBA

Tom Howell
Manager, State & Local Taxes
Pillsbury Company

David Lotocki
Manager, Benefits Communications
  and Analysis
Marriott Corporation

Robert C. Mitchell
Manager of Payroll Taxes
Sears, Roebuck & Company

Maurice Shapiro
Employment Security and Pension Manager
Labor Relations Staff
The Ford Motor Company

Richard Stifter
Assistant Director
Unemployment and Workers'
  Compensation Activity
General Motors Corporation

Cheryl Templeman
Unemployment Insurance Director
Interstate Conference of
  Employment Security Agencies, Inc.

Contents

List of Tables

List of Figures

1
Introduction

August 14, 1985 marked the golden anniversary of the federal-state unemployment compensation (UC) program. Such a milestone in the evolution of the employment security system invites both reflection on past successes and consideration of how the system might be improved to meet present and future challenges. Both UC benefit provisions and the labor market within which the program operates have changed significantly since the inception of the UC system. Increased coverage of unemployed workers, higher weekly benefits, and the introduction of various extended benefit programs have tended to increase UC program outlays for any given level of aggregate demand.[1] Substantial changes also have occurred in the composition of both the insured and total labor forces. The conceptual distinction between voluntary and involuntary unemployment—once thought to be quite clear—has become increasingly blurred. Furthermore, cyclical fluctuations have become more pronounced, with the two deepest recessions since the Great Depression recorded within the past 13 years.

In spite of the diverse challenges it has confronted, however, the UC system has retained many of its basic goals and organizational/operational features. Perhaps the most apparent impacts of the above changes have been reflected in the overall volume of UC benefit payments and in the consequent pressures on UC system solvency. In addition, there has been increased emphasis on assessing the labor market impacts of UC benefits

---

1. Over the past few years the proportion of all unemployed persons receiving UC support has declined, and the divergence between the total and insured unemployment rates has been a topic of increased attention. For a recent survey of this issue, see National Foundation for Unemployment Compensation & Workers' Compensation (1986b).

1

2 INTRODUCTION

and on determining the extent to which UC claimants are eligible for the support they actually receive.[2]

This study focuses on a number of issues related to UC eligibility criteria and the extent to which compliance with them has been and can be enforced. In addition to the program's 50th anniversary, several other events also suggest that a major reconsideration of UC eligibility criteria, enforcement provisions and administrative practices may be appropriate. For example, a number of UC reform proposals have been suggested within the past few years.[3] Beginning in 1984, the U.S. Department of Labor (USDOL) initiated an intensive effort to design a Quality Control (QC) program for the UC system; the core or initial component of this recently implemented program specifically relates to ascertaining the extent to which UC claimants are entitled to the benefits they receive.[4] Proposals for restructuring federal-state administrative funding relationships within the UC program also have been advanced recently, including the Reagan administration's 1985 "devolution" proposal that would place much greater responsibility on the states for the administrative financing of their UC systems.[5] The analysis in this study is intended to contribute to these already ongoing efforts to improve the UC system.

Study Background/Overview

As background for this investigation, it first is useful to clarify some terminology. *Payment errors* occur in the UC system when claimants receive benefit amounts that differ from those to which they are entitled, given the provisions of employment security

2. For example, see the following for three very recent analyses of claimant eligibility issues: Kingston and Burgess (1986); Kingston, Burgess and St. Louis (1986); and St. Louis, Burgess and Kingston (1986).

3. See for example Blaustein (1981).

4. The planning for this program was announced by USDOL to state UC agencies in March 1984. See U.S. Department of Labor (1984e).

5. Deborah L. Steelman, Special Assistant to the President, Office of Intergovernmental Affairs, announced this UC reform proposal at the 1985 national conference of the National Foundation for Unemployment Compensation & Workers' Compensation. See National Foundation for Unemployment Compensation & Workers' Compensation (1985a). For more recent details, see Cogan (1985).

law and policy. Consequently, payment errors include both overpayments and underpayments. UC overpayments are the focus of this study because of the availability of much better data on this type of payment error and because the available data suggest that overpayments are a more serious problem than underpayments. Nonetheless, this emphasis should not be interpreted to imply that underpayments are unimportant. As explained in more detail below, relatively little is known about the extent to which UC claimants are underpaid, although some research directed towards this issue is now underway. Finally, it should be emphasized that UC system overpayments are not synonymous with "fraud" or "abuse" of the UC program. Available evidence suggests that overpayments occur for a variety of reasons, many of which do not entail deliberate efforts by claimants to obtain benefits to which they are not entitled. Indeed, a central theme of this study is that many features of the present day UC system contribute to the erroneous payment of benefits, apart from any deliberate efforts claimants may make to obtain benefits to which they are not entitled.

Prior to 1980, accurate and substantive evidence on the extent of overpayments in the UC system was not available. Although concerns about overpayments frequently were expressed in the public press prior to 1980, the first valid estimates of UC system overpayments were produced by a study conducted by the authors for the National Commission on Unemployment Compensation during 1979 and 1980.[6] The overpayment estimates in that (Kingston-Burgess) study were developed for six major metropolitan areas on the basis of intensive eligibility verifications that were conducted for samples selected to represent the vast majority of UC payments made in those areas. The major findings of that initial study—that UC overpayment rates were much higher than even informed observers had expected, and that most overpayments were not likely to be detected by conventional program procedures—led USDOL to pilot test a modified, "operational" version of the Kingston-Burgess study in five statewide UC programs. An analysis of the results of this

---

6. See Kingston and Burgess (1981).

second study by Burgess, Kingston and St. Louis reinforced the
earlier findings about the existence of a potentially serious
overpayment problem in the UC program.[7] This evidence and
subsequent findings produced by the Random Audit (RA) system
prompted USDOL to expand the RA program to a total of 46
states by FY 1984, and to design an even more comprehensive
Quality Control program which was implemented in 1986.[8]

This sequence of events has focused both official and broader
public attention on the problem of overpayments in the UC
system. Such a focus may be somewhat appropriate because high
overpayment rates may, of themselves, be a major problem in
some state UC programs. However, a major theme of this study
is that high overpayment rates per se are not necessarily the most
fundamental issue requiring attention by policymakers and UC
program administrators. Rather, these rates may be symptomatic
of more basic problems that very likely represent important
issues for states with both low and high payment error rates.
Although the basis for this contention may not be immediately
obvious, the analysis in chapters 2-7 clearly indicates that three
fundamental problems confront the UC system: (1) adverse
incentives; (2) program complexity; and (3) partly because of the
first two problems, ineffective monitoring of claimant compliance with weekly UC eligibility criteria. These considerations
also indicate that the overall quality of state programs clearly
cannot be judged on the basis of overpayment rates alone. In
fact, it is quite conceivable that overall program quality could be
higher in certain states with high overpayment rates than in
certain other ones with low overpayment rates.

Economists emphasize how individuals, business firms and
government agencies respond to incentives in making various
decisions under whatever constraints apply. Accordingly, the
basic focus of this study is on how UC system participants are
likely to respond to the incentives they confront in that system.
In fact, the analysis indicates that adverse incentives characterize

7. See Burgess, Kingston and St. Louis (1982).
8. See U.S. Department of Labor (1984f) and U.S. Department of Labor (1984g). Even
though planning for the QC program began in 1984, implementation was delayed until April of
1986.

the decision environments of all major UC system participants. Adverse incentives include: (1) incentives in federal administrative funding procedures and performance criteria that adversely affect entire state UC systems; (2) incentives in individual state systems that fail to discourage and may even encourage claimant noncompliance with stated UC eligibility criteria; (3) very limited incentives for employers to monitor claimant compliance with eligibility criteria, especially those that must be satisfied on a weekly basis; and (4) limited incentives for state agency personnel either to monitor claimant compliance with eligibility criteria or to prevent/detect payment errors.[9]

The other two fundamental problems stressed in this study— program complexity and ineffective monitoring of claimant compliance with UC eligibility criteria—are interrelated issues which also affect and are affected by adverse incentives. Program complexity creates numerous undesirable impacts, including the possibilities of relatively high payment error rates, high administrative costs and substantial administrative discretion in applying UC eligibility criteria which may result in the inequitable treatment of claimants. Program complexity also creates a situation in which adverse incentives represent a more serious problem than would be the case in a less complex program. In turn, program complexity and adverse incentives contribute substantially to the difficulties of monitoring claimant compliance with the weekly eligibility criteria (e.g., nonrefusal of suitable work, availability for work and active job search). These monitoring problems imply that adverse incentives and program complexity are more serious issues than would be the case in a system in which claimant compliance with weekly eligibility criteria could be more easily and less expensively enforced.

The three fundamental problems—adverse incentives, program complexity and ineffective compliance monitoring—represent the building blocks around which the subsequent analysis is organized. The approach taken is to analyze the three problems

---

9. A related issue revolves around incentives for and detection of internal agency fraud, but that issue is not addressed in this study. However, it should be noted that this problem may represent a potentially important issue in some states, as perhaps is indicated by the increased emphasis by USDOL on this issue in recent years.

in separate chapters and then to provide some possible responses for dealing with the specific problems analyzed in those same chapters. The responses suggested typically are quite general in nature; in most cases, the specific details of these approaches would have to be formulated by state or federal policy-makers/program administrators. Furthermore, although a number of responses are suggested for the particular problems identified in individual chapters, it is important to emphasize that a systems approach should be taken in devising any overall set of reform proposals, either for federal-state relationships or for those within individual states. Because of the interactive nature of system components, apparently plausible responses to specific problems might well generate unintended and unacceptable side effects in terms of other program aspects. Consequently, it would be difficult even to evaluate the desirability of certain changes, except in the context of whatever overall changes might be implemented. Moreover, because of uncertainty about the exact impacts that most suggested changes would have, it is important to emphasize the need for further research and experimental pilot studies to fully evaluate many of the changes suggested by the analysis in this study.

Qualifications and Limitations of the Analysis

The UC system is an extremely complex one, with a variety of philosophical, social, legal and economic dimensions that merit study. Moreover, even the limited issues raised in this study could be approached in a number of different ways. Accordingly, it is important to emphasize the limited scope of this inquiry. Some fairly specific qualifications or limitations that apply to this study include, but certainly are not limited to, the following: (1) the problem of UC underpayments is not addressed in any substantive way; (2) little attention is directed to tracing the evolution of most of the system deficiencies analyzed, and no attempt is made to pinpoint responsibility for those deficiencies; (3) only within-system reform approaches that would maintain the fundamental features of the existing UC system are emphasized; (4) benefit financing and trust fund solvency issues are virtually ignored; (5) in many cases, indirect (v. direct) evidence is provided to support the analysis; (6) the specific applicability of particular aspects of the analysis to individual states varies with state-specific circumstances; (7) the most recent overpayment statistics from the Quality Control program were not available for this analysis; (8) the interstate benefit system is not analyzed; and (9) a general knowledge of UC system features is assumed.

Underpayments Not Emphasized

This study emphasizes overpayment errors and treats underpayments only in a tangential manner. This asymmetry reflects the absence of substantive evidence about the frequency or extent of total underpayment errors, the difficulties encountered in designing experiments to produce underpayment evidence, and the generally greater concerns that have been expressed about overpayments in the UC system. This emphasis on overpayments, however, should not be interpreted to imply that underpayments are unimportant. Some information on underpayments recently has become available as a result of the Random Audit programs which operated in as many as 46 states; evidence related to UC underpayments is summarized in the appendix to chapter 2. Unfortunately, however, this evidence reflects only underpayments in *benefits actually paid*, and excludes underpayments due to erroneous denials of UC claims for which no payments were made. Consequently, no comprehensive evidence is available to assess the magnitude of all types of underpayment errors in the UC system.

Evolution of and Responsibility for Existing Deficiencies

Virtually no attempt is made to trace the emergence or evolution of the existing UC system deficiencies analyzed in this study. There also is no attempt to pinpoint responsibility for these system deficiencies, since it is assumed that federal and state policymakers/program administrators did not deliberately set out to create a system with the adverse incentives and other problems emphasized in this study. In fact, at least some of these individuals probably still do not recognize the existence of a number of these adverse features. The very explicit analysis of adverse UC program characteristics is provided to clarify these issues, and is not intended as a criticism of those who have shaped or managed various parts of the federal-state UC system over the years. Given the interactive nature of the relationships among all system participants—including not only federal/state UC program personnel, covered employers and claimants, but also federal/state legislators, the federal/state judicial system, private sector firms that specialize in handling UC program matters for employers, organized labor, the academic community and yet other groups—it would be both futile and unproductive to attempt to place responsibility for existing system problems on certain groups.

Within-System Reform Emphasized The reforms or policy responses to the problems analyzed in this study are ones that could be implemented within the basic institutional framework and traditions of the existing UC system without fundamentally altering its basic features and assumptions. In this sense, the responses considered necessarily are somewhat limited. Less conventional reform approaches are not considered in this study.

The decision to limit reform approaches and policy responses to those that could be carried out within the existing system reflects two basic considerations. First, it reflects a consensus of opinion among many informed observers that such proposals would be much more likely to receive serious consideration than less conventional responses. Second, the research undertaken for this study now has convinced us that, contrary to our opinion at the outset, very significant improvements actually could be made without altering the basic philosophical approach and institutional framework of the existing UC system. Although many of the changes suggested in subsequent chapters likely will be considered to be very major ones (particularly by many federal and state UC program administrators), our view is that these proposals actually involve relatively minor changes, especially relative to proposals that would alter the foundations of the system itself.

From the perspective of within-system reform, it appears that emphasis should be placed on: (1) reducing the complexity of the existing UC system and also finding ways to improve the administration of existing (or less complex) provisions; (2) improving both federal administrative funding procedures and other federal incentives for state UC agencies; (3) improving claimant incentives for increased self-compliance with UC eligibility criteria; (4) improving the incentives of state UC agency personnel and, to a lesser extent, of covered employers to prevent and detect payment errors; and (5) improving the procedures used to monitor claimant compliance with weekly UC eligibility criteria. Many might question the political feasibility of taking effective action in some of these areas, but the subsequent discussion of the specific within-system responses analyzed in this study has not been limited by any attempt to consider only proposals likely to be politically popular. Apart from whatever may be the political feasibility of the suggestions, it is hoped the analysis of system deficiencies and policy options presented may serve to stimulate interest in UC system reform.

It very well could be that society's long-run interests ultimately might be better served by completely replacing the existing UC system with one that would be quite different from even a reformed version of the present system. However, a serious analysis of the many issues that would be involved in designing an optimal replacement for the existing system is completely beyond the scope of this study.

Benefit Financing and Trust Fund Solvency Issues Not Analyzed

The UC program experienced a financial crisis during the past 13 years which began with the 1974-1975 recession and became even more severe with the onset of back-to-back recessions in 1980 and 1982. By January 1, 1985, state UC systems had obtained loans from the federal government that totalled $23.5 billion.[10] As a result of these and other considerations, trust fund

---

10. Vroman (1985).

solvency and benefit financing issues recently have received substantial attention.[11] This study, however, was not motivated by these considerations. It is the case, of course, that the over-all volume of UC benefit payments (for a given level of aggregate demand) can be set at whatever level policymakers choose by simply altering eligibility criteria and benefit levels. Hence, some of the proposals considered in this study could have some implications for benefit financing issues because they could impact on the overall volume of UC program outlays (for a given level of aggregate demand). These impacts, however, are viewed primarily as side effects of policies intended to address the incentives or other issues that do constitute the focal point of this study. This approach reflects both the emphasis of our previous research and also our view that an analysis of the benefit payment side of the UC program ledger can make an important contribution in terms of improving the existing UC system.

Indirect v. Direct Evidence

In many cases, it is necessary to provide indirect evidence for the existence of some of the adverse features analyzed in this study. For example, there is no accepted basis for proving that the UC program is too complex, especially since certain features of existing complexity were specifically introduced by policymakers in the hopes of achieving certain goals. Further-more, merely documenting the existence of adverse incentives does not indicate the extent to which system participants actually respond to them. Nevertheless, even though much of the evidence offered in this study is indirect in nature, our opinion is that it provides a sufficient basis for the conclusions reached; others, however, will have to make such assessments for themselves. At several places throughout this study, we offer suggestions for additional research in areas in which more direct or substantive evidence may be useful.

---

11. Two recent studies by Vroman provide an excellent overview of the issues involved. See Vroman (1985) and (1986).

Applicability of Analysis to Individual States

The federal-state UC system includes 53 individual UC jurisdictions (the 50 states plus the District of Columbia, Puerto Rico and the Virgin Islands). The specific eligibility criteria applicable in each jurisdiction are determined by that jurisdiction, subject to conformity with broad federal guidelines. Administrative practices and operational procedures vary considerably among the states. Accordingly, the assessment of the UC system provided in this study is a generalization that may apply to varying degrees to individual UC jurisdictions. Because of the diversity of state UC systems, no attempt is made to indicate how each portion of the analysis applies to specific states. It is our view that the general thrust of most of the analysis would be applicable, at least to some degree, to nearly all state UC programs.

Unavailability of Recent Overpayment Evidence

Information on overpayment rates in as many as 46 statewide jurisdictions is available for FY 1983, FY 1984, FY 1985 and for a portion of FY 1986, but is not summarized or discussed in this study because the data had not been publicly released at the time this study was undertaken. Our judgment, however, is that this limitation does not significantly impact on the substance of the study. In fact, evidence released in 1987 for more recent periods is entirely consistent with the evidence analyzed in this study. Furthermore, the dominant themes of this study are related to issues, circumstances or relationships of which high UC overpayment rates are primarily symptomatic. In the absence of convincing evidence that fundamental changes have recently occurred with respect to the complexity, incentive and monitoring issues, there seems to be no strong basis for assuming the analysis would have been significantly altered by the availability of more recent data.

Interstate Benefit System Not Analyzed

About 5 percent of the UC benefits paid in the United States in recent years have been paid on an interstate basis.[12] Cooperative agreements among the UC jurisdictions permit the interstate payment of benefits. Claimants receive interstate benefits from the (liable) state in which they had worked and earned their qualifying wage credits, but file for those benefits from another (agent) state in which they have temporarily or permanently relocated.

The present study does not provide for a separate analysis of the interstate benefit (IB) payment system. No meaningful evidence currently is available on overpayment rates in the IB system, although USDOL apparently plans to encompass the interstate system in an expanded version of its recently implemented Quality Control program.[13] However, the fundamental problems that contribute to payment errors and reduced UC program quality with regard to intrastate benefits—adverse incentives, program complexity, and an inability to effectively monitor claimant compliance with UC eligibility criteria—almost certainly are even more pronounced problems in the IB system. In addition, shared administration of an IB claim between the liable (paying) state and the agent state clearly would be expected to introduce additional complexities and to provide for even more adverse incentives for payment accuracy than those which exist for intrastate payments.[14]

UC Program Knowledge Assumed

As is perhaps already apparent, it is assumed that the reader has at least a general understanding of the UC system. No attempt is made to provide any detailed description of the UC

---

12. This estimate was provided during 1985 by the Interstate Benefits unit in the National Office of the Unemployment Insurance Service of the U.S. Department of Labor.

13. See U.S. Department of Labor (1985e: I-C-4 through I-C-6).

14. For example, neither covered employers nor UC agency personnel in agent states would have strong incentives to deny IB claims because the benefits received by interstate claimants: (1) would be charged to out-of-state employers; and (2) likely would account for some increased spending within agent states, thereby creating additional sales, profits and employment opportunities.

system as it presently operates, although some background is provided in selected portions of the study for particularly complicated features of the system. It probably still is the case that even those with little general knowledge of the system can evaluate many of the adverse UC system features stressed in this study. In any case, a number of good sources are available for those who wish to supplement their UC system knowledge before considering the subsequent analysis.[15]

Organization of the Study

This investigation is organized in the following manner. Evidence of overpayments and some information on underpayments in the UC system are summarized in chapter 2. The sources and extent of complexities that characterize the UC program, especially those related to UC eligibility criteria, are documented in chapter 3. The major theme of this study—the importance of adverse incentives in affecting the behavior of UC system participants—is developed primarily in chapters 4, 5 and 6. The adverse incentives confronted by state UC agencies with respect to federal-state administrative funding issues are discussed in chapter 4, whereas issues related to state compliance with federal performance criteria are considered in chapter 5. In chapter 6, the incentives faced by UC claimants, covered employers and state UC agency personnel are examined, especially as they relate to the extent of claimant compliance with UC eligibility criteria. In chapter 7, the difficulties of monitoring claimant compliance with weekly UC eligibility criteria, particularly worksearch requirements, are analyzed in detail. Possible responses to the problems identified in chapters 3–7 are analyzed in each chapter. The final chapter contains principal findings, policy recommendations and a brief summary of the entire study.

---

15. See for example Haber and Murray (1966) and Hamermesh (1977).

2
Evidence on Overpayments
in the UC System

Prior to 1980, information on UC overpayments consisted primarily of official statistics based on overpayments both detected and officially processed (i.e., "established") by state UC agencies. Later studies indicated that these data tended to understate, perhaps by a substantial margin, the true extent of payment errors in the UC system. Also, prior to 1980 much of the public debate about improper UC payments tended to equate "overpayments" with "fraud" and "abuse" and generally was expressed in emotionally charged terms.[1] Much more accurate estimates and objective assessments of UC overpayment rates became available in 1980. Analysis of this more recent evidence motivated the assessment of the UC program presented in this study.

This chapter is organized in the following manner. First, the information on overpayments available prior to 1980 is summarized, followed by somewhat more detail on the two major studies that have provided much more factual evidence. A brief discussion of even more recent (but very fragmentary) evidence on UC overpayments from USDOL's Random Audit program is presented next. Some concluding comments close the discussion. Information developed since 1980 on UC underpayments is summarized in the appendix to this chapter.

---

1. Becker's 1953 study represents a clear exception to this characterization of early studies of UC fraud and abuse as "emotional" in nature. Drawing on the limited factual evidence available to him, Becker provided a logical assessment of the extent of abuse of the UC program. Another exception to this characterization is the work of Adams (1971).

15

Information on UC Program Overpayments Prior to 1980

The first major study of overpayments in the UC program was undertaken by Joseph Becker in 1953. In assessing the extent of knowledge about improper payments over the first decade or so of the program's operations, Becker stated:

> Yet at no time since the system was established has anyone been in a position to offer a reasonably accurate estimate of the amount of improper payments. In 1945, ten years after the Social Security Act was passed, not one of the forty-eight States had adequate evidence of the proportion of claims and claimants it was paying but would not pay if it knew all the relevant facts—that is, claims and claimants improper by the first and simplest norm, the norm of the State's own law and interpretation. Only three or four States had reasonably accurate information regarding even their working violators, the easier to detect of the two groups of violators, as also the smaller and less important. As regards nonworking violators—there was nothing.[2]

Becker further explained why so little information about overpayments was available at that time: the UC program was a young one, and the states were much more involved in the essential tasks of collecting taxes and paying benefits than in detecting program abuses. Although the Interstate Conference of Employment Security Agencies appointed a committee to study program abuse as early as 1941, World War II intervened, so that the task of obtaining information on improper payments had not yet seriously begun by 1948. Some hesitancy on the part of the Bureau of Employment Security to give high priority to benefit payment control activities, as well as a hesitancy of the states to respond positively to those incentives that were provided, further limited the development of factual data on overpayments in the UC system.[3]

Public concern about improper payments did increase during the 1945-1947 reconversion from a wartime to a peacetime

2. Becker (1953: 319).
3. Becker (1953: 321–322).

economy. In 1946, the *Baltimore Sun* won a Pulitzer Prize for a series of articles on the issue of UC program abuse, and the paper was credited with the ''most meritorious public service rendered by an American newspaper during the year.''[4] Several factors likely did contribute to a decline in the integrity of the UC program's payment system during this interval, including: (1) the large increase in the number of claims filed; (2) the limited ability and interest of program administrators in controlling overpayments; (3) lack of cooperation between the UC system and the Employment Service; and (4) frequent attempts by workers to obtain benefits even if they did not qualify.[5] Furthermore, benefit charges to employers during the war years were so low that employers apparently became much less interested in the issue of claimant compliance. In addition, state UC agencies generally lacked the trained staff required to effectively conduct benefit payment control activities.[6]

During the first one-and-one-half decades of the program's operation, relatively little factual evidence on UC overpayments was available. In assessing the evidence related to the frequency with which benefits had been properly paid during this interval, Becker concluded that:

The favorable evidence produced by the investigation will impress different readers differently. It will probably suffice for most of them to conclude that even in the reconversion period the system as such was not discredited. . . . Whether one finds the favorable evidence sufficient for coming to some conclusion depends very much on what advantages one sees in a system of unemployment benefits.[7]

With respect to the evidence related to the improper payment of benefits, Becker reported that:

On the subject of willful violations—that is, the proportion of working violators who are cheaters—the most intelligent state-

---

4. Becker (1953: xvii).
5. Becker (1953: 154–160).
6. Becker (1953: 155–156).
7. Becker (1953: 304).

ment that can be made is that no one knows. . . . The figures are
even less certain for non-working violators. . . . [8]

Despite public concerns about improper payments and abuse in the
early years of the program (especially in the immediate postwar
period), no factual basis existed to evaluate these claims or to guide
policymakers.

Several expressions of public concern about the UC program
also surfaced during the 1960s. A nationwide poll undertaken by
the University of Michigan in 1961 to determine the extent of
public support of nine domestic programs revealed that only 29
percent of those polled favored higher unemployment compensation benefits, and that unemployment compensation ranked
seventh in terms of public support, followed only by parks and
recreational facilities and support for agriculture.[9] In a similar
vein, the results of a 1965 Gallup Poll indicated that three-fourths
of the respondents believed that the insured unemployed collected benefits even though they could find work; nearly seven-
tenths of those surveyed supported making UC benefit laws more
strict.[10]

Other indications of public concerns about the UC program
during the 1960s emanated from the popular press. A series of
articles appeared in *Reader's Digest*, with similar articles ap-
pearing in *Harper's* and *Atlantic Monthly*.[11] Among the concerns
raised in these articles were: (1) abuse of the program by those
who did *not* want to return to work and by those who had *not* lost
their jobs through no fault of their own; (2) the encouragement
by the Bureau of Employment Security that states exclude the
specific requirement that claimants "actively seek work;" (3)
inadequate screening of claimants with respect to the reasons for
their unemployment; and (4) inadequate efforts to prosecute
fraud overpayments when they were detected.[12] The U.S.
Department of Labor responded that these allegations were
essentially unfounded. In his response to the initial *Reader's*

8. Becker (1953: 310–311).
9. Adams (1971: 20).
10. Adams (1971:21).
11. These articles are all cited by Adams (1971: 27).
12. Adams (1971: 27–28).

Digest article, Assistant Secretary of Labor Newell Brown stated that, during the 1956-1968 interval, fraud overpayments constituted only about 0.2 percent of UC program benefits.[13] He further stated:

> . . . I am convinced that, for the most part, the allegations are a distortion of facts. By innuendo and half-truths a wholly inaccurate picture of the program has been presented.
>
> Just criticisms and suggestions as to where improvements might be made in the program are always welcome. But baseless attacks on the soundness of a public program or the actions of public administrators do not, I believe, make much of a contribution to the public interest.[14]

The integrity of the UC payment system also was defended by UC program administrators surveyed by Adams in 1970 about the problems of fraud and abuse. The consensus view of this group was that public perceptions of UC program abuse were due primarily to misinformation on the part of employers, claimants and the general public. Two common problems cited by these administrators were the tendencies of the public to confuse unemployment insurance with welfare and to believe that UC claimants did not have a real desire to return to work.[15] Overall, however, those surveyed believed that the UC program was well-accepted by the public and that abuse of the program was not a serious problem. A similar positive assessment of the program was provided by Adams who, on the basis of a detailed review of the evidence over the first 25 years of the program, concluded that:

> . . . the problem of claimant abuse of the UI program was less significant at the end of the decade of the 1960s than it was during the immediate post-World War II period when Becker made his study. Furthermore, it is likely that the extent of abuse was less

---

13. Adams (1971: 29).
14. Adams (1971: 29).
15. Adams (1971: 56).

than the general public thought it was when the Gallup Poll was taken in 1965. It is probably less than most people, who are not familiar with the facts, are inclined to believe.[16]

During the decade of the 1970s, however, extraordinary pressures were placed on the UC system. UC benefits that had averaged only $2.65 billion annually during the 1960s increased to an annual average of $8.6 billion during the 1970s.[17] By 1979, the trust funds of 15 states had become depleted, resulting in an indebtedness to the federal government of about $3.8 billion.[18] The reasons for this dramatic rise in UC program outlays included: substantially higher unemployment rates; implementation of several extended benefit programs (that provided for up to a total of 65 weeks of regular and extended benefits combined during some periods); increases in the size of weekly benefit payments; expansions of program coverage; and labor force growth. These events tended to heighten public concerns about the potential for fraud and abuse in the UC system. Perhaps the most notable of the expressions of public concern was the *60 Minutes* broadcast aired on CBS television on April 25, 1976 that included a segment on abuse of the UC program. Several articles quite critical of the UC program also appeared in the popular press during the late 1970s.[19]

Notwithstanding these expressions of public concern about improper payments and abuse of the UC program, relatively little factual evidence was available even in the late 1970s to document the existence of such problems. In fact, the official reports submitted by state UC agencies to the U.S. Department of Labor on overpayments actually detected and established for the years 1975 through 1978 indicated that the combined total of fraud plus nonfraud overpayments amounted to between 0.5 percent and 1.5

---

16. Adams (1971: 92).
17. National Commission on Unemployment Compensation (1980: 74).
18. National Commission on Unemployment Compensation (1980: 74).
19. For example, see "Confessions of an Unemployment Cheat," in the May, 1977 issue of *The Washington Monthly*; "Crackdown on Cheaters Who Draw Jobless Pay," in the May 15, 1978 issue of *U.S. News and World Report*; and "Unemployment Comp is Middle-Class Welfare," in the February 19, 1977 issue of *The New Republic*.

percent of total benefits paid.[20] USDOL also reported that efforts to control overpayments had been expanded during this period, the number of positions designated for benefit payment control activities in state UC programs had been increased by 72 percent, and additional steps had been taken to assist the states in their efforts to detect and recover overpayments.[21]

The above survey of information and public perceptions about improper payments in the UC program prior to 1980 reveals that little documentation was available to support the frequently expressed public concerns about fraud, abuse or poor administrative performance. Lacking factual evidence to the contrary, those most familiar with the program continued to believe that the integrity of the UC payment system was fundamentally intact, even though some problems likely had existed in the immediate postwar period. Over the first 45 years of the UC program's history, the absence of adequate factual data severely hampered efforts to accurately identify or respond to any overpayment problem that may have existed.

The Kingston-Burgess Overpayment Study[22]

As a part of the Unemployment Compensation Amendments of 1976 (Public Law 94-566), Congress established the National Commission on Unemployment Compensation (NCUC). In response to some of the concerns expressed about the problems of fraud and overpayments in the UC program, the NCUC commissioned an experimental overpayment study to be conducted in six major metropolitan areas. This investigation, denoted as the Kingston-Burgess (K-B) study, provided the first relatively accurate estimates of overpayments in the UC program ever available. Its principal features are considered in some detail.

---

20. U.S. Department of Labor (1979: 16).
21. U.S. Department of Labor (1979: 5).
22. This section draws heavily on Burgess and Kingston (1980), Kingston and Burgess (1981b) and Kingston, Burgess and St. Louis (1981).

Objectives and Design

The K-B study had two fundamental objectives. The first was to obtain accurate estimates of the amounts and rates of overpayments to fill the informational void with respect to the actual magnitude of the overpayment problem during the first 45 years of the program's operation. The second objective was to obtain statistically valid estimates of the overpayments *detected by routine operating procedures* to provide a basis for assessing the extent to which the overpayment statistics routinely reported by USDOL accurately reflected actual overpayment rates in the UC program.

The K-B study was conducted during the fourth quarter of 1979 and the first quarter of 1980 in the following metropolitan areas: Buffalo, Oklahoma City, Phoenix, Pittsburgh, the Queens Borough of New York City, and Salt Lake City.[23] In each city, a probability sample of UC *payments* (not claims) was selected each week and these sampled payments (each for a single week of unemployment) were subjected to a detailed audit. Because appropriate sampling techniques were utilized, it was possible to use the results of these reviews to estimate on a quarterly basis the amount and rate of overpayments in these cities.

The procedures used to investigate a claimant's eligibility for the week of unemployment for which UC benefits had been paid—denoted as the "key week"—were extremely thorough and involved verification of a claimant's compliance with all aspects of UC eligibility criteria.[24] Factors to be considered in a

---

23. The city of Nashville, Tennessee also was included in the study at the outset of the project, but it was eliminated because severe problems in selecting an appropriate sample never were resolved by the Tennessee agency. See Kingston and Burgess (1981: 4).

24. A fairly detailed description of UC eligibility criteria is included in chapter 3. Generally, UC claimants must satisfy three types of eligibility requirements. First, claimants must be monetarily eligible for benefits; such eligibility is determined by the claimant's earnings (and in some states weeks of work) in UC-covered employment in a one-year period prior to the filing of a first claim for UC support. These requirements are established to ensure that benefits are paid to persons who have demonstrated a sufficiently strong previous work attachment. Second, a claimant must have separated from his/her previous employer for a nondisqualifying reason; typically, those laid off due to lack of work are eligible for benefits, but those who separate for other reasons may qualify for benefits in some states (sometimes only after penalty provisions have been satisfied). Third, claimants also must satisfy a set of continuing or weekly eligibility criteria. For each week for which UC support is paid, claimants must be able to work, available for work, and (in most states) actively seeking work. In addition, during each week for which

typical review of a claimant's eligibility included: (1) the claimant's prior earnings and employment (to determine if the claimant satisfied all monetary eligibility criteria); (2) the reason why the claimant separated from his/her previous employer (to detect separation eligibility issues); (3) whether the claimant was both able to work and available for work during the key week, as required; (4) whether the claimant was actively seeking work during the key week (if required by the state's law or policy); (5) whether the claimant had refused an offer of suitable work during the key week (a disqualifying act); and (6) whether the claimant had any disqualifying earnings or employment during the key week.

The special investigative procedures developed for the K-B study to assess compliance with the above criteria included a "desk review" of all UC agency files related to the claimant whose eligibility for key week benefits was under review, and an in-person interview with the claimant. This personal interview included the completion of a detailed questionnaire which focused on many aspects of the claimant's eligibility for UC program support for the key week. Thereafter, the investigator attempted to obtain third-party verification from employers and other interested parties to substantiate relevant material facts related to the claimant's eligibility. The benefit eligibility verification process continued until all issues uncovered by the investigation had been resolved. In this sense, the investigations were conducted with virtually no time or resource constraints. On average, between 8 and 13 hours of direct investigative case time were devoted to each sampled case in the K-B study. In sharp contrast, UC local office personnel working under normal operating conditions probably would process an average of *at least* 50 times more claims for payments during a period of 8-13 hours.[25]

In addition to the above procedures, postaudits also were conducted to detect UC claimants who continued to draw

---

benefits are paid claimants must not refuse suitable work or have earnings (or days of work, in some states) beyond limits established by the individual states.

25. In New York, for the years 1980-1984, for example, cost-model funding was provided for up to about eight minutes for processing a continued claim. See Dunn and Griffin (1984: 16).

benefits while working. Postaudits involve the matching of the social security numbers of those who receive UC benefits in a calendar quarter against the social security numbers associated with the wages reported on a quarterly basis by employers in wage-reporting states.[26] If a match is found, additional information is then requested from the employer(s) to determine the particular weeks during the quarter in which the wages were earned. On the basis of the week-by-week comparisons of earnings and UC benefit payments made in these postaudits, it is possible to determine whether claimants receive benefits to which they are not entitled because of unreported earnings.

Limitations

Despite the thoroughness of the benefit eligibility verifications undertaken in the K-B study, the results very likely tend to *understate* the extent of true overpayments in the study cities. First, the initial presumption at the time a case was selected for review was that the claimant *was* entitled to the payment received for that week; this presumption resulted from the fact that the payment already had been processed through the routine UC program operating system, and that the claimant had been found eligible for UC support by that process. As a result, this initial presumption was not reversed unless documented evidence to the contrary was obtained during the course of the investigation. In some instances, such evidence was difficult to obtain simply because the benefit eligibility verifications had to be conducted many weeks following the key weeks for which UC payments had been made. Thus, some true overpayment cases undoubtedly were classified as proper payments in the K-B

---

26. In wage-reporting states, covered employers routinely submit to the state UC agency information on wages earned by all of their employees during the quarter, whether or not this information is needed at that time to determine whether a particular worker is eligible for UC support. By way of contrast, in request-reporting states firms submit wage information to the state UC agency only upon request. These requests occur when a former employee of a firm files for benefits and his/her eligibility may depend on earnings with that firm. Postaudit procedures are facilitated by the types of wage information generally available in wage-reporting states, but other sources of wage data or other procedures to detect working violators are used in request-reporting states. USDOL has mandated that all states adopt wage-reporting procedures.

study simply because sufficient documentation to establish an overpayment could not be obtained.

A second reason why overpayments were underestimated in the K-B study relates to the problems associated with detecting those who receive UC support while working. The postaudit procedures are effective *only* if unreported earnings occur in *UC-covered* employment. Unreported earnings in the "cash economy" or in the "underground economy" are unlikely to be detected by such procedures and thereby constitute a potentially significant source of undetected overpayments. Because over-payments due to unreported earnings are more likely to be established as fraud than nonfraud overpayments, this tendency towards underestimation of overpayments is much more likely to have affected the estimates of fraud than nonfraud overpay-ments.[27] Nonetheless, the results produced by the K-B study clearly represented the most reliable information produced up to that date on the extent and incidence of overpayments in the UC program.

Findings

The most conservative measure of overpayments used in the K-B study included only those cases in which official actions were taken by state agencies as a result of the findings of the investigative teams.[28] By this measure, the percentage of total UC benefits overpaid in the six cities ranged from 3.8 percent in City 1 to 24.3 percent in City 6 (see column 2 of table 2–1). Estimated overpayment rates exceeded 13 percent of all benefits paid in four of the six cities, and at least $1 in $12 of UC benefits were overpaid in five of the six cities during the six-month study

---

27. In contrast to the tendencies for understating true overpayment rates discussed in the text, it is conceivable that the inclusion of only timely payments in the K-B study may have tended to slightly overstate true overpayments. This would be the case if the excluded weeks were less likely than included weeks to be overpaid because of the extra UC agency scrutiny associated with at least some of the delayed payments excluded from the study. Timely weeks were those paid (or processed, for waiting weeks) within seven (fourteen) calendar days of the week-ending date of the compensated week of unemployment in states where certifications for benefits were filed on a weekly (biweekly) basis. See Kingston and Burgess (1981b: 21–25).

28. Two more broadly defined measures of overpayments/improper payments in the K-B study included additional cases that could be considered improper payments, even though no official UI agency actions were taken. For further details, see Kingston and Burgess (1981b:13-15).

TABLE 2–1
Kingston-Burgess Study Overpayment Rates
October, 1979–March, 1980

| City[b] | Estimated Overpayment Rates for Total Dollars of Benefits Paid:[a] | |
	All Overpayments[c]	Fraud Only[d]
1	3.8%	0.8%
2	8.6%	3.4%
3	13.3%	2.5%
4	16.7%	4.6%
5	16.8%	0.8%
6	24.3%	1.6%
Simple 6-City Average	13.9%	2.3%

Source: Kingston and Burgess (1981: 34).

[a] These rates are estimates for each city's total dollars of UI payments made to intrastate claimants.

[b] Cities are arrayed in ascending order from 1–6 on the basis of total overpayment rates. Cities are not identified by name in accordance with an agreement reached with participating state UC agencies at the outset of the study.

[c] Based on overpayments actually established against the weeks of unemployment as a result of the K-B Study investigations. Claimants had available to them the usual formal appeals process to dispute any of these overpayments.

[d] Although the specific definitions vary somewhat among the states, willful misrepresentation of facts by claimants to obtain benefits typically is the distinguishing characteristic of a fraudulent overpayment.

period. Overall, the simple average of the overpayment rates for the six cities amounted to 13.9 percent. For the six cities taken together, the most frequent cause of overpayments—accounting for more than one-third of the total of weeks overpaid—was the failure of claimants to satisfy the availability-for-work and the active worksearch criteria.

The K-B study estimates of fraud overpayments ranged from less than 1 percent of all dollars paid to a high of 4.6 percent, and these rates exceeded 2.5 percent in half of the project cities (see column 3 of table 2-1). The simple average of the fraud rates for the six cities was 2.3 percent. As noted above, however, an important but unanswered question is the extent of undetected overpayments in these six cities due to unreported earnings in the cash economy; if detected, such violations very likely would have been established as fraud overpayments.

TABLE 2–2
Kingston-Burgess Study vs. Routine State Agency Overpayment Rates
October–December, 1979[a]

| City[c] | Estimated Total Overpayment Rates: Percent of Total Dollars of Benefits Paid[b] | |
	K-B Study Rate	Routinely Detected UC Agency Rate[d]
1	2.3%	0.5%
2	7.0%	1.7%
3	14.5%	6.0%
4	14.1%	2.0%
5	20.1%	2.8%
6	25.4%	0.6%
Simple 6-City Average	13.9%	2.3%

Source: Kingston and Burgess (1981: 46).

[a] Comparisons are confined to the last quarter of 1979 because sufficient data for the first quarter of 1980 were not available.

[b] These rates are estimates for each city's total dollars of UI payments made to intrastate claimants.

[c] Cities are arrayed in ascending order from 1–6 on the basis of total overpayment rates. Cities are not identified by name in accordance with an agreement reached with participating state UC agencies at the outset of the study.

[d] For two cities, the entire postaudit process had not been completed at the time overpayment files were reviewed. Thus, two of the rates (which include completed postaudit results) reported in this column might be slight underestimates.

Strong evidence that actual overpayment rates greatly exceed those detected by routine state UC program procedures also was provided by the K-B study findings. For the fourth quarter of 1979, the percentage of dollars paid in UC benefits that were both overpaid and detected through normal benefit payment control procedures was calculated for each city and compared to the dollar overpayment rate estimated for the same period by the K-B study (see table 2-2). For the city with the smallest difference (City 3), the K-B study overpayment rate was 2.4 times larger than the routine state agency rate. For the city with the largest difference (City 6), the K-B study overpayment rate was 42 times the rate of overpayments detected by routine state agency procedures. Overall for the six cities, the simple average of the K-B study rates of 13.9 percent was more than six times the simple average of the routine state UC agency overpayment rates of 2.3 percent. These findings clearly suggest that accurate information about actual overpayment rates in the UC program is *not* provided by the reports submitted by the states to USDOL.

Reactions to the K-B Study

The findings of the K-B study were submitted in April of 1980 to the National Commission on Unemployment Compensation in the form of an interim report,[29] so that the results could be used by the Commission in preparing its recommendations to the Congress. On the basis of this report and other findings presented to the Commission, the following recommendations were forwarded to the Congress by the NCUC: (1) comprehensive audits of selected cases should become a regular feature of the UC program; (2) USDOL should begin a national study of different approaches to establish quality controls consistent with the prompt payment of benefits, minimum error rates and cost effectiveness; and (3) the Secretary of Labor should include, as a part of the audit of state UC agency administrative allocations or as part of performance evaluations, provisions for a randomized audit of all functions that have an impact on the incidence and control of error and fraud.[30]

Burgess-Kingston-St. Louis Analysis of Random Audit Program Pilot Tests

One response of USDOL to the K-B study findings was to refine and pilot test the K-B study methodology in five statewide UC programs for an entire year. At the conclusion of these tests, the findings were analyzed by Burgess, Kingston and St. Louis (B-K-S) and a series of reports summarizing the methodology, findings and implications of the Random Audit program pilot tests were prepared for USDOL. These reports contain the most comprehensive evidence available on payment errors in the UC

---

29. Burgess and Kingston (1980).
30. National Commission on Unemployment Compensation (1980: 109–110).

program. The principal features of the RA program pilot tests and of the B-K-S analysis are considered in some detail below.

Overview of the RA Program

The Random Audit program pilot tests were conducted for a one-year period beginning April 1981 in the States of Illinois, Kansas, Louisiana, New Jersey and Washington.[31] Specially trained UC program investigators were selected to conduct the benefit eligibility verifications for the weekly samples of state-wide UC payments selected in each of the five states. The investigative methodology was closely patterned after that used in the K-B overpayment study undertaken for the NCUC. Lengthy interviews with claimants, the completion of a detailed questionnaire related to various aspects of the claimant's eligibility for benefits during the key week, and comprehensive third-party verifications of claimant statements and certifications related to benefit eligibility were conducted. With the exception that no postaudits were routinely conducted, these investigations were at least as thorough, if not more so, than those conducted in the K-B overpayment study.

Principal Findings and Interpretations

In contrast with the K-B study, the B-K-S analysis provided some information on underpayments, as well as overpayments, in state UC programs. These underpayment estimates, which are reported in the appendix table, indicate that underpayments occurred in as few as 0.9 percent of the weeks paid statewide (in Kansas) and in as many as 13.9 percent of the weeks paid statewide (in New Jersey). The simple average of these underpayment rates for weeks paid for the five states combined is 6.3 percent. Underpayment rates measured in terms of weeks underpaid, however, do not accurately reflect the magnitude of such underpayment errors in terms of dollars paid. The dollar amounts

---

31. See Burgess, Kingston and St. Louis (1982) for a much more comprehensive report on these pilot tests; Burgess, Kingston and St. Louis (1984) for a convenient summary of some of the major study findings; and Kingston, Burgess and St. Louis (1986) for an analysis of some of the major implications of the study findings.

of the underpayment errors typically were quite small; expressed as a percentage of all UC benefits paid statewide, they did not exceed 1 percent in any of the five pilot test states. The frequency of underpayments of small dollar amounts was due primarily to errors in the reporting or recording of claimants' qualifying earnings in a one-year period prior to the unemployment spell. It should be emphasized, however, that even though the underpayment rates expressed as a percentage of dollars paid tended to be quite small, they exclude a potentially important source of additional UC underpayments: erroneous denials of benefits (for which no benefits are paid). Consequently, further research on underpayments will be required before the actual magnitude of all UC system underpayments can be accurately estimated. Some additional details on underpayments are provided in the appendix to this chapter.[32]

The focal point of the B-K-S analysis of the RA pilot tests was UC overpayments, rather than underpayments. The percentage of *weeks paid* statewide that were overpaid during the one-year pilot test period ranged from 10.5 percent to 38.2 percent in these five B-K-S study states (see table 2–3). As was the case for underpayments, the estimated overpayment rates in each state were somewhat lower for *dollars* of benefits paid than for *weeks* of benefits paid: the simple average overpayment rate for dollars of benefits paid for these five states was 13.1 percent, compared with the simple average overpayment rate for weeks of benefits paid of 19.8 percent. Overpayment rates for weeks paid exceed those for dollars paid mainly because of a number of sampled weeks with overpayments of small dollar amounts.[33] As was the case for underpayments, errors in reporting or recording base

32. Also see Burgess, Kingston and St. Louis (1982: 33 and 48–49) for further discussion of this issue.
33. For example, if an employer misreported a claimant's base period wages so that a error occurred in the calculation of the claimant's weekly benefit payment, that (entire) week would be counted as an overpayment in calculating the overpayment rate for weeks of benefits paid, but only the single dollar overpaid would be counted as an overpayment in calculating the overpayment rate for dollars of benefits paid. See Burgess, Kingston and St. Louis (1982: 48-52) and Kingston, Burgess and St. Louis (1986: 325) for a discussion of the circumstances in several of the RA states that resulted in frequent overpayments of small dollar amounts.

TABLE 2–3
Kingston-Burgess-St. Louis Study Overpayment Rates
April, 1981–March, 1982

State	Estimated Percentage Overpayment Rates For:[a]			
	Weeks Paid (Total)	Dollars Paid (Total)	Dollars Paid (Work search violations)	Dollars Paid (Fraud)
Illinois	16.0%	11.9%	5.7%	1.2%
Kansas	14.1%	12.9%	10.3%	0.2%
Louisiana	10.5%	7.3%	3.6%	2.7%
New Jersey	38.2%	24.3%	17.3%	1.9%
Washington	20.0%	9.3%	4.6%	2.1%
Simple 5-State Average	19.8%	13.1%	8.3%	1.6%

Source: Burgess, Kingston and St. Louis (1982: 47, 58).
[a] These rates are point estimates for each state's population of UC payments made to intrastate claimants. The rates are based on overpayments actually established by the participating state agencies against the sampled weeks investigated. Claimants had available to them the usual formal appeal process to dispute any of these overpayments.

period wages also were the most frequent cause of overpayments of small dollar amounts.[34]

Information provided in table 2–3 also indicates that violations of the worksearch requirement accounted for a substantial proportion of all UC dollars overpaid in these five states. The percentage of total dollars of UC benefits overpaid due to violations of the worksearch requirement ranged from 3.6 percent to 17.3 percent, with a simple average for the five states combined of 8.3 percent. In each of the states, nearly half or more of the total of dollars overpaid resulted from failures of claimants to satisfy worksearch requirements. Because of the importance of worksearch violations, this topic is discussed in considerably more detail in chapter 7.

Estimates of the dollar rates of fraud overpayments also are provided in table 2-3; these rates ranged from only 0.2 percent to 2.7 percent in the five states, and the simple average of these rates is 1.6 percent. Although the average fraud rate is much lower than the average total overpayment rate estimated for the

---

34. Burgess, Kingston and St. Louis (1982: 49–52).

five states, it actually exceeds the rate of overpayments for fraud and nonfraud cases *combined* (of 1.28 percent) reported by USDOL for the UC system as a whole for a nearly comparable one-year period.[35] In view of the fact that the B-K-S study estimates are based on investigations that did *not* include postaudits to detect instances of unreported earnings—the most frequent basis for establishing fraud overpayments—these results strongly reinforce the findings of the K-B study that the official overpayment rates (especially for fraud cases) published by USDOL tend to substantially understate actual overpayment rates. The difficulties involved in detecting instances of unreported earnings in the "cash economy" clearly indicate that the overpayment rate estimates reported both by USDOL and in the B-K-S study understate true overpayment rates, especially fraud overpayment rates.

Additional factors also tended to produce low estimates of actual overpayment rates in the B-K-S study. The ex post nature of the investigations and the initial presumption that key weeks were properly paid both contribute to such an underestimation, as they did in the K-B study. Also, two of the B-K-S study states required that overpayments could not be established for violations of the worksearch requirement unless claimants previously had received formal warnings (usually in writing) that their job-seeking efforts were deficient. Other state-specific circumstances also contributed to an underestimation of actual overpayment rates[36] and to the diversity of the estimated rates.[37]

The above considerations indicate that the overpayment rates in table 2-3 understate actual overpayment rates in these states. Overall, the existence of an overpayment problem of substantial proportions for the UC system as a whole is strongly suggested by the findings in this section. In fact, the estimated total dollars overpaid just in the five pilot test states during the one-year study period ($392 million) actually exceed by 60 percent the total of all UC overpayments officially reported by USDOL for the entire

35. U.S. Department of Labor (1982a:3).
36. See Kingston, Burgess and St. Louis (1986: 326) for further details.
37. Burgess, Kingston and St. Louis (1982: 60).

nationwide UC system for approximately the same one-year period.[38]

More Recent Evidence on UC Overpayments

Even before the B-K-S evaluation of the RA program pilot tests had been completed, USDOL had determined that the RA program would be continued as an operational feature of the UC system. In 1982, 10 additional states agreed to participate in the program and, as of 1984, a total of 46 jurisdictions were included. As a result, much more evidence on overpayments in state UC programs currently is available, but relatively little of that information has been released by USDOL.[39] However, in May of 1987 USDOL released data for the 46 states that participated in the Random Audit program during FY 1985. The unweighted average overpayment rate for these states was 15.6 percent.[40] Based on approximately $14.3 billion of UC benefit payments during FY 1985, USDOL estimated that overpayments could have amounted to as much as $2.2 billion during that one-year period.[41] Furthermore, if UC program outlays average $16 billion per year over the next four years, as USDOL recently has projected, a 15 percent overpayment rate would result in overpayments during this interval of about $9.6 billion.[42] These estimates indicate the potential magnitude of the overpayment problem in the UC program.

Summary and Conclusions

Relatively little factual information was available on overpayments in the UC program prior to 1980. Throughout the first 45

---

38. The benefit payment control procedures routinely used by state UC agencies resulted in a total of $239.4 million in overpayments that were established and reported by all UC jurisdictions combined from July 1981 through June 1982 [see U.S. Department of Labor (1982a)]. This one-year interval overlaps much of the April 1981 through March 1982 Random Audit program pilot test period. Both of the above overpayment figures relate to overpayments in regular state UC programs and exclude extended duration and special UC programs.

39. It is the position of USDOL that, because the states that participated in the Random Audit program were "volunteers," decisions about the public release of RA program data were (and are) to be made by state, not federal, authorities.

40. U.S. Department of Labor (1987: III-J-49).

41. U.S. Department of Labor (1987: III-J-49).

42. U.S. Department of Labor (1987: III-J-53).

years of the program's history, allegations of UC fraud and abuse appeared periodically, but no solid basis existed to substantiate such claims. Those closest to the UC program—federal and state UC program administrators and those who had seriously attempted to gather and evaluate evidence on UC overpayments—generally agreed that, with the possible exception of the 1945-1947 reconversion period, the program had not been subject to excessive overpayments or abuse. Official statistics on overpayments actually detected and established by state UC agencies tended to support these optimistic pre-1980 views. By way of contrast, those less familar with the program and the public at-large expressed greater concerns about fraud, overpayments and abuse of the UC system; the lack of supporting documentation, however, tended to erode the substance of these concerns.

More reliable evidence on the actual extent of payment errors in the UC system has become available since 1980. Findings from the K-B and B-K-S studies, in conjunction with the limited additional information released by USDOL on overpayments detected by the Random Audit program since 1982, provide a strong basis for the view that relatively high overpayment rates may exist in many statewide UC programs. For example, current USDOL estimates indicate overpayments could amount to more than $9 billion over the next four years. Such an estimate indicates the existence of a potentially major overpayment problem in the nationwide UC system. Although overpayments are problems in and of themselves, however, they are symptomatic of more fundamental defects in the current UC system. The analysis in the next five chapters addresses these more fundamental issues.

Appendix to Chapter 2
SUMMARY OF UNDERPAYMENT EVIDENCE FROM THE B-K-S STUDY

This study does not focus on underpayments in the UC system. Nonetheless, some information is available from the B-K-S analysis of the RA program pilot tests that indicates the frequency and magnitude of underpayment errors in the population of UC payments *actually made* [see Burgess, Kingston and St. Louis (1982: 45-46)]. It should be emphasized, however, that these statistics *exclude* underpayments that occur because of erroneous denials of benefits (for which no payments are made). Consequently, the information available from the B-K-S study is quite limited and may exclude an important proportion of total underpayments in the UC program.

Underpayment information for the B-K-S study is summarized in the appendix table. The percentages of weeks paid in which underpayments occurred ranged from 0.9 percent to 13.9 percent for the five B-K-S states. The simple average of these underpayment rates was 6.3 percent. However, the relatively frequent underpayment errors in two of the states, New Jersey and Washington, merit additional comment.

The relatively high percentage of underpaid weeks in New Jersey likely reflects the "request-reporting" system used in that state (but not in the other four pilot test states) to obtain information from employers on the qualifying wage credits of potential UC claimants; under this system, covered employers report such wage information only upon request by the state UC agency at the time a potential UC claimant files for benefits. Delays and inaccuracies that occur in employer responses to such requests or inaccuracies in claimant estimates of prior wages tend to result in more frequent payment errors because of incorrect monetary determinations than would be expected in "wage reporting" states (in which employers routinely submit wage information on all covered employees on a quarterly basis).

The relatively high underpayment error rate estimated for Washington likely resulted from an inconsistency in employment security law that required wages to be reported on the basis of the amount *earned* per period, while weekly UC benefit amounts were calculated on the amounts *paid* per period. Following the B-K-S study pilot test period, this inconsistency was corrected.

Of particular importance in appendix table 1 is the fact that underpayments expressed in terms of *dollars paid* were much smaller than those expressed in terms of *weeks paid*. For example, in New Jersey 13.9 percent of the weeks paid but only 1.0 percent of the *dollars paid* were overpaid. Similarly, in Washington 11.7 percent of the weeks paid but only 1.0 percent of the dollars paid were overpaid. This large difference is due to the fact that many (most) underpayments in these states involved very small dollar amounts and were primarily due to errors in the reporting of qualifying wage credits by employers. In terms of dollars of UC benefits paid, the simple five-state average rate of underpayments was only 0.6 percent. Consequently, in terms of the dollar volume of payment errors, the evidence presented here tends to suggest that underpayments are much smaller than overpayments. It should again be emphasized, however, that these comparisons are based on weekly samples of UC *payments*, not UC *claims*. As a result, a potentially significant source of underpayments (claims erroneously denied) is excluded from this comparison.

As noted in chapter 1, some efforts now are underway to estimate underpayments in the population of UC claims filed. As one part of USDOL's new Quality Control program, several research designs have been developed for pilot tests of methodologies to estimate UC system underpayments. However, estimating underpayment errors tends to be more complex than estimating overpayments. For example, some potential claimants may receive erroneous information that discourages them from even filing a claim for benefits, and such "underpayments" are virtually impossible to detect. In some states, computerized files of denied claims also are either unavailable or difficult to access. Difficulties in estimating underpayments also arise because of the sequence of eligibility criteria that must be satisfied by UC claimants. For example, even if a claimant were mistakenly denied benefits because of allegedly insufficient prior earnings

APPENDIX TABLE 1
Kingston-Burgess-St. Louis Study Underpayment Rates
April, 1981–March, 1982

State	Estimated Percentage Underpayment Rate For:[a]	
	Total Weeks Paid	Total Dollars Paid
Illinois	3.1%	0.8%
Kansas	0.9%	0.1%
Louisiana	1.7%	0.1%
New Jersey	13.9%	1.0%
Washington	11.7%	1.0%
Simple Average	6.3%	0.6%

Source: Burgess, Kingston and St. Louis (1982: 47).
[a] These rates are point estimates for each state's population of UC payments made to intrastate claimants. The rates are based on underpayments detected for the sampled weeks investigated in the B-K-S study. Underpayment rates in the "weeks paid" column reflect the percentage of total weeks paid that were underpaid by some amount. Underpayment rates in the "dollars paid" column reflect the ratio of total dollars underpaid to total dollars paid, expressed as a percentage. Underpayments that occur because of an erroneous denial of benefits (in which no benefits are paid) are *not* included in the above tabulations.

or employment, one can not be certain that this claimant would have satisfied all other eligibility criteria (e.g., an appropriate reason for separating from employment); consequently, an erroneous denial of benefits at one point may or may not ultimately lead to an underpayment of benefits. As the results of these USDOL-sponsored studies become available and are combined with information on underpayments in the population of UC benefits paid, a more accurate assessment of UC system underpayments will be possible.

3
UC System Complexity
Adverse Effects and Responses

The UC system may not be an excessively complex payment system compared to many other government programs, such as defense contracting, public welfare programs or state worker compensation programs. Moreover, complexity per se is not necessarily an undesirable feature of a social payment system. In fact, the current level of complexity in the UC system obviously reflects the interactions of economic, social, judicial and political considerations that have shaped the evolution of the system over the past 50 years. The complexity of any social payment system is, of course, a relative concept which requires some basis for evaluation. Appropriate criteria for such an evaluation include efficiency and equity considerations, and also the maximum level of real resources likely to be committed for administering program provisions.

What makes UC program complexity a serious problem is that it results in a number of adverse impacts, including: (1) high payment error rates; (2) unequal treatment of claimants and employers who interact with the system under similar circumstances; (3) inefficiencies in administering program provisions; and (4) public misunderstanding and confusion that may weaken support for desirable program goals. In addition, complex program provisions necessarily place some discretionary power in the hands of state agency personnel who must interpret and administer such provisions in the numerous specific circumstances that arise. Some of the decisions made by different agency personnel under widely differing circumstances undoubtedly result in de facto policy decisions contrary to the legislative intent. Given these adverse impacts, and in light of any equity or other benefits that existing levels of complexity are believed to produce, it is our judgment that the present UC system is unduly complex.

The existing level of UC system complexity can be traced to a number of factors. Partly, it reflects the results of a multitude of political compromises made over the past half century at both the federal and state levels to accommodate the conflicting interests of employers and workers. Complexity also can be traced to a number of federal requirements imposed on state UC programs, partly as a result of certain judicial decisions (some of which are discussed in chapter 5). Other causes of existing complexity reflect attempts by legislators and UC administrative agencies to make subtle distinctions about particular claimant circumstances. Complexity also has resulted from the increasing emphasis in recent years on ''legalism'' in the administrative procedures of social programs and on ensuring due process for social program participants, partly as a result of federal and state court decisions. The evolution of UC program complexity is an interesting topic in itself, and one that has been dealt with by Haber and Murray as well as Rubin.[1] The purpose here, however, is to analyze the implications of and responses to system complexity.

There are three obvious approaches for dealing with the adverse effects of program complexity: increase the resources for administering the existing UC system; reduce the level of complexity within the current system; or devise better methods for administering existing (or reduced) levels of complexity. Because it does not appear that substantially increased administrative funding would be either feasible or cost effective, only the latter two responses to program complexity are analyzed in this chapter.

The chapter is organized as follows. First, evidence that the existing system is a complex one is presented. Second, some major impacts and implications of that complexity are briefly

---

1. Haber and Murray (1966) and Rubin (1983).

discussed. Then, some possible responses to those impacts are considered. A conclusion completes the chapter.[2]

Evidence of System Complexity

The UC program is generally complex with regard to benefit eligibility determinations. This section provides a few illustrations of such complexity, including: (1) a simple flowchart of the UC eligibility determination process; (2) an example of the written guidelines many states use in attempting to concretely define UC law/policy in the large variety of different situations that arise in determining claimant eligibility for benefits; (3) the complexities added to the UC system by federal laws, standards and programs; and (4) the time required to verify the eligibility of claimants for benefits.

UC Eligibility Criteria Overview

The UC system is designed to provide benefits to workers who have recent work experience, who become unemployed through no fault of their own, who are able to work, who are currently unemployed, and who are available for employment. All state systems have eligibility criteria that can be grouped into three basic categories: (1) monetary requirements that specify a minimum level and acceptable pattern of earnings (or employment) prior to unemployment; (2) job separation requirements that specify acceptable reasons for leaving prior jobs; and (3) current unemployment, ability-to-work and availability-for-work requirements that specify the weekly conditions under which workers are entitled to continue receiving support. Although the details included in state systems for each of these three categories vary substantially, the categories provide a useful framework for reviewing general UC system eligibility criteria.[3]

---

2. We are indebted to Saul J. Blaustein (1986) and H. Allan Hunt of the W.E. Upjohn Institute for substantial assistance in clarifying the issues and organizing the discussion in this chapter.
3. See The National Foundation for Unemployment Compensation & Workers' Compensation

42 CHAPTER 3

Analysis of just the main UC eligibility concepts mentioned in the three categories above could be quite complicated, but particular state provisions actually involve many additional issues that must be addressed in applying these concepts. The flowchart presented in figure 3–1 provides a simplified illustration of the specific provisions of claimant eligibility criteria that are quite typical of the major features of most state programs. The issues involved in processing particular cases often would be much more complicated still.[4]

Monetary Eligibility. All states require that claimants meet certain minimums for earnings or employment in order to be eligible for benefits. A major rationale for such requirements is that UC benefits are intended only for unemployed persons who have demonstrated adequate work attachment in terms of employment in the recent past. The specific requirements vary considerably among the states, but generally involve steps 1–4 in figure 3–1. In some cases, particularly for claimants who have only one employer in their base periods and who file in quarterly wage-report states (where wages are routinely reported to the state UC agency by employers), the entire monetary determination process can be a relatively simple one.

Even the conceptually simple monetary determination process can result in errors for a variety of reasons, however. Errors can arise, for example, in determining whether a particular job actually involved employment and earnings covered by a state's law. Also, errors in entering either claimant social security numbers or wage/employment credits by employers or agency personnel can result in payment errors. Multiple employers for individual claimants obviously contribute to the complexity of accurately determining monetary eligibility to some extent. Given that millions of wage items are processed annually by even relatively small states, some data entry errors would be expected even in states with meticulous data verification

---

(1985c or 1986a) for a very convenient and annually updated reference for comparing various eligibility provisions among the states.

4. For example, the administrator of Arizona's UC program has strongly emphasized how simplified figure 3–1 is in terms of reflecting all of the potential issues in processing claimants in Arizona. See Vaughn (1985).

FIGURE 3 - 1

**SIMPLIFIED FLOWCHART OF CLAIMANT INTERACTIONS
WITH ARIZONA'S UMEMPLOYMENT COMPENSATION PROGRAM**

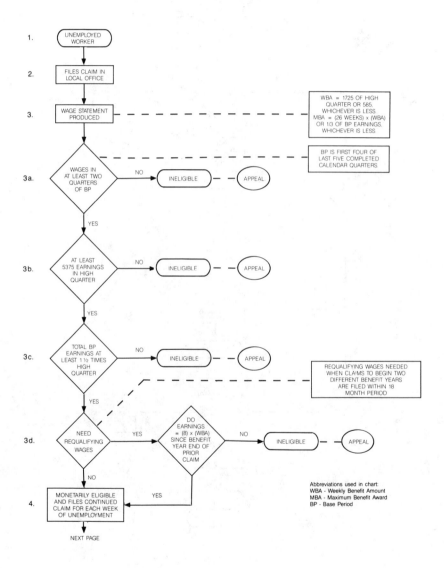

Figure 3-1 (continued)

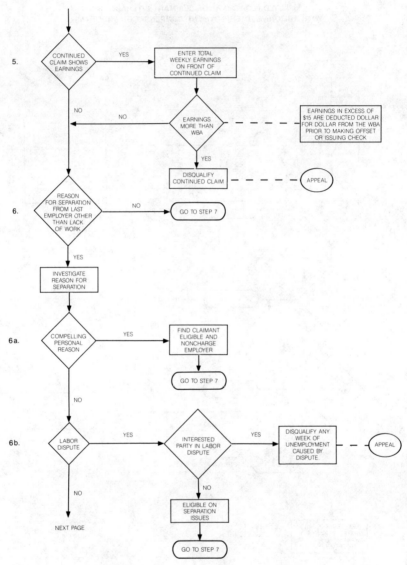

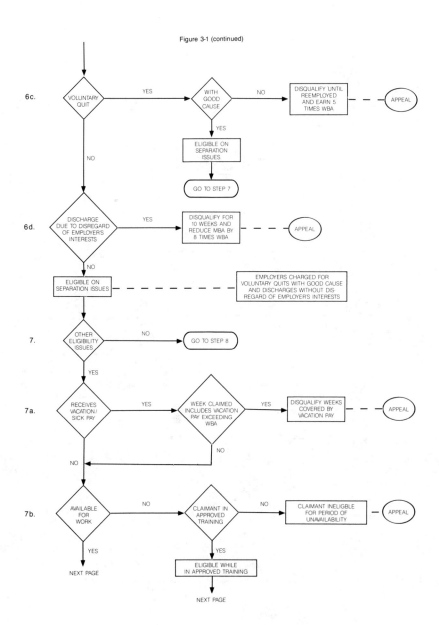

Figure 3-1 (continued)

Figure 3-1 (continued)

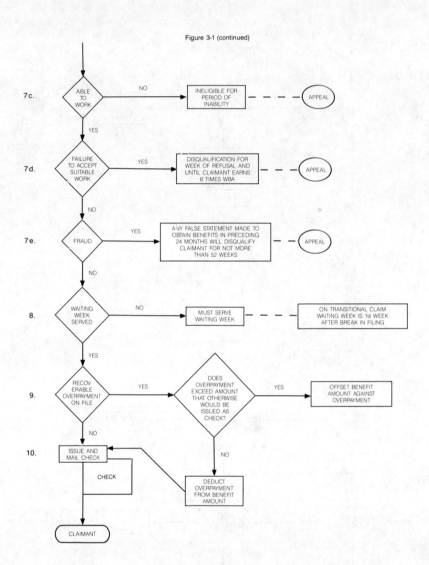

Source: Adapted for Anderson et al. (1977) The specific provisions in this
flowchart were included in Arizona's law as of June, 1977.

procedures.[5] In addition, wage-reporting errors may result from complex reporting forms.[6] Because of the difficulty of accurately determining benefit amounts in a timely manner for claimants in states with wage-request (rather than wage-report) systems, higher monetary determination error rates would be expected in these states; consistent with this expectation, the one wage-request state included in the B-K-S study had a much higher monetary determination error rate than any of the other four states.[7] As another example, an inconsistency was found in one of the B-K-S study states which required employers to report wages *when paid* but required benefit determinations to be based on wages *when earned*.[8]

The brief discussion above indicates that even the potentially simple process of determining a claimant's monetary eligibility for benefits can entail a number of possible complexities which can result in either overpayments or underpayments. Some evidence about the frequency with which monetary errors occur is available from the B-K-S study. For example, the simple averages for weeks with monetary errors in the five statewide study populations are: 14.8 percent for errors in weekly benefit amounts; 18.9 percent for errors in maximum benefit awards; and 31.3 percent for errors in base period wages.[9] Although all of these errors clearly cannot be attributed to complexity,[10] their numbers might be reduced to some extent by reducing the complexity of the monetary determination process.

Job Separation Issues. A second general category of eligibility

---

5. For example, about 1.5 million UC wage items had to be processed in the relatively small state of Arizona in a recent year. See Vaughn (1985).

6. For example, Raymond Thorne, the Employment Division administrator for Oregon, believes that wage reporting errors may result from complex forms. As a result, Oregon has redesigned its wage-report forms to reduce such errors. Experience with these revised forms indicates that errors have been reduced. See Thorne (1985a and 1985b).

7. New Jersey was the only wage-request state included in the B-K-S study. It was found that 36.1 percent of the cases in New Jersey had incorrectly calculated weekly benefit amounts, compared to a simple average of 9.5 percent of the cases in the other four states. See Burgess, Kingston and St. Louis (1982: 49-50).

8. Burgess, Kingston and St. Louis (1982: 51-52). On the basis of these findings, Washington subsequently changed its law to rectify the inconsistency noted in the text.

9. Burgess, Kingston and St. Louis (1982: 49–50).

10. Special circumstances in both Washington and New Jersey accounted for the unusually high error rates found in those states.

criteria includes provisions intended to target benefit payments to persons who have become involuntarily unemployed through no fault of their own. In contrast with the relatively objective monetary eligibility determination, attempting to determine why workers have become unemployed is an elusive issue approached in most states by complicated criteria that can only be measured subjectively.[11] Although the general concept that UC recipients should be unemployed through no fault of their own is a relatively simple one, making the specific distinctions required to implement the concept is a difficult task. For persons unemployed for reasons other than a layoff due to lack of work, some additional review of job separation circumstances usually is required prior to the payment of UC benefits (see step 6 of figure 3-1). This review is designed to deal with the numerous exceptions which distinguish disqualifying and nondisqualifying separations from employment.

One example of the complexity of job separation issues is the seemingly simple concept of a voluntary quit. Most might agree that people who voluntarily quit their jobs should not be entitled to receive UC benefits, at least not immediately after they quit their jobs. However, even if agreement were reached on that concept, how would UC personnel determine the difference between a voluntary and an involuntary quit? Moreover, identifying voluntary quits necessarily raises the difficult issue of whether employees were forced to quit for "good cause" because of employer actions. What would constitute the difference between "good" causes and other causes in such cases (see step 6c of figure 3-1)? Obviously, the validity of a cause for quitting will depend on subjective judgments to some extent, even though state laws/policies attempt to distinguish between "good" and other causes for quitting. For example, some states pay benefits to workers who voluntarily quit their jobs if their actions were the result of compelling personal reasons (see step 6a of figure 3-1.)[12] In fact, as of January 1, 1985, most states

---

11. Packard (1972) provides a good discussion of these issues.

12. One of several such exceptions in Arizona was made for persons who were compelled to quit their jobs to accompany their spouses who were moving out of state to accept new employment. See Anderson et al. (1977: 13–14).

recognized some such exceptions to the general rule that a claimant who voluntarily quits a job is not entitled to receive UC benefits.[13]

Another dimension of the complexity in evaluating job separation circumstances is that workers who are discharged for "willful misconduct" or "disregard of an employer's interests" are not eligible for benefits (see step 6d of figure 3-1). Such issues can be particularly difficult to evaluate because of the difficulty of correctly identifying the elements that comprise willful misconduct. In fact, Packard contends that such issues represent the "most mysterious area" of unemployment compensation.[14]

Another example of a difficult job separation issue is provided by the labor dispute provisions that are contained in all state laws (see step 6b of figure 3-1). "Interested parties" to a labor dispute oftentimes are not entitled to receive UC benefits for any week of unemployment caused by the dispute. Although it might not seem to be a difficult matter to make the required determinations, substantial complexity actually could arise in determining who initiated the labor dispute, whether a particular claimant has a "direct interest" in a dispute and in deciding other issues that arise in adjudicating labor dispute issues.[15]

Weekly Eligibility Criteria. Assuming that a claimant were monetarily eligible for benefits and had become unemployed for a nondisqualifying reason, then a number of other criteria must be satisfied on a weekly basis in order to remain eligible for benefits. Included among these weekly requirements are provisions that are intended to ensure that claimants receive benefits only if they: (1) continue to remain unemployed (rather than become reemployed); (2) are available for work, including an active job search in most states; (3) are able to work; and (4) do not refuse offers of suitable employment. Each of these weekly eligibility requirements is briefly discussed below.

All states specify that during the week for which they claim

---

13. National Foundation for Unemployment Compensation & Workers' Compensation (1985: 55–58).
14. Packard (1972: 644).
15. See Anderson et al. (1977: 14) for a brief discussion of some of these issues.

benefits, claimants shall not have worked or, if they did have some limited employment, shall not have earned over a specified amount of wages (see step 5 of figure 3–1). All states allow for partial weekly benefits by reducing the full weekly benefit payable by a portion of any wages earned during the week.[16] To correctly enforce such provisions, it is necessary, on a *weekly basis*, to accurately: record the amount of any earnings reported by the claimant; apply the state formula to determine the amount of the deduction to be made from the full weekly benefit amount; and calculate the partial benefit payable, if any. The main difficulties involved in monitoring claimant compliance with weekly reporting criteria obviously relate to detecting earnings or employment, not to making the calculations necessary. However, detecting employment that claimants wish to conceal is an especially difficult task for the UC system, with the exception that unreported earnings in UC-covered employment can be detected easily through the postaudit procedures described in chapter 2.[17]

Another major requirement for weekly benefit eligibility in all states is that claimants be *available* for work (see step 7b in figure 3–1). Enforcing this requirement is one of the most difficult administrative tasks confronted by state programs,[18] because availability for employment depends largely on a claim-

---

16. The discussion in the text does not address the differential treatment accorded to claimants under a relatively new concept—work sharing—provided for in seven states (including Arizona) as of January 1985. Under such programs, claimants put on reduced hours (rather than on layoffs) by employers with reduced workloads may qualify for UC benefits to compensate for the hours lost. See National Foundation for Unemployment Compensation & Workers' Compensation (1985: 50-51).

17. Another issue that revolves around the unemployment v. employment issue is the treatment of vacation or sick pay that is received after a worker leaves his/her job (see step 7a in figure 3–1).

18. An extreme and somewhat bizarre, yet illuminating, example of the difficulties that can be involved in determining claimant availability is provided by the issues that arose during the more than five years that elapsed before the eligibility of an opera singer who resided in Arizona was finally settled. The issues involved in this case included: (1) her education and experience as an opera singer over an eight-year period; (2) how and where she practiced her voice lessons; (3) whether she was qualified for lead roles or supporting roles; (4) whether the appropriate worksearch area for her was local or international; (5) her attempts to find work in Spain, Germany and elsewhere in Europe; (6) her auditions before a leading conductor in the United States and for an opera company in her local community; (7) the agencies where she was registered for work; and (8) her access to transportation for finding work. See Arizona Department of Economic Security (1982).

ant's state of mind. As a result, a variety of provisions designed to test claimant availability for work are included in state programs. For example, all states require that most claimants register with state Job Service offices as one determinant of availability for work.[19] In addition, as of 1985, an active job search requirement was included in the UC laws of 40 states as a test of claimant availability for work,[20] but this provision is extremely difficult to administer. As noted in chapter 2, the major source of overpayments found in both the K-B and B-K-S studies was the failure of claimants to satisfy active search/availability requirements, and there can be little doubt that the complexity involved in defining and enforcing these requirements is an important contributor to such overpayments. Moreover, certain adverse incentives contained in state laws/policies also contribute to the difficulty of enforcing availability/search requirements. In fact, this latter issue is such a major one that it is dealt with in considerable detail in chapter 7.

Another requirement for weekly benefit eligibility is that claimants be able to work (see step 7c of figure 3–1). Although this requirement may be somewhat easier to administer than the availability requirements just discussed, a number of fairly complicated issues still may arise in particular cases.[21] For example, questions may arise with respect to the nature of the work the claimant is expected to perform. Some states require that claimants be able to perform "suitable" work, but the nature of potential employment is not specified in other states. Other dimensions of the ability issue may relate to whether work is full time or part time, whether certain health-related restrictions are relevant and whether claimants are considered able to work

19. Even the apparently simple concept of Job Service registration involves a number of potential exceptions in applying this requirement. For example, union members who seek work solely through hiring halls often are excused from Job Service registration. Similarly, workers on short-term layoffs with definite recall dates normally are excused from Job Service registration. There are many other potential exceptions. Including the various possibilities involved in this issue in figure 3–1 would result in adding several decision points to the flowchart, emphasizing the point that figure 3–1 is an extremely simplified overview of the decisions actually involved.

20. U.S. Department of Labor (1985a: Table 400). Some of the states without a statuatory worksearch requirement, however, included this criterion in their Benefit Policy Rules (e.g., Arizona).

21. For a good discussion of some of these issues, see Roche (1973: 77–79).

during illnesses or disabilities. In short, ability-to-work provisions can be much more complex to administer than might appear to be the case.

Consistent with the philosophy of paying benefits only to involuntarily unemployed individuals, all states require disqualifications for claimants who refuse to accept "suitable work without good cause." Moreover, because such a disqualification is viewed as a serious matter, the penalties imposed for refusing suitable work typically are quite substantial and may include benefit postponements, benefit reductions and requirements that claimants first work and earn given amounts before receiving future UC benefits.[22] Although the rationale for imposing fairly substantial penalties for refusing suitable work can be easily understood, it actually can be quite difficult to determine precisely what constitutes an offer of suitable work. For example, in some states, a disqualification for a refusal of suitable work could not be established without first showing that a job offer was "outright, unequivocal and genuine."[23] A few of the other factors that may be involved in the concept of suitable work include: how a job affects the health and safety of a worker; how long an individual has been unemployed; whether the claimant has voluntarily left or previously refused a similar position; the wages, hours and potential employment duration of the job; and the job requirements as they relate to a claimant's education and job experience.[24] As a result, determining whether a claimant has refused suitable work often becomes a complex and subjective process.[25]

A claimant who meets all of the eligibility criteria in steps 1-7 of figure 3-1 would be eligible for one week of UC support. However, as indicated in step 8 of figure 3-1, an Arizona claimant served a "waiting week," the first week of unemployment for which no UC benefits were paid but in which all

---

22. For a summary of state disqualification penalties, see National Foundation for Unemployment Compensation & Workers' Compensation (1985c: 62–64).

23. Arizona Department of Economic Security (n.d.: Section 533330).

24. See for example Felder (1979: 12) and Arizona Department of Economic Security (n.d.: Article 53).

25. Roche (1973: 74).

eligibility criteria were satisfied. Such a waiting period was included in the laws of 43 states as of January 1985.[26] It also should be noted that, once a claimant meets all of the criteria for actually receiving a payment in most states, either a portion or all of the weekly UC benefit amount that otherwise would be paid could be used to offset any recoverable overpayments owed by the claimant (step 9 in figure 3-1).[27] Otherwise, a check would be issued to the claimant (step 10).

Claimant Appeals of Adverse Decisions. The Social Security Act requires all states to make available fair hearings for appeals by persons whose claims for benefits are denied.[28] Claimants are entitled to appeal adverse decisions at various points in the eligibility determination process. Although a system of appealing adverse decisions obviously is a desirable feature of any social payment system, it necessarily adds to UC program complexity, particularly given the possibility that appeal decisions may conflict with general practice within the operational UC payment system. As shown in figure 3-1, the possibilities for claimants to appeal adverse decisions add many possible "detours" to the process. Moreover, although not shown in figure 3-1 because of its focus on claimant interactions with the UC system, employers also can appeal adverse decisions at several of the points. The process of obtaining a final appeal decision may last for years because of the built-in complexities and delays, particularly if formal court proceedings become involved.

Conclusions. The above summary indicates the significance of complexity in the UC program. With perhaps a few technical exceptions, the separation and monetary eligibility issues in steps 1-4 and 6 (and waiting-week provisions in step 8) of figure 3-1 must be reviewed only once for one benefit year or for a single

---

26. National Foundation for Unemployment Compensation & Workers' Compensation (1985c: 43).

27. State agencies distinguish between recoverable overpayments subject to repayment by claimants who receive them and nonrecoverable overpayments that are not subject to such repayment. Overpayments that result from administrative errors by UC agency personnel typically would be included in the latter category.

28. For a good discussion of the fair hearing provision contained in the Social Security Act, including the minimum due process safeguards required, see Rubin (1983: 50-54).

spell of compensated unemployment. However, the eligibility criteria in steps 5 and 7 (and overpayment offsets in step 9) must be evaluated for each week of compensated unemployment claimed. Moreover, it should be emphasized again that correctly adjudicating many of the individual steps can be an extremely complex and subjective process and may involve disagreements even among well-trained personnel.

Written Guidelines For Interpreting Eligibility Criteria

A second illustration of the complexity of UC eligibility criteria is provided by a review of the written guidelines many states utilize to provide specific interpretations of the general provisions of their state laws for personnel who must evaluate eligibility issues. As indicated by the discussion in the prior section, the potential number of issues and circumstances for inclusion in such guidelines is extremely large. So many subtle variations can arise in applying typical state laws/policies that it would be nearly impossible to account for all possibilities, even in such guidelines. Nonetheless, the alternative to providing detailed guidelines likely is a situation in which many of the hundreds or thousands of ad hoc decisions made each day by UC personnel would be mutually inconsistent and sometimes contrary to law or UC agency policy.

An examination of the actual guidelines for particular states illustrates further the UC program's complexity. As an example, the topical content and extensive detail of selected portions of the written guidelines for interpreting Arizona's eligibility criteria during the 1979-1980 K-B study period are shown in table 3-1. The five major eligibility issues included in this table—voluntary leaving, misconduct, able/available, refusal of work and labor disputes—involved 79 major sections, 147 subsections and 148 pages of text in Arizona's manual of "benefit policy rules" or BPR manual.

A simple listing of the main section and selected subsection titles from Arizona's BPR manual for just one of the eligibility issues—voluntary leaving—includes 7 major sections: termination of employment; time; union relations; voluntary; wages; definition of work; and working conditions. The following nine

TABLE 3–1
Selected Portions of Written Guidelines for Interpreting
Arizona's Eligibility Criteria During K-B Study Period

Topic	Number of Major Sections	Number of Subsections	Number of Text Pages
Voluntary Leaving	7	31	45
Misconduct	19	44	29
Able/Available	25	30	38
Refusal of Work	17	24	20
Labor Disputes	11	18	16
Totals	79	147	148

Source: Arizona Department of Economic Security (n.d.).

subsections are included to further define the major section on time: general; days of week; hours; irregular employment; layoff imminent; leave of absence or holiday; overtime; part-time work; and shift-work. Even within each of these time subsections, further detail occurs as illustrated by the following five categories included in the subsection for hours: general; irregular hours; long or short hours; night work; and prevailing standards. The large number of items involved in such apparently simple concepts illustrates the complexity that arises in attempting to precisely specify how general provisions of UC law are to be administered. Regardless of whether states have written guidelines, there can be little doubt that such complexity is a characteristic of most, if not all, state systems.

Federal Laws, Standards, and Programs

The federal element of the UC system also adds to the complexity of the program in each state. As Rubin notes in a recent analysis of the federal-state relationship, Congress has adopted a diverse set of federal standards, which reflect no consistency in terms of underlying principles.[29] In fact, the federal standards that have resulted from the original Social Security Act plus the more than 40 subsequent pieces of federal legislation, summarized in the appendix to this chapter, have

29. Rubin (1983: 20).

affected the unemployment compensation program in a variety of ways. The end result has been a complex array of federal standards, and effective state enforcement of many of them probably could not be realistically expected by even the most zealous advocate of federal standards. Explaining the content and administration of these federal standards is such a complex undertaking that it comprises 102 pages of Rubin's extensive analysis of the federal-state UC relationship.[30]

One illustration of the complexity created by federal standards at the state level is the instructions USDOL produced as guidance to states on how to administer the worksearch requirements revised by Congress for the federal-state shared Extended Benefit program:

> Section 202(a)(3)(C) defines "suitable work" for the purposes of those provisions as meaning any work within the unemployed individual's capabilities. There is an exception to the determination of work's suitability as so defined; however, if the individual's prospects for obtaining work in his customary occupation "within a reasonably short period" are good, in which case suitability will be determined under provisions of the State law applicable to regular benefit claimants.
>
> In GAL 21-81 and UIPL 14-81, the recommendation was made that the prospects for obtaining work in an individual's customary occupation be determined with reference to a period not exceeding four weeks beginning with the first week for which extended benefits are claimed. If classified as having good prospects but they are not realized by the end of the period specified as reasonably short, the individual's prospects may be determined again with respect to an additional reasonably short period. In Change 2 to UIPL 14-81, the recommendation was replaced by a requirement that the period not exceed four weeks.
>
> Experience with administration of the "suitable work" provisions of Section 202(a)(3)(C) of SESAs for over a year has indicated the desirability of allowing States to determine the meaning of the phrase "a reasonably short period" flexibly in the

---

30. Rubin (1983: 69–170).

context of their respective patterns of employment and unemployment during particular economic cycles. Accordingly, "a reasonably short period" will be, for these purposes, the number of weeks specified by or pursuant to State law in the extended benefit eligibility period applicable to each claimant. We continue to recommend that the period be limited to four weeks beginning with the first week for which extended benefits are claimed. Such a limitation will no longer be deemed a requirement, however.

The foregoing relaxation of the period established for determining whether an individual's prospects for obtaining work in his customary occupation are good does not constitute an exemption from the requirement to make such a determination in every case. It merely allows flexibility in determining the length of the period that may be considered "reasonably short" for purposes of Section 202(a)(3)(C). In addition, when an issue arises with respect to failure to apply for or to accept an offer of suitable work, an appealable determination must be made of the correctness of the classification of the individual's job prospects as good or not good. Whatever the classification, it continues to have an impact on the determination with respect to failure to "actively engage in seeking work" in Section 202(a)(3)(A).

Under Section 202(a)(6) these same requirements apply with respect to regular benefits for which the State may be entitled to claim Federal sharing in the costs. This change of position does not affect other modifications to UIPL 14-81 announced in Change 2.[31]

These detailed instructions are cited at length to convey some sense of the difficulties that state programs are likely to have in following federal guidelines.[32]

A significant aspect of the impact of federal intervention on state programs is that it has become increasingly frequent in recent years. One indication of this trend is provided in the summary of federal legislation contained in the appendix to this chapter. Dur-

---

31. U.S. Department of Labor (1982b). It perhaps should be noted that Golding (1985) contends this is a worst-case example of the complexity created by federal standards.

32. A second illustration is provided by the nearly 30 pages of instructions issued by the Unemployment Insurance Service to implement congressionally mandated restrictions on paying benefits to certain aliens. See Rubin (1983: 86–88).

ing the first quarter of a century after enactment of the Social Security Act (through 1959): (1) only 14 major pieces of legislation directly affecting the UC system were passed; (2) less than one page is required to summarize the major changes included in the laws enacted; and (3) five of the 14 laws enacted can be primarily attributed to either wartime impacts or to providing benefits to veterans. In contrast, during the second quarter of a century after the enactment of the Social Security Act (1960-1984): (1) more than 30 major pieces of federal legislation that directly affected the UC system were passed; (2) over two pages are required to summarize the major changes included in the laws enacted; (3) only one of the more than 30 laws can be primarily attributed to wartime impacts or to providing benefits to veterans; and (4) during just the years from 1980 through 1984, 13 separate pieces of federal legislation were enacted (only one fewer than the number enacted during the first quarter century of the program), and these acts alone require over a page to summarize. It should be noted that the U.S. Department of Labor (USDOL) also recognizes the increasing impact of federal legislation on state UC programs. For example, USDOL estimated in February 1985 that 77 changes in federal law since 1981 have resulted in an approximate total of 2,000 changes in the laws of the 53 UC jurisdictions.[33]

In addition to paying regular claims covered by its own law/policy and dealing with the federal standards just discussed, each state also has the responsibility of paying benefits under various federal programs, including permanent federal programs established for ex-armed forces personnel (the UCX program) and for other former federal employees (the UCFE program). The states also have paid benefits under numerous other federal programs, including the federal-state shared Extended Benefit (EB) program permanently enacted in 1970 and the Federal Supplemental Compensation (FSC) program that expired in March 1985.[34] Complexity is increased by these additional

---

33. O'Keefe (1985:4).

34. Examples of other programs include the Trade Adjustment Assistance and Special Unemployment Assistance programs. These and several other programs are referenced in the summary of federal legislation in the appendix to this chapter.

programs because certain eligibility provisions in them differ from those in regular state programs. The complexity created by attempting to administer federal programs and initiatives (only a few of which are mentioned above), combined with relatively limited administrative funding levels, adds to the possibility of payment errors both in these additional programs and in regular state programs.[35]

Time Required for Eligibility Verifications

Perhaps the most striking indication of the effects of UC program complexities is the average time required in both the K-B and B-K-S studies to determine as fully as possible whether one claimant was eligible for a single week of compensated unemployment. An average claim took somewhere between 8 and 13 hours of *direct case time* to complete in these two special studies. As noted in chapter 2, typical case loads for personnel routinely processing continued claims in the operational UC system probably would be at least 50 times the case loads assigned to UC personnel in these special studies.[36] Even given the intensive verifications involved in the K-B and B-K-S studies, some payment errors were likely not detected in those studies. Thus, it hardly is surprising that UC agency personnel frequently make payment errors in processing claims, given the time constraints under which they must operate.

Some Impacts and Implications of Complexity

Many adverse consequences of existing UC system complexity were neither intended nor anticipated by policymakers or UC

---

35. Oregon's Employment Division administrator contends that the "overlay of complex, constantly changing" federal programs contributes to overpayments in both such federal programs and also in regular state programs. See Thorne (1985b).

36. It also should be noted that the case loads in the two special studies may tend to overstate the resource commitment required to ascertain a claimant's compliance with the criteria for a single week. The potential overstatement arises because a complete review of the original monetary determination and separation circumstances was a standard part of the investigation in these special studies, whereas compliance with only the weekly eligibility criteria would be assessed in routine processing.

program administrators. Nonetheless, these consequences do occur and merit serious consideration.

First, the complexity of the system means that it would be extremely costly to fully administer and completely verify claimant compliance with existing provisions. It seems neither socially desirable nor likely that administrative funding allocations will be increased sufficiently to provide for effective enforcement of existing UC program provisions. An obvious implication of this is less effective program administration than could be achieved in a less complex system.

A second consequence of existing complexity is that neither claimants nor UC program personnel know with certainty whether payments should be made in many cases because of uncertainties about the appropriate interpretation of existing requirements. Both the K-B and B-K-S studies found instances where trained experts within a particular state disagreed on the correct interpretation of particular cases.

A third result of system complexity is that higher payment error rates for both overpayments and underpayments are likely. Viewed in this light, the relatively high payment error rates found in the K-B and B-K-S studies certainly are not as unexpected as they might otherwise seem. Some payment errors clearly are inevitable because of incorrect interpretations of UC law/policy in complex cases. Given other system characteristics and administrative funding limitations, it would be expected that payment errors, which result from both accidental and intentional misreporting, would be more frequent in more complex systems. This expected impact on payment accuracy also has been emphasized by others familiar with the UC system. For example, Dunn and Griffin state:

> The key element in *effective control* over payments and other elements within the unemployment insurance system is adequate numbers of trained, properly supervised, permanent staff who are fully aware of the criteria which govern the establishment of eligibility, the determination of benefit rates, and the other elements which underlie the minimum requirements for unemployment insurance eligibility. The *complexity* of the program and

the factors which underlie determinations of eligibility mandate that the individuals have adequate training to attain the background necessary for this function. In most instances a minimum of six to twelve months is required before a claims examiner can be considered to be fully trained.[37] (emphasis added)

A fourth result of UC system complexity is that administrators and other "front-line" agency personnel may be either forced or permitted to exercise considerable discretion in interpreting legislative intent. These persons may respond to either perceived or real public and political pressures to alter the UC eligibility and payment process in certain ways. It is obvious that the subjective judgments resulting from this process cannot be made consistently across either all states (for federal laws/policies) or among all employees within a state (for state laws/policies). Inconsistencies almost necessarily will arise, both because of confusion and because of philosophical differences in interpreting complex criteria.[38] Moreover, it may well be that policymakers are not fully aware of the extent to which control of UC system policy is subject to administrative discretion necessarily exercised by UC personnel. An important result of a less complex system would be an increased likelihood that administrative outcomes would reflect the intentions of policymakers, rather than sometimes reflecting judgments made by UC program personnel.

A fifth result of such a complex UC system is that horizontal inequities are more likely. This effect is a further consequence of the discretion exercised by administrative personnel and the inconsistencies in their judgments. Employers and claimants who interact with the UC system under similar circumstances are not all accorded similar treatment in terms of the ultimate outcomes of those interactions. Such adverse impacts of program complexity also have been emphasized recently by Corson, Hershey, and Kerachsky.[39]

---

37. Dunn and Griffin (1984: 12–13).
38. Corson et al. (1986: 133–34) also emphasize the substantial discretion that can be exercised by agency personnel in the existing UC system.
39. Corson et al. (1986: 133–34).

A sixth impact of program complexity is that it reduces incentives for UC system participants to ensure claimant compliance with stated criteria because of the high costs involved in monitoring such compliance. It is reasonable to assume that state agency personnel are less motivated to prevent or detect overpayments because UC eligibility criteria may be perceived as too complex for effective or equitable enforcement. Also, claimants clearly would find it both more difficult and costly to engage in self-compliance efforts in a system with relatively complex provisions. Similarly, it seems reasonable to assume that the relatively high costs of attempting to monitor claimant compliance with relatively complex requirements tends to discourage employer monitoring efforts. In fact, incentives for UC system participants to engage in relatively little monitoring is such an important issue that it is dealt with in considerable detail in chapter 6.

A seventh potential impact of UC program complexity is much more speculative. Although no study has been conducted that would allow definitive conclusions, it seems likely that complexity has two opposite effects on the propensities of potential claimants to file for UC benefits.[40] On the one hand, complexity probably encourages some ineligible claimants to file claims because the capacity of the system to enforce its complex requirements is very limited. More generally, voluntary claimant compliance with stated criteria undoubtedly is reduced and claim filing by ineligible claimants probably is increased by perceptions that stated and effective eligibility criteria differ markedly. In contrast, it also seems reasonable that some potentially eligible claimants do not file for benefits because they are unwilling to incur the costs of interacting with a system as complex as the existing one.

---

40. It should be noted that USDOL has questioned the existence of this seventh impact, and also has suggested that substantive evidence should be provided on any such claim filing effects (see Golding 1985). Although anecdotal evidence may be found to support the existence of such claim filing effects, the studies required to document their existence and magnitudes have not yet been designed or conducted.

Responses to Effects of System Complexity

Effective treatment of the adverse consequences of program complexity is a difficult task. One approach would be to simply acknowledge and accept the consequences of administering a relatively complicated system with limited resources. Making the reasonable assumption that some measures to deal with UC system complexity should be undertaken, at least three general options appear to merit consideration. The first would be to provide a large increase in the resources devoted to administering the existing UC system (without simplifying that system). As noted earlier, however, the existing level of UC program complexity would require perhaps a fiftyfold increase in the time currently devoted to eligibility verification. Given competing claims for society's scarce resources, it appears to be a virtual certainty that such a large increase would not be considered acceptable. The more feasible alternatives would be to devise acceptable ways of reducing the complexity of the system and to develop better techniques for administering whatever level of complexity remains. Because these alternatives are both more feasible and more desirable in terms of both equity and efficiency considerations, they are the only possibilities discussed in the remainder of this chapter. The issue of designing and conducting pilot tests of proposals for either reduced complexity or improved administration also is discussed.

Reducing Program Complexity

The previous discussion of the system's existing complexity and its adverse consequences is intended to encourage consideration of acceptable methods of reducing that complexity. Although many policymakers and program administrators are at least partially aware of the program's complexity and its effects, it may prove to be extremely difficult to reduce that complexity.

Even with the goal of reducing system complexity, a number of difficult questions would remain about which program features should be changed. Certainly, simplicity per se should not be accepted as a necessarily desirable end result, independent of the benefits and costs of particular changes. For example, one of the costs of reducing the complexity of UC eligibility criteria is that some of the subtle distinctions in the current system would have to be removed; it is possible that policymakers may not be willing to incur the costs associated with the elimination of these distinctions. Such practical realities have caused several UC system experts to suggest that advocating program simplification may represent a naive, impossible dream.[41] Moreover, as one of them recently pointed out, merely recommending program simplification will not remove the public pressures—particularly by legislators and the courts—that have contributed to current system complexity.[42]

Reducing program complexity could either decrease or increase UC benefit outlays. Such cost considerations would be relevant in evaluating proposals for specific changes. Furthermore, changes implemented in some UC jurisdictions may not be appropriate for all others. Hence, the judgments required to evaluate the desirability of certain changes must be made by policymakers and others familiar with the state-specific circumstances in particular UC jurisdictions.

Contributions to reducing program complexity by both legislators and UC program administrators are briefly discussed below. However, a full benefit/cost evaluation has not been undertaken to assess the equity, claims filing or other impacts of such changes. Consequently, no judgments about the relative merits of these approaches are offered. The examples simply illustrate a few of the reductions in UC program complexity that could be considered.

Legislative Contributions. Contributions to a less complex system could be made by both federal and state legislative bodies. It would be helpful for both the Congress and state legislatures to carefully evaluate proposed programs and initiatives for their impacts on UC system complexity and administrative feasibility, particularly given the relatively limited administrative funding provided to state programs. Obviously, more

---

41. The difficulty of UC program simplification has been emphasized by a number of UC system experts, including Saul Blaustein and H. Allan Hunt of the W.E. Upjohn Institute, Carolyn Golding of USDOL, and Sally Ward of the Illinois Department of Employment Security.
42. Ward (1985).

complex programs are more expensive to administer effectively than less complex ones, other things equal. Hence, although legislated program complexity may not be inappropriate in the context of overall policy decisions,[43] administrative funding and the feasibility of proposed initiatives should be at least important considerations. For example, the guidelines for implementing congressionally-mandated EB worksearch requirements—discussed earlier in this chapter—suggest that program complexity and administrative feasibility/costs were accorded little or no weight in the decisions that led to the legislation. At the state level, reductions in the complexities of legal provisions, such as the elimination of the difference between wages reported by employers for tax purposes and the wages used for claimant benefit determinations, would be important in many instances. Elimination of dependents' allowances that require verification of family circumstances not otherwise related to the UC eligibility process also merits consideration by state legislators. Serious consideration also could be given to reducing the complexity of separation provisions and other features of UC eligibility criteria.

Administrative Contributions. Both USDOL and state program administrators also could make some contributions to reduced program complexity. At the federal level, the administrative funding process utilized by USDOL could be simplified substantially, as is discussed in detail in chapter 4. Also, USDOL could reduce the complexity of some of the guidelines issued to implement the legislative intent of the Congress.

State program administrators also have considerable administrative flexibility to reduce the complexity of policies and procedures they devise to implement state laws. Some states have found that complex reporting forms result in payment errors that could be reduced by appropriate state actions. Also, state administrative actions could lead to revisions of the benefit policy rules related to reasons for job separations. For example, the complexity of provisions for ''compelling personal reasons''

---

43. For example, Golding (1985) has suggested that existing complexity created at the federal level may well be justified in terms of the judgments made by presidential and congressional decisions through the years.

and perhaps other voluntary quit disqualification exceptions could be considered. As another example, administrative actions could be taken in some states to eliminate or otherwise modify the active search provisions devised to test claimant availability for work. This is discussed in much more detail in chapter 7.[44]

Improving Program Administration

Some degree of complexity is inevitable in any social payment system that does not simply provide benefits to any who apply as a matter of right. Even a UC system that reflected substantial reductions in current complexity probably could be significantly improved by developing more effective techniques for consistently applying law/policy within a given state.

Accordingly, it may be more important, in terms of improving the existing system, to consider how any given level of complexity could be more effectively administered than to focus just on reducing system complexity. Undoubtedly, many states could implement a variety of relatively minor operational improvements, but the focus in this section is on more general approaches. The general approach most strongly emphasized in this study is the provision of appropriate incentives for all UC system participants, but that issue is dealt with in detail in chapters 4 through 7. The approaches discussed in this chapter are: (1) clearly specifying legislative intent at the state level; (2) providing detailed, written guidelines to agency personnel for applying law/policy; (3) computerization of eligibility determinations; and (4) computerized profiles for targeting administrative resources on "high-risk" claimants.

Clarifying Legislative Intent. More clearly specifying the legislative intent of particular laws could facilitate improved administration in at least some states. In the absence of clear legislative intent, state UC program administrators are forced to determine what they believe the intent to be and to develop (often

---

44. In many states, active search requirements are administratively required as a test of availability provisions included in state laws. Accordingly, modification or elimination of the search requirement is mentioned in the text as an administrative change. However, in some states an active worksearch is specified in state laws.

complex) procedures for implementing it. This problem may be partially attributed to the fact that legislative intent at the state level often is not as clearly developed through extensive and documented hearings as is typical at the federal level. For example, one legal scholar contends:

> In applying disqualifications for voluntary leaving and misconduct, an effort is being made to find objective standards and proof in place of the apparent ambiguity and subjective tests of present statutes. In the process, courts and administrative agencies sometimes invent doctrines, presumptions and rules which ignore or exceed the legislative intent. The necessity for such inventiveness flows from the practical difficulty of processing and deciding numerous claims promptly, and from the dual role of the various administrative agencies to assist the unemployed in a time of need, yet to protect a limited fund from ineligible claimants so that an employer's reserve account is not unfairly charged. While the difficulty may not be desirable, it is one commonly found in the area of administrative law. The solution lies not in greater procedural formality, but rather in a return to the legislative intent and in demanding a minimum quantum of competent evidence before disallowing a claim. The main purpose of the legislative scheme, the integrity of the system itself and fairness to the unsophisticated claimant will thus be better served.[45]

Written Guidelines for Administering Law/Policy. A general suggestion that follows from the previous analysis of complexity would be for those states that do not currently have detailed, written instructions for administering UC law/policy to develop them. In order to facilitate the development of such guidelines, it also would be helpful to develop either a more detailed flowchart of UC law/policy than that provided in figure 3–1 or some similar device for summarizing law/policy in a particular state. A recent six-state study of eligibility decisions also has strongly emphasized the importance of providing written guidelines to increase the consistency of eligibility decisions. Corson, Hershey and Kerachsky state:

---

45. Packard (1972: 653–654).

The states we visited varied dramatically in the extent to which they made UI policies and procedures available in a clear, organized form, or even consistently recognized in more informal ways. . . . Not surprisingly, we found that in states that had more comprehensive and detailed written policy and procedures, the staff's understanding of state policy was more accurate and more consistent.

Detailed and specific policies tend to restrict the amount of discretion that can be exercised by claims staff in considering each claimant's case . . . .

However, detailed and specific program guidelines need not prompt claims staff to undertake unreasonable enforcement activities, and probably provide greater protection for claimants than do nebulous and unwritten rules . . . . In contrast, the lack of clearly written rules makes it more difficult for adjudicators to justify their decisions, and more difficult for claimants to understand the standards they must meet and to prepare arguments in their defense. *Agency adjudicators then apply unwritten standards which may be understood and interpreted quite differently by different adjudicators,* and leave claimants with no reasonable basis for predicting the relationship between their behavior and the adjudication outcome. In such circumstances, *high standards of due process may be difficult to achieve.*[46] (emphasis added)

The availability of detailed, written guidelines should also facilitate the benefit/cost analyses that would be appropriate for making decisions about which aspects of UC law or policy could be eliminated or simplified.

Computerizing Benefit Eligibility Determinations. Another way to increase consistency in applying UC law/policy and to reduce associated administrative costs would be for the states to increase the use of computers in making benefit eligibility determinations. Computerized monetary determinations already are a common feature of many state programs, but recent developments in computer software suggest that computer-assisted decisions could be made for other eligibility criteria as

---

46. Corson et al. (1986: 133–34).

well. This approach would involve the use of "expert systems" that have evolved from many years of research in the artificial intelligence area of computer science. Although no state UC agency has yet implemented such an approach, Nagy, DiSciullo and Crosslin completed an experimental study during 1983 that was funded by USDOL to explore the potential of such an approach for one "relatively simple" eligibility issue—labor disputes.[47] Even though their expert system for labor disputes has never been operationally implemented by any state agency, the results of their study and the use of expert systems for handling other, relatively complicated issues in other applications[48] show that such an approach holds considerable potential for the operational UC system. Because existing computer software programs clearly could be adapted for utilization in the UC system and because of the potential benefits of expert systems as a method of inexpensively improving UC program administration, some important implications of that study are discussed in considerable detail below.

In evaluating the expert system approach for UC eligibility decisions, Nagy, DiSciullo and Crosslin conclude that important advantages include: (1) the need for little or no retraining to account for policy changes implemented through changes in an expert system's program; (2) the ease of implementing policy changes; (3) the "common sense" of expert systems to ask only necessary questions and to follow efficient lines of questioning; (4) a reduction in the time required for making determinations (and a consequent increase in the timeliness with which they are made); (5) an increase in the consistency of determinations and a corresponding reduction in erroneous determinations (because

---

47. Nagy et al. (1983) provide an excellent discussion of the use of expert systems in the UC program, including how such systems have evolved from research on artificial intelligence. The discussion of expert systems in this section is based primarily on their study.

48. For example, expert systems are becoming fairly common in the private sector for handling complicated underwriting decisions that are required to assign risks and determine rates for various types of insurance coverage, as illustrated by the work of Decisions & Designs, Inc. of McClean, Virginia. As other examples, work has been undertaken on profiling both health cost containment and worker compensation risks. The interested reader may obtain additional information on this latter work by contacting the International Association of Accident Boards and Councils in Jackson, Mississippi; the National Council on Compensation Insurance in New York City; and Medstat Systems, Inc. in Ann Arbor, Michigan.

all determinations would be based on "the same knowledge base and inference mechanism"); (6) the possibility that existing technology is sufficient for expert systems to "reliably handle" between one-half and four-fifths of nonmonetary adjudications; (7) largely as a reflection of the above advantages, reduced costs of making nonmonetary determinations; and (8) an overall improvement in the service claimants receive.[49]

The essence of utilizing (computerized) expert systems can be easily understood in terms of how human experts currently make decisions on whether particular claimants are eligible for UC support. Under ideal circumstances, highly trained individuals gather facts about particular cases, sift through the evidence, and then draw upon their knowledge of UC law/policy to determine whether claimants are eligible for benefits. Unfortunately, the staff with the training and experience required to make such decisions often is so small, relative to the number of decisions that must be made, that many decisions actually are made by persons with less training and experience than that necessary to obtain accurate decisions. If equipped with expert system technology, however, relatively inexperienced staff should be able to make better decisions than are often made under the present system about whether claims should be paid, denied or referred for further evaluation by human experts.

In order to develop the computer-assisted approach outlined above, it would be necessary to develop a sequence of questions to cover most (ideally, all) possible situations relevant to each eligibility criterion. The detailed written guidelines suggested in the prior section probably would be a necessary input into the process of developing the required questions. Also, it should be noted that the less complex the eligibility criteria, the easier it would be to develop the required questions.

Eligibility determinations from an expert system would be based on responses to questions input (by trained clerks, rather than eligibility adjudicators) through a computerized, interactive question-answer process. The inference mechanism of the expert system would be able to sort cases into three categories: (1) those

---

49. Nagy et al. (1983: 75, 78, 80, 82, 91, 92 and 93).

in which the issues involved exceed the capabilities of the (computer) expert system and should be referred to human experts for adjudication; (2) those in which the claimant is eligible to receive benefits for the week in question; or (3) those in which the claimant is not eligible for benefits. For those eligible for benefits, the preparation of a check could be triggered by the expert system. In contrast, claimants identified as ineligible for benefits would receive a computer-generated eligibility determination that would provide the facts, reasoning, conclusions and documentation involved in the determination. If UC eligibility criteria were sufficiently simplified, then the number of cases in category 1 probably would be relatively small, given the current state of expert-system technology.

The above discussion indicates the potential benefits of applying expert systems for at least some UC eligibility criteria in experimental, if not operational, settings. Assuming further experience with this approach proved to be at least as positive as the conclusions reached by Nagy, DiSciullo and Crosslin, expert systems could represent an important source of improvement for the existing UC system. The initial explorations of implementing expert systems in an operational setting reported by the states of Nevada and Utah are encouraging.[50]

Computerized Profiles for Targeting Administrative Resources. Another application of computerized technology to facilitate administration of eligibility determinations would be to develop claimant screening profiles for use in targeting compliance verification. Such an approach might distinguish between "high-risk" and "low-risk" claimants, so that administrative resources could be focused on the high-risk group exclusively. The low-risk group might be processed and paid almost solely on the basis of claimant certifications. Screening profiles also might be used for determining which claimants to routinely process through the computerized expert system and which claimants to review more frequently by other methods. In any case, the thrust

---

50. Hanna (1985) reports that the Region IX Office of USDOL and the state of Nevada are continuing their attempts to obtain funding for an operational feasibility study of the expert-system approach. Also, the state of Utah has explored the possibility of implementing an expert-system approach for some eligibility determinations.

of implementing computerized profiling would be to more effectively use administrative resources both to prevent and detect overpayments.

A number of issues arise in considering the technical and administrative potential of computerized profiling. Most of these are dealt with extensively in chapters 6 and 7 and elsewhere.[51] However, it may be noted that the critical technical issue in this regard is whether high-risk and low-risk claimants can be effectively identified by analyzing differences in characteristics between claimants with and without overpayments from historical data taken from the intensive eligibility verifications conducted in the Random Audit or Quality Control programs.[52] If the overpaid and properly paid groups of claimants within a particular state differ substantially with respect to certain labor market or demographic characteristics, it then would be possible to develop a screening profile (on the basis of historical data) to identify claimants with relatively high overpayment likelihoods in that state. In this regard, Kingston and Burgess noted recently that experimental results for five states indicate that:

> The development and use of statistical profiles, on the other hand, appears to be a technically feasible approach that could significantly improve the allocation of UC program administrative resources. This approach would require no increase in the (real) level of resources devoted to UC program administration and could be implemented with existing or revised eligibility criteria. Furthermore, increased claimant self-compliance with UC eligibility criteria would be induced. Also, the technical feasibility of utilizing such profiles on an operational basis has been greatly enhanced by the availability of Random Audit program data in most states, and by the availability of Quality Control program data in all states, starting in April 1986.

---

51. In addition to the discussion in chapters 6 and 7, see Burgess, Kingston, St. Louis and DePippo (1983); Kingston and Burgess (1986); Porterfield, St. Louis, Burgess and Kingston (1980); and St. Louis, Burgess and Kingston (1986).

52. The development of such profiles should not be based on routine operational data because such data (incorrectly) include many claimants who actually receive overpayments in the group considered to be properly paid. Thus, accurate screening profiles cannot be developed from such data. See Burgess, Kingston, St. Louis and DePippo (1983) for a discussion of this issue.

Notwithstanding these considerations, statistical profiling has received very little consideration to date. The rather limited profiling efforts analyzed in this paper, however, illustrate the potential contributions of such an approach.

It seems quite certain that futher estimation efforts, based on either Random Audit or Quality Control program data, would result in more powerful statistical profiles than those discussed in this paper. Hence, further investigation of this approach appears warranted.[53]

Nonetheless, it should be emphasized that most of the work in this area to date relates to availability/worksearch issues or to unreported earnings. It remains an open question whether statistical profiles also might be effective for other eligibility issues.

Pilot Tests

A systems approach is important in devising and evaluating responses to the problems analyzed throughout this study, including the adverse effects of complexity addressed in this chapter. The importance of such an approach arises from the interactive nature of the various components and relationships that comprise the existing UC system. The interrelationships within the system mean that even apparently plausible responses to particular problems, such as complex eligibility criteria, may result in unintended and undesirable side effects. As a result, it is difficult to overemphasize the importance of further research and experimental pilot studies for assessing the overall costs and benefits of particular responses to system problems.

Given existing federal-state relationships, administrative funding arrangements, and the lack of well trained research personnel in some state agencies, there obviously is an important leadership role for USDOL in supporting and encouraging pilot studies to assess approaches for reducing program complexity and improving program administration. USDOL-supported pilot tests appear to be particularly appropriate because many of the approaches that might be considered in a particular state could be

---

53. Kingston and Burgess (1986: 40).

relevant for many other state programs as well. Conducting pilot programs for small sets of states could avoid the expensive duplication of pitfalls that are almost inevitable in applying new procedures and would provide valuable insights and refinements for all states.

Although USDOL leadership in promoting pilot studies is vital, states must also take lead roles in identifying and operating appropriate pilot studies, since most changes would have to be implemented by the states themselves. Also, individual states or groups of states probably will want to explore some possible changes not included in whatever research effort may be initiated by USDOL for the UC system as a whole. Individual state analyses of data available from the Random Audit and Quality Control programs, as well as from other sources, undoubtedly would provide valuable guidance in determining: the further research and pilot tests that might be useful; the desirability of possible reductions in the complexity of UC provisions and administrative procedures; and the desirability of suggestions for improved administration. In short, the individual states necessarily will play a critical role in designing and evaluating most of the important changes that might be made in the existing UC system. Moreover, interstate cooperation in such efforts—through the Interstate Conference of Employment Security Agencies, other organizations or smaller groups of states with similar problems or interested in similar issues—would greatly facilitate responses to the issues discussed in this chapter.

Although efforts to analyze, test, and evaluate the various kinds of responses to the adverse effects of program complexity might seem very difficult, some extremely encouraging progress has been made in these areas, including the following three developments: (1) USDOL provision of specific guidelines, as part of the recently implemented Quality Control program, for evaluating and funding special studies that state agencies may wish to conduct; (2) the start of a study entitled the "Quality Improvement Project" undertaken in a number of western states; and (3) the initiation of the "Quality Unemployment Insurance Project" by a consortium of state agencies and the authors.

Although some of these projects have other objectives, they also represent attempts to reduce program complexity or to improve administrative effectiveness. A very brief overview is provided below of some major features of each of these developments, with no attempt to summarize their entire scope.

USDOL Guidelines for Special Studies. USDOL issued formal guidelines to the states in April 1986 for the preparation of funding proposals for special studies within the context of the Quality Control program.[54] Funding for special studies under these guidelines is a potentially important step towards a broader pilot test effort that could contribute to a significantly improved program. It also appears, however, that these guidelines are somewhat restrictive in scope in that the emphasis clearly is on various approaches to conducting the Quality Control program, rather than on encouraging studies designed to improve the UC system itself. Obviously, fundamental UC system improvement is more likely to result from the latter types of studies. In addition, there is room for less rigorous studies designed for the diagnosis and correction of selected problems in particular states. It is hoped that USDOL will expand its guidelines in light of these considerations in order to encourage pilot studies related to a broad range of possible program improvements. Such an expansion could represent a very important addition to the initiative already taken by USDOL.

Quality Improvement Project. The Quality Improvement Project was initiated in 1985 by USDOL's regional office in Seattle and the States of Alaska, Idaho, Oregon and Washington. Its purposes include identifying benefit payment error sources, why errors occur and whether such errors can be corrected at a reasonable cost.[55] The project emphasizes various agency data sources—including Random Audit (and Quality Control) data, routine benefit payment control information and the results of local office quality reviews—for identifying potential payment errors. The project seeks specifically to determine whether particular errors are symptomatic of general system weaknesses,

---

54. U.S. Department of Labor (1986b).
55. Johnson (1985).

and to carefully evaluate the costs of corrective actions against the anticipated benefits of those actions. Based on this analysis, priorities can be suggested to rank the importance of various changes that might be considered.

Quality Unemployment Insurance Project. The Quality Unemployment Insurance Project (QUIP) was initiated in August 1985 by the authors and the following 10 state employment securities agencies—Arizona, Illinois, Louisiana, Missouri, New Jersey, New York, North Dakota, Oklahoma, Pennsylvania and Utah. Alaska joined the QUIP consortium in August 1986. Except for Arizona and Louisiana, these QUIP states have continued to work as a group on UC program improvements during 1987. The project was designed to provide a forum for analyzing system problems and exchanging ideas on how each state might improve its UC system, particularly given severe funding constraints in recent years. The importance of the project relates to the efforts of these states to either reduce program complexity or to improve law, policy and administrative procedures. Most of the participating states have formed task forces or work groups of key agency personnel to assess possible system weaknesses and to evaluate various possibilities for law/policy changes or improved administrative procedures. As part of this process, each state has conducted case-by-case analyses of the Random Audit or Quality Control cases it has processed to identify any general patterns or system weaknesses that may suggest the need for corrective actions. No attempt is made to catalog the large number of specific findings and actions taken by the QUIP states, but some are particularly consistent with the types of complexity responses suggested earlier in this chapter. The following few examples will serve to illustrate some findings and responses of these QUIP states:

1. Reducing program complexity or improving administration requires detailed analyses of existing procedures, policies and problems. Although all states have undertaken some analyses, the flowcharting of law/policy by New York and the detailed, computerized analysis of Random Audit cases by Pennsylvania

illustrate the suggestions in this chapter for pinpointing potential problems.

2. Several states have addressed the worksearch issue during the QUIP project. Missouri's special study of claimants, employers and local office personnel found considerable confusion about the precise nature of this requirement. Missouri found that employers strongly favored *verifiable* search efforts by claimants, but the employers also conceded that it was difficult to suggest concrete guidelines that were administratively feasible, and they generally did not favor the employer recordkeeping that would be necessary for comprehensive verification. Illinois found that telephone verification of job contacts may be as effective and much less costly than in-person verification by agency personnel. Perhaps surprisingly, Illinois also concluded that in-person eligibility reviews with claimants did not seem to improve their worksearch efforts. Oklahoma is experimenting with sorting claimants into various categories in terms of required search activities. New Jersey has instructed claimants that they must contact "hiring officers," not just any employee of the firms they contact. Missouri, New Jersey and Oklahoma have implemented law/policy changes designed to improve claimant worksearch and job finding activities.

3. Difficulties with coordinating Job Service and unemployment insurance efforts to return claimants to work have been highlighted in studies undertaken in both Oklahoma and New Jersey, with a special pilot test to improve such efforts implemented in New Jersey during 1986.

4. Utah has implemented an experimental claimant screening profile to improve the targeting of administrative resources on "high-risk" claimants. Alaska, Illinois and New Jersey are in the process of conducting the research needed to evaluate whether such an approach might be feasible in their states.

5. Alaska and New Jersey are conducting special studies to determine whether claimants who collect UC benefits while working can be inexpensively identified by using computerized screening profiles.

6. Utah is attempting to determine whether an expert system approach would be cost effective for administering some portions of its eligibility criteria.

7. Both Louisiana and Missouri found that partial claims appear to be a particular problem in terms of overpayments. Their detailed analysis of this problem has resulted in new forms, procedures and policies for dealing with partial claims in both states.

8. Programs for improving reviews designed to assist local offices have been conducted by Oklahoma and Pennsylvania. For example, Oklahoma has initiated a new procedure that requires local offices to routinely utilize a "quality checklist" in order to identify error sources and initiate immediate corrective actions.

9. Oklahoma also has conducted a special study of employer tax audits and has found some employer wage reporting errors and also some independent contractors that were not paying UC taxes they owed.

10. Alaska and Illinois are conducting special studies to determine whether employers who misreport claimant earnings can be effectively targeted for tax audits by using computerized screening profiles.

11. Louisiana found that its system for auditing claimants for unreported earnings could be improved through a revision of its employer wage-reporting forms.

12. Overall oversight and quality evaluation functions have been improved by better integrating and coordinating a variety of functions designed to enhance program quality by Arizona, New York and Pennsylvania.[56]

Conclusions

The evidence presented in this chapter does not necessarily prove that the UC program is excessively complex. All social payment systems must have eligibility criteria to regulate the volume of payments and to determine those who will or will not

---

56. These findings and activities have been reported on at four meetings held by the QUIP states during 1985 and 1986. The summary in the text is based on the authors' meeting notes and the sources referenced below, since no comprehensive report or summary of QUIP state activities has yet been developed. For details on any of these projects, contact the relevant state agencies. Also see Missouri Division of Employment Security (1986) for the worksearch survey; Murrie (1986) for the Oklahoma "quality checklist" and revised worksearch requirements; and Utah Department of Employment Security (1986) for the worksearch profile.

be paid. The extent of program complexity required to accomplish this goal obviously is an issue about which informed individuals may disagree. On the basis of equity/efficiency criteria and the maximum level of real resources likely to be allocated to UC program administration, however, our judgment is that the present system is unduly complex—that the costs implied for the adverse effects of current complexity, as detailed in this chapter, exceed any realistic expectation of what the benefits of that complexity might be.

Responses to the negative impacts of program complexity could include a substantial increase in administrative funding, a reduction in program complexity or improved methods of administering any given level of program complexity. Because a substantial increase in administrative funding seems neither likely nor even desirable, particularly in the absence of other changes discussed in this study, this chapter focused on reducing program complexity or improving administration.

Reducing program complexity would require policymakers and UC program administrators to confront the issue of which subtle distinctions (with regard to eligibility criteria, for example) they are willing to eliminate. Considerable controversy is likely to occur. Such controversy should be evaluated, however, in light of the costs and difficulties involved in attempting to administer relatively complex eligibility distinctions.

Even though the benefits of a less complex UC system might be substantial, political realities are likely to constrain overall system simplification. Accordingly, implementing better policies and procedures for administering any given level of program complexity could represent an important contribution to an improved UC system. Three such approaches were emphasized in this chapter. First, the development of detailed, written guidelines for administering state law/policy could be helpful in states that do not currently have such guidelines. Second, computerized expert systems might improve the administration of UC eligibility criteria. Third, computerized screening profiles may represent an effective technique for identifying high-risk claimants, so that claimant compliance can be increased by targeting administrative resources more heavily on this group.

Finally, it should be emphasized that further research and pilot tests of the potential responses to the adverse effects of program complexity would be very important in evaluating their overall costs and benefits, particularly because of the likelihood that many proposals could result in unintended side effects. The recent leadership shown by several state agencies and USDOL in initiating research and experimental studies is particularly encouraging.

APPENDIX 3A

CHRONOLOGY OF MAJOR CHANGES IN FEDERAL UNEMPLOYMENT COMPENSATION LAWS

Source: *Reprinted from National Foundation for Unemployment Compensation & Workers' Compensation (1985c: 76–78).*

CHRONOLOGY OF MAJOR CHANGES IN FEDERAL UNEMPLOYMENT COMPENSATION LAWS

August 1935	(P.L. 74-271, App. 8/14/35) Enactment of Social Security Act. Declared constitutional May 24, 1937. Creation of Federal unemployment tax; credit for employers against Federal tax for taxes paid under a State law that meets Federal law requirements; Federal financing of administrative costs; State autonomy over substantive elements of State UC programs.
June 1938	(P.L. 75-722, App. 6-25-38) Enactment of Railroad Retirement Act (Federal system of unemployment insurance for railroad industry).
February 1939	(P.L. 76-1, App. 2/10/39) Taxing provisions in Title IX of Social Security Act transferred to Internal Revenue Code—Federal Unemployment Tax Act (FUTA).
August 1939	(P.L. 76-379, App. 8/10/39) FUTA taxable wage base limited to first $3,000 of a worker's earnings; States required to establish merit systems for personnel who administer UC programs; coverage extended to certain Federal instrumentalities.
September 1944	(P.L. 78-346) Servicemen's Readjustment Act of 1944 (G.I. Bill). Readjustment allowances of $20 a week for a maximum of 52 weeks.
October 1944	(P.L. 78-458, App. 10/3/44) established the George Loan Fund for Federal loans to States in anticipation of heavy reconversion costs.
August 1946	(P.L. 79-719, App. 8/10/46) Extended coverage to maritime service; permitted States to withdraw employee contributions from fund for payment of benefits under a temporary disability insurance program; provided reconversion unemployment benefits for seamen employed by the War Shipping Administration.
July 1947	(P.L. 80-226, App. 7/24/47) Voluntary contributions permitted in employer rate computations.
June 1948	(P.L. 80-642, App. 6/14/48) Supreme Court decision resulted in the term "employee" in the FUTA being limited to employees under the common law rule of "master-servant" retroactive to 1939. Federal coverage withdrawn from 500,000, including outside salesmen.
October 1952	(P.L. 82-550) Veterans Readjustment Act of 1952 (UCV program) provided up to 26 weeks of benefits at $26 a week ($676) to unemployed veterans of the Korean conflict.
August 1954	(P.L. 83-567, App. 8/5/54) The Employment Security Administrative Financing Act of 1954 (Reed Act) earmarked all proceeds of the unemployment tax to UC purposes by appropriating to the Federal Unemployment Trust Fund any annual excess of Federal tax receipts over employment security expenditures approved by Congress. Bill created loan fund; provided for return to the States of any excess over a $200 million reserve in the loan fund to be used for benefits and State administrative expenses, including buildings.
September 1954	(P.L. 83-767, App. 9/1/54) Coverage: established Unemployment Compensation for Federal Employees—(UCFE) program; extended coverage (eff. 1/1/56) to employers of 4 (instead of 8) or more workers in 20 weeks in a calendar year. Tax: States permitted to allow reduced rates to employers with 1 (instead of 3) years' experience.
June 1958	(P.L. 85-441, App. 6/4/58) Established Temporary Unemployment Compensation Act of 1958 (TUC). Provided up to 13 weeks of extended benefits to individuals who had exhausted regular entitlement after June 30, 1957 and before April 1, 1959. Financed by Federal loans to States. State participation optional.
October 1958	(P.L. 85-848, App. 8/28/58) Permanent program providing benefits to veterans under law of State in which claim was filed. Ex-servicemen's Unemployment Act of 1958 (UCX).
September 1960	(P.L. 86-778, App. 9/13/60) Federal tax increased from 3 to 3.1 % without a change in the 2.7% offset credit, thus increasing Federal share from 0.3% to 0.4%; permitted advances from loan fund only to States unable to meet benefit costs in current or following month; extended coverage to Federal Reserve Banks, land banks, and credit unions. Puerto Rico brought into system. Effective 1/1/62, coverage extended to employees on American aircraft working outside U.S.; nonprofit organizations not exempt from income tax, feeder organizations of nonprofit organizations.
March 1961	(P.L. 87-6, App. 3/24/61) Established Temporary Extended Unemployment Compensation Act of 1961 (TEUC). Provided up to 13 weeks of extended benefits to workers who exhausted benefits after June 30, 1960 and before April 1, 1962. Financed by a temporary additional Federal unemployment tax of 0.4% for 1962 and 0.25% for 1963. Mandatory for all states.
August 1970	(P.L. 91-373, App. 8/10/70) Tax: wage base increased from $3,000 to $4,200, eff. 1/1/72; Federal tax rate increased from 3.1% to 3.2%; new employers permitted reduced rate on basis other than experience. Created Extended Unemployment Compensation Program providing up to 13 weeks of extended benefits financed 50-50 Federal-State to claimants who exhausted regular entitlement during periods of high unemployment nationwide or in their State: nationwide, whenever seasonally adjusted insured unemployment rate is 4.5% or more for 3 consecutive months; State; whenever State's insured unemployment rate averaged 4% or more for 13 consecutive weeks and was at least 20% higher than the average of such rates for the corresponding 13-week periods in the preceding 2 years. Extended benefit period ends when conditions no longer exist, but must remain in effect at least 13 weeks. Coverage extended, eff. 1/1/72, to employers with 1 or more employees in 20 weeks or a quarterly payroll of $1,500; nonprofit organizations of 4 or more employees; State hospitals and

institutions of higher education; outside salesmen, agents and commission drivers; certain agricultural processing workers; U.S. citizens employed by American firms outside the U.S. New State requirements added; nonprofits must be given right to finance benefit costs by straight reimbursement instead of tax; certain professional employees of colleges must be denied benefits between school terms if they have a contract to work both terms; benefits may not be paid any claimant for a second successive benefit year unless he has worked since beginning of the preceding benefit year; benefits may not be denied claimants in approved training; benefits may not be denied because a person files a claim in another State or Canada; required participation in interstate plan for combining a claimant's wage credits when his earnings are in more than one State; prohibits cancelling wage credits or totally reducing benefit rights except for misconduct in connection with the work, fraud in connection with a claim, receipt of disqualifying income.

December 1971	(P.L. 92-224, App. 12/29/71) Enacted the Emergency Compensation Act of 1971, providing additional extended benefits of up to 13 weeks to claimants in States with an insured unemployment rate plus an adjustment rate for exhaustees of 6.5%, provided extended benefits had already triggered on in the State. Act was effective between January 30, 1972 and September 30, 1972.
June 1972	(P.L. 92-329, App. 6/30/72) Extended Emergency Compensation Act of 1971 to March 31, 1973. Financed by increase in Federal tax rate for 1973 from 3.2% to 3.28%.
October 1972–October 1976	Several bills enacted temporarily suspending the requirement that a State must have both an insured unemployment rate of at least 4% and the rate must be 120% higher than the average of the rates for the corresponding period in the 2 preceding years. Most such bills permitted States to waive the 120% requirement.
December 1974	(P.L. 93-567, App. 12/31/74) The Emergency Jobs and Unemployment Assistance Act provided a temporary program of Special Unemployment Assistance (SUA) to individuals with work experience but no benefit rights under regular unemployment compensation programs because their jobs were not covered.
December 1974	(P.L. 93-572, App. 12/31/74) Created emergency benefits program providing up to 13 weeks of Federal Supplemental Benefits (FSB) to individuals who had exhausted all regular and extended benefit entitlement. Payable between January 1, 1975 and December 31, 1976 on the basis of same triggers as in the extended benefits program.
March 1975	(P.L. 94-12, App. 3/29/75) Increased maximum number of weeks payable under FSB from 13 to 26 until January 1, 1976.
June 1975	(P.L. 94-45, App. 6/30/75) Changed FSB trigger to require insured unemployment rate of at least 5%; limited FSB benefits to 13 weeks duration; extended the program until March 31, 1977; provided for a 3-year deferral of the tax credit reduction provisions applicable to borrowing States, provided they met conditions prescribed by Secretary of Labor.
October 1976	(P.L. 94-444, App. 10/1/76) Provides for Federal reimbursement to the States for unemployment compensation paid to individuals separated from CETA public service jobs.
October 1976	(P.L. 94-566, App. 10/20/76) Financing: increased tax base from $4,200 to $6,000, effective 1/1/78; increased net Federal tax rate from 0.5% to 0.7% to return to 0.5% after all advances for the Federal share of extended benefits have been repaid. Coverage: extended to State and local government employees; household workers who are paid $1,000 or more in any calendar quarter for such services; agricultural labor for employers having 10 or more workers in 20 weeks of paying $20,000 or more in wages in any calendar quarter; employees of nonprofit elementary and secondary schools; Virgin Islands admitted to the system. Extended benefits: change in triggers—National, seasonally adjusted insured unemployment rate of 4.5% during a 13-week period; State, the 4% unadjusted rate and the 120% requirement retained, but the latter may be waived by the State whenever the unadjusted rate is 5% or more. Standards: disqualification on basis of pregnancy is prohibited; payment prohibited to professional athletes between successive seasons and to aliens not legally admitted to U.S. for permanent residence; to individuals receiving a pension. Payment based on service for a school by a professional must be denied between school terms if individual has reasonable assurance of reemployment. States permitted to apply same denial to nonprofessionals employed by schools. Establishes a National Study Commission to study and report on the unemployment compensation program.
April 1977	(P.L. 95-19, App. 4/12/77) Reduced length of FSB emergency benefit period from 26 to 13 weeks; extended FSB program to November 1977 for new claims; added special disqualifications for refusal of suitable work and defined suitable work for FSB claimants; provided general revenue financing of FSB beginning April 1, 1977; extended the deferral period for borrowing States for 2 years; clarified the required denial of benefits to undocumented aliens; permitted States to extend the required denial of benefits to school employees to vacation periods and holiday recesses in addition to the period occurring between school terms.
December 1977	(P.L. 95-216, App. 12/20/77) Required State UC agencies to provide wage information to welfare agencies on request; for annual rather than quarterly reporting of FICA wages.
November 1978	(P.L. 95-600, App. 11/6/78) The Revenue Act of 1978 subjected unemployment benefits to taxation for those whose total income exceeds certain amounts.
October 1979	(P.L. 96-84, App. 10/10/79) Extended exclusion from the FUTA of certain alien farmworkers for 2 years but provided that these workers shall be counted for determining if a farm operator has enough workers or payroll to be subject to FUTA coverage.
September 1980	(P.L. 96-364, App. 9/26/80) Amended pension standard to require deduction of pension payments only in specified circumstances and to allow States to consider an individual's contribution to the pension in determining the amount to be deducted from unemployment benefits; required States to prohibit payment of extended benefits beyond 2 weeks to an interstate claimant if the claim was

filed in an agent State where an extended benefit period was not in effect; required exservice-members to have one year instead of 90 days of active service before they can be eligible for benefits.

December 1980 (P.L. 96-499, App. 12/5/80) Terminated Federal funding of unemployment benefits paid to CETA/PSE workers; eliminated Federal share of the first week of extended benefits in any State that does not have a noncompensable waiting week requirement for regular benefits; required denial of extended benefits to individuals who fail to meet certain specified requirements concerning application for suitable work, or who fail to actively engage in seeking work; prohibited States from paying extended benefits unless State law provided duration of unemployment disqualifications for the 3 major causes for EB claimants.

August 1981 (P.L. 97-35, App. 8/13/81) Eliminated natinal EB trigger; increased from 4% to 5% the State EB trigger (and from 5% to 6% the optional trigger if a State waives the 120% requirement); disqualified ex-servicemembers who separate from the service when they had an opportunity to re-enlist; required offsetting of unemployment benefits by amount of child support owed by a claimant; prohibited States from granting extended benefits to any claimant who qualified for regular benefits with fewer than 20 weeks of work (or the equivalent) in his base period.

August 1982 (P.L. 97-248, App. 9/2/82) Increased FUTA taxable wage base from $6,000 to $7,000 and net Federal tax rate from 0.7% to 0.8% (eff. 1/1/83); increased the gross Federal tax rate from 3.4% to 6.2% (eff. 1/1/85) including 0.2% temporary tax until EUCA debt is repaid. 90% offset credit applies to 6.0% yielding net Federal tax of 0.8%. Allocation of Federal taxes was revised with 60% to ESSA account and 40% to EUCA account until debt is repaid. Fifth year added tax credit reduction for debtor states was amended to eliminate cost rate/tax rate comparison in qualifying states. Lowered the earnings level at which the U.C. benefits are taxable from $20,000 to $12,000 for singles and from $25,000 to $18,000 for married individuals. Debtor states were permitted to make repayments from experience rated trust fund moneys. States with very high insured unemployment rate allowed to defer a portion of their interest payments. Wages paid certain student interns were exempted from FUTA. Initiated a temporary program of Federal Supplemental Compensation providing for 6-10 weeks of benefits with program terminating 3/31/83. Extended for 1982-83, the FUTA exemption on wages paid certain alien farmworkers. Directed USDL to assist states desiring to adopt short-time compensation. Extended the Reed Act for 10 years permitting states to restore depleted Reed funds if state has solvent trust fund.

October 1982 (P.L. 97-362, Miscellaneous Tax Act of 1982, App. 10/1/82) Extended for two years FUTA exclusion of services performed on fishing vessels with crews of fewer than 10; amended UCX program to provide that ex-servicepersons may qualify if they leave the service after a full term of enlistment; imposed a 4-week waiting period on UCX benefits; limited UCX duration (including extended benefits) to a maximum of 13 weeks; required UCX payments to be charged to Department of Defense after 10/1/83.

December 1982 (P.L. 97-424, App. 1/6/83) Provided for an additional 2-6 weeks of Federal Supplemental Compensation for each state, according to insured unemployment levels.

January 1983 (P.L. 97-424, Surface Transportation Assistance Act of 1982, App. 1/6/83) Revised triggers and duration of benefits under Federal Supplemental Unemployment Compensation Act of 1982.

April 1983 (P.L. 98-21, Social Security Amendments of 1983, App. 4/20/83) Extended FSC program 6 months to 9/30/83. Modified conditions debtor States must meet to avoid FUTA tax increase. Established new conditions under which interest may be deferred. Required States to provide that nonprofessional employees of schools and colleges be denied benefits between terms and during holidays and vacation periods. Gave States option to extend denial to individuals performing services for or on behalf of schools, even though not employees of those schools. Permitted States to deduct from an individual's unemployment check amounts for health insurance if individual agrees. Allowed States to modify availability requirements for EB claimants to take account of jury duty or hospitalization if such exemptions also apply to regular claimants. Removed from FUTA "wage" exclusions, begin ning January 1985, certain employer payments relating to employee retirement benefits and sick pay.

October 1983 (P.L. 98-135, Federal Supplemental Compensation Amendments of 1983, App. 10/24/83) Extended provisions of Act to 3/31/85. Revised triggers and duration of FSC; added exclusion from taxable wages of any payment made by an employer to a survivor or estate of a former employee after the calendar year in which the employee dies; extended for two years, to 12/31/85, exclusion from coverage of wages paid certain alien farmworkers under contract for fixed periods; directs Secretary of Labor to make special reports on feasibility of area triggers for extended benefits, structural unemployment among claimants, eligibility of federal retirees and federal prisoners for benefits.

July 1984 (P.L. 98-369, Deficit Reduction Act of 1984, App. 7/18/84) Extended definition of "wages" to all tips reported by employee to employer, including tips made by credit cards as well as cash; extended for 2 years (to December 31, 1984) the exclusion of services performed on fishing vessels with crews of fewer than 10 whose remuneration involves a share in the catch; required that State UI agencies provide for exchange of information with agencies administering other programs for purposes of income and eligibility verification; required all States to require employers to make quarterly reports of wages to a State agency.

October 1984 (P.L. 98-601, Small Business Unemployment Tax Act, App. 10/30/84) Permitted State UI laws to provide certain small businesses (quarterly total wages of under $50,000) opportunity for phasing in to a maximum tax rate of 5.4%, from 1985 to 1989. (Parallels a similar phase-in provision in P.L. 97-248 applicable to certain industries subject to a uniform State rate above 2.7%.)

October 1984 (P.L. 98-611, App. 10/31/84) Provided a 2-year (1984 and 1985) extension of an employer credit against FUTA and FICA taxes for employer-paid costs of education assistance for employees.

October 1984 (P.L. 98-612, App. 10/31/84) Provided a 1-year (1985) extension of an employer credit against FUTA and FICA taxes for employer-paid costs of group legal services for employees.

4
Adverse Impacts of Federal Administrative Funding Procedures

Each state is responsible for determining its eligibility criteria and benefit levels, and also for raising the tax revenue necessary to fund its benefit payments. However, state administrative costs are financed by Federal Unemployment Tax Act (FUTA) receipts collected from taxpaying employers in all states.[1]

This federal funding process is one of the major features of the federal-state partnership in the UC system. USDOL applies administrative funding allocation procedures that affect state programs by creating various incentives and disincentives to which states respond. After providing a brief overview of the USDOL administrative funding process, this chapter analyzes the adverse incentives and impacts of that process on payment accuracy and overall UC program quality. Then, some possible improvements in the administrative funding process are discussed.

---

1. As of 1985, the FUTA tax rate on employers was 6.2 percent of the first $7,000 paid to each covered employee, but employers may receive a credit of 5.4 percent of this tax for taxes paid under state UC laws (to fund benefit payments). Thus, the net federal tax on employers is 0.8 percent. Both federal and state UC program administrative costs are paid from appropriations made annually by Congress out of funds accumulated from net FUTA tax receipts. In addition to funding federal and state administrative costs, the net federal tax is used to finance the federal share (50 percent) of federal-state extended benefits and to provide a loan fund for states that deplete the reserves available for benefit payments. For details on the federal tax (including details on the "flow of funds" from the 0.8 percent net federal tax), see the excellent summary provided in National Foundation for Unemployment Compensation & Workers' Compensation (1986a).

Background

Control of administrative funding represents a substantial source of federal authority over state UC programs. In fact, Rubin contends that:

> The source of this authority is the federal control over the distribution of administrative grants and the power to establish standards "designed to insure competence and probity."
>
> Under the Social Security Act, administrative grants are permitted only if the state law provides "such methods of administration as are found by the Secretary (of Labor) to be reasonably calculated to insure full payment of compensation when due." A second provision permits expenditure of administrative grants by a state only in the amounts and for the purposes found necessary by the Secretary for proper and efficient administration.
>
> The virtually unqualified authority of DOL to allocate administrative grants regularly collides with the states' responsibilities to administer their own laws. Control over allocation has translated into federal dictation of priorities, limitations on state flexibility, friction, and cooperation. The conflicts have produced state recommendations either for some share of the authority over allocations or for independent sources of administrative funds without federal control.[2]

Individual state UC programs receive administrative funding from the federal government on the basis of allocations by USDOL.[3] Initially, detailed line item budgeting was utilized for all budgetary items, but in 1941 this approach was replaced by a system of "functional" budgeting, under which administrative financing was provided for the specific costs of performing various UC functions (e.g., the maintenance of employer wage

---

2. Rubin (1983: 27–28).
3. For a recent and excellent discussion of the administrative funding process, see House Committee on Appropriations (1985). This chapter draws heavily on this source. For recent analyses of financing issues in terms of state trust fund solvency for paying UC benefits to claimants, see Vroman (1985 and 1986).

records).[4] This functional budgeting system eventually evolved into one in which funding for direct UC operations, such as benefit payment procedures, depended on "standard" times per unit of work performed in each state.

Because of difficulties with its functional budgeting system, which included an inability to explain or justify cost variations among the states, USDOL initiated a major research and development project in 1971 that was intended to result in an improved administrative funding system.[5] The result of this effort was the Cost Model Management System implemented in the mid-1970s and used through at least FY 1987, although some changes were made for FY 1987 allocations. Because some familiarity with this system is essential for understanding existing, past and probably future administrative funding impacts and problems, it is briefly explained below.

At the very outset, it is important to emphasize that USDOL already has responded positively to some of the adverse funding impacts analyzed in this chapter. In particular, USDOL implemented some potentially significant changes that affected FY 1987 allocations to the states, as discussed in a subsequent section.[6] Nonetheless, because the funding process described below is essential to understanding adverse federal impacts on state programs from the mid-1970s through at least FY 1987, and because many features of that funding process may be retained in future years, it is important to provide further background.[7]

The Cost Model Management System is based upon work measurement and time studies of the various functions involved in processing UC claims in each state. Statistical sampling techniques are used to analyze sample work stations in order to estimate the (statewide average) time required to perform the major UC functions in each state.[8] These time factors are

---

4. National Governors' Association (1983: 9).

5. House Committee on Appropriations (1985: 7).

6. See Semerad (1986), Jones (1986) and Balcer (1986).

7. It should be noted that, although such funding procedures are not discussed in the text, USDOL also provides separate funding to the states for certain special purpose projects, such as the operation of the Cost Model System itself. Nonetheless, most administrative funding for state programs has been provided through the funding process discussed in the text.

8. A number of potential issues arise because of the use of "sample" work stations for

denoted as "minutes per unit" (MPUs) and have been developed
for a number of major cost model components, including: initial
claims, weeks claimed, nonmonetary determinations, appeals,
wage records and tax functions.[9] MPUs for 17 different workload
activities were used in the administrative funding allocation
process for FY 1985.[10]

On the basis of the MPUs developed from the Cost Model
System and forecasts of future workloads, the total staff positions required by each state to process its predicted workload for
each year are estimated. One of the major problems that led to
the development of the Cost Model System—the inability to
justify or explain cost differences among the states—has continued as an unresolved problem, however. In fact, as early as FY
1977, only two years after implementation of the Cost Model,
the Office of Management and Budget began to cut USDOL's
annual budget requests for administrative financing because of
unexplainable variances in administrative costs among the
states.[11]

A recent summary of the Cost Model System by Dunn and
Griffin provides a convenient overview of a number of administrative financing issues frequently raised by the states:

> The primary elements in financing the administration of the
> nation's unemployment insurance program are the *estimated
> workloads* for the forthcoming fiscal period and the time factors
> established as necessary to maintain a fully effective program for
> the prompt payment of benefits and the prevention of fraud and
> other abuses. As a hedge against inaccurate estimates (which are
> made initially 21 months before the end of the fiscal period) only
> a portion of the estimated workloads (the base) is funded in
> advance—the rest (the contingency) will be funded only if and
> when the additional workloads occur.

relatively short periods to estimate the average (statewide) time required to perform particular
tasks. Obvious issues include the statistical validity of the selection procedures for the sample
work stations and the extent to which "gaming" strategies may be utilized by states to affect the
Cost Model estimates. However, these and other potential Cost Model design issues are not
addressed in this study because the authors have no substantive basis for evaluating such issues.

9. National Governors' Association (1983: 9).
10. See Brown (1984) and House Committee on Appropriations (1985: 24).
11. House Committee on Appropriations (1985: 10).

. . . *Base funding* presupposes a sufficiency of resources to support the minimum number of experienced staff who will provide a continuity of operations and stability, regardless of workload fluctuations.

In contrast, *additional contingency funding* presupposes that when workloads exceed base entitlements, temporary, part-time and transitional staff (usually lower salaried) will be added to handle this excess workload on an as-needed basis. The proportion of total expected workload which is funded at "base" is critical since the *allowances for salary and NPS [Non-Personal Services]* are lower for the contingency workloads than for those in the base. One major difficulty is that for the past several years, *the base workloads nationwide have been arbitrarily fixed,* while the actual number of claims processed has varied widely during the same period.[12] (emphasis added)

Four issues noted in the above summary of funding procedures require further clarification: (1) workload projections, (2) the underfunding of state UC program operations, (3) "base" v. "contingency" funding, and (4) the funding for nonpersonal services.

Workload Projections

One of the major determinants of the level of administrative funding for state programs in any year is the projected (national) workload. The accuracy of these projections is essential to the overall adequacy of administrative funding because, as discussed below, it affects the extent to which funding is provided on a base or a contingency basis.[13] Accurately projecting the national workloads for particular years would be extremely difficult, even if such projections were based solely on objective factors. However, political considerations affect the objectivity of these forecasts, since USDOL and the Office of Management and Budget utilize the administration's official economic assump-

---

12. Dunn and Griffin (1984: 7 and 3).
13. Dunn and Griffin (1984 or 1985) and House Committee on Appropriations (1985: 17).

tions in determining workload projections.[14] Relatively inaccurate workload estimates that consistently understate actual workloads have been used by USDOL in its administrative funding process in recent years. Actual UC workloads were greater than projected workloads for FY 1976 through FY 1980.[15] More recently, the Interstate Conference of Employment Security Agencies has found that USDOL's projected annual workload estimate was never more than 80 percent of the actual workload from FY 1980 through FY 1984, with the exception of one year.[16]

Underfunding of State Programs

One issue that has aroused strong state objections, especially in recent years, has been the practice of underfunding states for the number of positions indicated by the Cost Model MPU studies.[17] The underfunding issue partly reflects the fact that congressional appropriations (which determine the total funds from FUTA collections available to USDOL for state programs) have not been sufficient to fully fund all positions indicated by the Cost Model System, although underfunding actually predates the Cost Model System. According to a report prepared by the Interstate Conference of Employment Security Agencies and Macro Systems, Inc., numerous methods have been used to reduce the number of positions implied by the Cost Model and workload estimates to the number of base positions that could be supported with available resources.[18] As a result, states often have received different percentage reductions in allowable MPUs for different functions.

---

14. See House Committee on Appropriations (1985: 17–23) and Interstate Conference of Employment Security Agencies and Macro Systems, Inc. (1980: 607).

15. House Committee on Appropriations (1985: 17).

16. Cited in House Committee on Appropriations (1985: 17–18).

17. UC program personnel also often contend that the Job Service underfunds programs related to placing UC claimants in jobs. The issue arises because Job Service operations receive specific funding from FUTA collections deposited into the Employment Security Administration Account for serving UC claimants. However, UC program personnel often contend they do not receive service for their claimants commensurate with the funding provided to the Job Service from these FUTA collections.

18. Interstate Conference of Employment Security Agencies and Macro Systems, Inc. (1979: III-9).

The states with the highest MPUs for a given function usually have the funding for those MPUs reduced by the largest percentage amounts; in most instances, these MPU funding reductions become progressively smaller for states with lower MPUs. Full MPU funding has been unusual in recent years. During the FY 1985 allocation process, USDOL fully funded the MPUs in each of the workload components for only the five states with the lowest MPUs.[19] Overall, USDOL funded only about 84 percent of the state needs indicated by the Cost Model studies during fiscal years 1984 and 1985, with this percentage evidently falling to about 82 percent for FY 1986.[20]

The practice of not fully funding state MPUs has aroused overwhelming, if not unanimous, opposition by the states. In fact, a recent analysis by the House Committee on Appropriations found that nearly all states surveyed supported the Cost Model as "a theoretically sound approach to accurately determining the time needed to accomplish specific UI functions,"[21] and most states also believed that USDOL's reductions for the MPUs indicated by the Cost Model studies have been arbitrary.[22] These state concerns are summarized well by Dunn and Griffin:

The MPUs identified for each state are revised downward by the Secretary of Labor to assure that the number of positions allocated to states does not exceed the number of positions which have been included in the President's annual budget request. These adjustments seriously affect the funding each state actually receives. The program needs have been methodically documented and justified through the cost model/workload estimating process. These needs nevertheless are modified arbitrarily by ETA to fit within a total funding ceiling.[23]

---

19. House Committee on Appropriations (1985: 24).
20. See House Committee on Appropriations (1985: 24) for the estimates for fiscal years 1984 and 1985. The estimates for FY 1986 were provided by New York's former UC administrator, Gerald Dunn.
21. House Committee on Appropriations (1985: 20).
22. For a summary of state views, see House Committee on Appropriations (1985: 24). Also, see Dunn and Griffin (1984 or 1985).
23. Dunn and Griffin (1984: 3).

USDOL generally believes nationwide funding for the administration of state programs is adequate, despite the fact that full funding for Cost Model MPUs is not provided.[24] This may explain why many states maintain that USDOL does not make as strong a case to Congress for full funding of Cost Model MPUs as the states believe is appropriate. A recent analysis by the House Committee on Appropriations concluded that USDOL could not support its conclusion or "adequately demonstrate that Cost Model results were improperly prepared or were inaccurate."[25]

Base v. Contingency Funding

Another administrative funding issue is that overall funding adequacy partly depends on the proportion of total funding provided to a state as "base," rather than "contingency," funding. The need for such a distinction in the funding process arises because claim loads can fluctuate sharply from quarter to quarter in any state. The base allocations are supposed to provide funding for a sufficient number of permanent staff to effectively operate a state's program during relatively low volume periods. In contrast, contingency funding is supposed to make it possible to effectively process claims during higher volume periods by allowing states to supplement their permanent (base) staffs with temporary/seasonal employees. However, in addition to the tendency of USDOL to underestimate base staff needs, there are at least three interrelated issues that complicate the apparently simple distinction between base and contingency funding: (1) differential funding levels for a given number of positions, depending on whether they are funded as base or contingency positions; (2) the problems states confront because of the distinction between positions "earned" and "used" for particular calendar quarters; and (3) the allocation constraints imposed for base staff gains and losses in particular states. Each of these issues is briefly discussed below.

---

24. House Committee on Appropriations (1985: 20).
25. House Committee on Appropriations (1985: 19).

An implicit assumption of the Cost Model System is that the efficiency of permanent and temporary employees is the same. No adjustment is explicitly made in the MPUs for a state on the basis of the proportion of its workload processed with permanent v. temporary employees. At the same time, however, USDOL provides lower funding levels to a state for contingency than for base positions to reflect the lower wage and employment costs supposedly associated with temporary v. permanent employees. Thus, a state would receive a smaller (larger) administrative funding allocation if it had fewer (more) of a given number of total positions funded as base positions; as explained earlier in this chapter, USDOL has consistently underestimated base workloads in recent years.

Funding generally has been provided to a state for base positions only if it has "used" all of the positions it "earned" for a particular calendar quarter; excess positions earned typically have been recaptured by USDOL at the end of each calendar quarter. In contrast, contingency or other extra funding generally has *not* been provided to a state in past years if it has used more positions than it has earned for a particular calendar quarter. As a result, the adequacy of funding has depended partly on how accurately states could forecast the exact staff size required to process quarterly workloads, since the states typically have been funded for the lower of earned or used staff positions. In addition, it can be extremely difficult to vary staffing rapidly enough during particular calendar quarters, even given accurate annual workload forecasts, to keep actual (or "used") staffing exactly matched to "earned" staffing. In apparent recognition of these problems, USDOL recently changed its policy to allow states to make accounting carry-overs of earned but not used positions from the first to the second quarter in a year, and for FY 1987 USDOL decided to allow states to continue such carry-overs for base positions for the entire fiscal year.[26] Moreover, at least for FY 1987, the states could be paid for earned contingency positions, even if they were not used during

---

26. For the earlier change, see House Committee on Appropriations (1985: 30). For the more recent changes, see Jones (1986).

the year.[27] However, it still is not clear whether these recent changes will be continued in future years, and they certainly do not fully address the other base v. contingency funding issues discussed above.

Another dimension of the underfunding of base positions is that the allocation procedures in recent years appear to penalize states that experience extremely sharp increases in claim loads from one year to the next. This occurs because USDOL generally has modified the allocation of base staff positions for certain functions indicated by MPU/workload estimates to constrain the increase in such positions for any state from one year to the next.[28] The effect of such constraints obviously is to increase the relative underfunding of states that have rapidly growing claim loads, as has been emphasized by the Florida UC agency.[29] The relative underfunding imposed on such "loser" states by this zero-sum reallocation process (that benefits some "gainer" states) would be expected to contribute to quality problems in "loser" states.

Funding for Nonpersonal Services[30]

The funding of nonpersonal services (NPS) is another major feature of the existing administrative funding system. The NPS category consists of nonstaff items such as supplies, communications, travel, equipment, premises and various purchased services that may include data processing. Prior to 1981, funding for such costs was based mainly on historical funding levels, adjusted for numerous special factors relevant in particular states. Because of historical difficulties encountered in equitably funding differential NPS costs among the states, a special model intended to account for wide variations in NPS costs among the states was developed in 1981.[31] This special model was soon discarded in favor of existing NPS funding procedures.

---

27. Balcer (1986).
28. For example, see Brown (1984).
29. Burnett and Pendleton (1985).
30. For an excellent and extremely detailed analysis of NPS funding issues, see House Committee on Appropriations (1985: 36–62). The discussion in this section draws heavily on that source.
31. National Governors' Association (1983: 15).

In recent years, NPS funding has been closely tied to actual workloads (and staffing costs), even though many NPS costs (e.g., premises) represent fixed or quasi-fixed costs that vary little (if at all) with actual workloads, particularly on a quarterly basis.[32] A particular problem with this NPS funding process is that capital-intensive states, especially those with highly auto-mated systems, tend to receive less adequate funding than labor-intensive states, especially those with relatively high MPUs and salary levels. Other difficult issues that must be confronted by USDOL in attempting to equitably fund NPS costs among the states include: (1) the substantial differences in NPS costs among the states in a given year; (2) differences in NPS costs within a state from year to year; (3) the fact that state decisions can alter both the amount and mix of NPS costs; and (4) the fact that the extent and duration of the fixed component of NPS costs varies substantially among the states.[33] However, it is quite clear that USDOL's NPS funding procedure[34]—to fund NPS costs attrib-uted to contingency staffing at a much lower rate than the rate used for NPS costs attributed to base staffing—has created serious difficulties for state programs. In particular, the consis-tent underestimates of base workloads result in lower NPS funding allocations because less NPS funding is provided for contingency than for base positions.[35]

It also appears that the difficulties states have in fully covering their NPS costs have accelerated in recent years. According to a survey conducted by the Interstate Conference of Employment Security Agencies, which obtained responses from 47 state agencies, the number of states that reported NPS deficits increased from 18 to 40 between 1980 and 1983.[36] USDOL has contended that the shortfall in NPS funding alleged by the states

---

32. For example, see Dunn and Griffin (1984: 4) and House Committee on Appropriations (1985: 36–44).

33. House Committee on Appropriations (1985: 36–62).

34. House Committee on Appropriations (1985: 36 and 50).

35. An additional dimension of the NPS underfunding issue is the shortfall in NPS funds for the UC program that resulted from the split in NPS funding for the UC and ES programs mandated in the 1982 Wagner-Peyser Act amendments. This issue is not addressed here, but it is discussed in House Committee on Appropriations (1985: 46-49).

36. House Committee on Appropriations (1985: 55).

is due to state accounting procedures rather than to inadequate funding.[37] Nonetheless, most states and the Interstate Conference of Employment Security Agencies view the shortfall as indeed a real one; this position evidently was accepted by the Congress in at least two recent years, as reflected by the fact that portions of supplemental appropriations for the UC system for FY 1984 and 1985 were earmarked specifically for NPS funding.[38] In addition, the evidence and substantive analysis provided by the states, the Interstate Conference of Employment Security Agencies, the House Committee on Appropriations, and even USDOL certainly appears to be much more supportive of the state position than of USDOL's position.[39]

Funding Impacts on Payment Accuracy and Program Quality

The overview of the funding process in the prior section provides a basis for analyzing how the administrative funding procedures utilized from the mid-1970s through at least FY 1987 likely have impacted on both payment accuracy and overall UC program quality. Although the effects analyzed obviously are interrelated, at least eight somewhat distinct impacts or issues can be identified: (1) the inherent complexity of the funding process; (2) the overall underfunding of state UC program operations; (3) the base v. contingency funding procedures; (4) the underfunding of nonpersonal services; (5) the likelihood the funding process discourages general innovations in state operations; (6) disincentives for states to automate their operations; (7) the absence of direct incentives to encourage administrative cost efficiency, including a lack of incentives for reducing program complexity; and (8) the absence of appropriate incentives to encourage states to prevent payment errors or to detect/recover overpayments.

---

37. House Committee on Appropriations (1985: 47).
    38. House Committee on Appropriations (1985: 47–62) and International Association of Personnel in Employment Security (1985).
    39. For a summary of the arguments and evidence for several states, see House Committee on Appropriations (1985: 47–62). Also, several individual states have documented their NPS shortfalls. For example, see Dunn and Griffin (1984).

It should be emphasized that USDOL has disputed the existence of some of these impacts. Nonetheless, a December 1984 internal study prepared by USDOL's own Administrative Finance Workgroup severely criticized the funding system and explicitly acknowledged most of the adverse impacts listed above.[40] Moreover, in evaluating these adverse impacts, it is important to emphasize that USDOL already has implemented some changes in that system. After obtaining substantial input on reforming its administrative funding process, USDOL implemented some short-term reforms in May 1986.[41] At the same time, USDOL announced that there would be continuing public discussion of long-term revisions in its administrative funding procedures.[42] Although there continues to be controversy about the importance of the short-term revisions that were implemented during FY 1987, it certainly appears to the authors that these changes represent an important step towards a much better administrative funding process. Probably the most important of these short-term changes is that USDOL has provided the states much more flexibility in determining how to allocate the administrative funding they receive among various cost categories. In addition to increasing the flexibility of state spending decisions, the FY 1987 changes implemented by USDOL include: (1) an emphasis on monitoring state performance outcomes, rather than expenditures by detailed cost categories; (2) a reduction and simplification of fiscal reporting; (3) the replacement of the quarterly recapture of unused funding for base positions with only the annual recapture of such funds; and (4) evidently for FY 1987 only, contingency funding for positions states earn, instead of funding for the lesser of earned or used positions.[43] Thus, USDOL already is in the process of improving its past administrative funding system. Accordingly, although the full impact of these recent changes cannot yet be evaluated, their apparent contribution to a better funding system

---

40. Cited in House Committee on Appropriations (1985: 73–74).
41. Jones (1986).
42. Jones (1986).
43. Jones (1986) and Balcer (1986).

will be noted in the relevant sections of the subsequent
discussion of the eight issues identified above.

Funding Process Complexity

The inherent complexity of USDOL's funding process becomes evident from a careful examination of the intricate details
of the system. In a study prepared in 1980 at the request of the
National Commission on Unemployment Compensation, the
undue complexity of the administrative funding mechanism was
identified as a major problem:

> Congress appropriates Grants-to-States resources to states in three
> categories: UI, Employment Service, and contingency. In recent
> years, however, the allocation of these resources to the States has
> become increasingly complex and restrictive as well as being
> constantly under revision. This complex of mechanisms has
> resulted in increased confusion and frustration in understanding
> funding concepts, incentives, and mechanisms. . . . [44]

Although the funding system has been revised since the above study
was completed, it is very clear that the process subsequently utilized
still was a complex one.[45]

The funding process makes it difficult for states to undertake
effective long-range planning on the basis of reasonably stable
funding, even assuming constant workloads. The complexity of
the funding process also makes it difficult to understand or
explain either existing funding allocations among the states or
how changes in a particular state would affect its allocation. In
fact, a conclusion of an internal ETA study dated December
1984 is that the administrative funding process was "unneces-
sarily costly," "highly complex," and resulted in "incongru-
ities" between resources and workloads "that are difficult to

44. Interstate Conference of Employment Security Agencies and Macro Systems, Inc. (1980: 606).
45. For an excellent discussion of some complexities involved in allocating administrative funds among the states, see Brown (1984).

understand and explain."[46] A recent and detailed comparison of various components of the FY 1986 administrative funding allocations among the states by the Arizona UC agency also finds "that there are radical relative differences between states for which logical explanations do not come to mind."[47] Fortunately, it appears that USDOL now has somewhat reduced the complexity of the administrative funding process, at least for FY 1987 allocations.[48]

Overall Underfunding of State UC Program Operations

State UC program administrators have strongly contended that USDOL underfunds the administrative costs that would be associated with "quality" programs, since full funding is not provided for the MPUs indicated by USDOL's own Cost Model System.[49] For example, Dunn and Griffin contend:

Virtually all states support the use of objectively developed Cost Model MPU's as indicators of the time necessary to accomplish program goals.
. . . When the Cost Model-developed MPUs are reduced to fit within the funds included in the President's Annual Budget request, the quality of administrative operations in each state, and each state's ability to minimize fraud, waste, and abuse in the unemployment insurance program, is eroded.[50]

Even more recently, the Quality Control Subcommittee of the Interstate Conference of Employment Security Agencies argued that, given underfunded state programs, allocating funds for a system to detect/measure UC payment errors (in USDOL's Quality Control program) does not make sense because without adequate staffing "the same errors will occur despite any amount of statistics collected."[51] It also should be noted that concerns about the administrative underfund-

46. Cited in House Committee on Appropriations (1985: 73–74).
47. Arizona Unemployment Insurance Administration (1985: Cover Sheet).
48. Jones (1986).
49. House Committee on Appropriations (1985: 13).
50. Dunn and Griffin (1984: 8 and 11).
51. Quality Control Subcommittee (1985: 8).

ing of state programs are not recent or isolated. The National Commission on Unemployment Compensation recommended an increase in administrative funding for state programs, including provisions for fully funding state MPUs, on the basis that such an increase in funding would allow states to maintain prompt payments with low error rates.[52]

The underfunding concerns expressed by state program administrators, the Interstate Conference of Employment Security Agencies, the National Commission on Unemployment Compensation and others evidently have not convinced USDOL that underfunding represents a real problem. In fact, a recently completed investigation by the House Committee on Appropriations found that USDOL officials "were quick to blame the states for the funding problems they were experiencing."[53] Although USDOL officials tended to attribute financial problems to the "inability or reluctance to make prudent managerial cost-cutting decisions" by state officials, the House study found that this conclusion was in "direct conflict with an internal study report prepared by ETA's own Administrative Finance Workgroup."[54]

The analysis in chapter 3 of this study suggests that the underfunding of state programs could be greatly reduced and perhaps eliminated, without any increase in funding, if states would reduce the complexity of their programs. However, it must be recognized that state legislators have little incentive to reduce program complexity because they are not involved in funding the administrative costs of the laws they enact. There is little doubt that administrative funding is far short of the levels required for states to fully and accurately administer their *existing* laws/policies. As discussed subsequently in this chapter, however, the large increase in funding that would be required for states to fully administer their existing programs does not appear to be desirable. Nonetheless, it still must be recognized that payment accuracy and overall program quality undoubtedly are adversely affected because of inadequate funding to fully administer the complex state UC programs that currently exist.

---

52. National Commission on Unemployment Compensation (1980: 130).
53. House Committee on Appropriations (1985: 72).
54. House Committee on Appropriations (1985: 72).

Base v. Contingency Funding Issues

The administrative funding procedures used by USDOL virtually guarantee that states often will be forced to rely on temporary or seasonal employees to process substantial proportions of their workloads; such staffing patterns have been particularly evident in recent years. At the same time, USDOL also has continued to emphasize the importance of timely benefit processing and payments, even during peak workload periods. These time pressures, in conjunction with the problems caused by staffing variability and substantial reliance on temporary employees, would be expected to contribute to quality problems and high payment error rates, particularly during high volume periods. This conclusion was supported by the responses to the 1980 K-B study, in which highly trained UC personnel in six states were asked to express the extent of their agreement or disagreement with statements about the prevention and detection of overpayments in their states. The respondents were virtually unanimous in *either disagreeing or strongly disagreeing* with both of the following statements:

1. In your state, adequate training in overpayment *prevention* is provided to local office personnel who are hired as ''temporary'' or ''seasonal'' employees.
2. In your state, adequate training in overpayment *detection* is provided to local office personnel who are hired as ''temporary'' or ''seasonal'' employees.[55]

The difficulties created by base/contingency funding differences and the reliance on temporary employees were also strongly emphasized in Dunn and Griffin's recent analysis:

This [base/contingency funding] theory works fairly well when the base workload is reasonably close to the total workload . . .

---

55. Kingston and Burgess (1981b: 58). Those surveyed did not represent a cross-section of all UC program personnel. For example, UC program administrators were not included in the survey. Nevertheless, the results presented in the text represent the judgments of knowledgeable and highly trained UC program personnel. Accordingly, we believe these survey results merit serious consideration.

Problems arise, however, when the total workloads experienced for the full year greatly exceed the base. With as much as half of the claims loads in many states in the above-base category, this means that at least half the local office staff responsible for claims processing, screening for eligibility issues, and enforcing work-search requirements are temporary staff who are recruited quickly and who have little training or experience.

. . .Since permanent staff[ing] is primarily determined by base workloads, a low proportion of base workloads to estimated total workloads is reflected directly in the quality of claims control. This results in a greater number of overpayments than would occur if a higher proportion of the state's total staff were permanent.[56]

In their recent study of six state UC systems, Corson, Hershey and Kerachsky also stress the adverse impacts of relying on poorly trained temporary employees.[57] Apparently, an additional problem in managing variations in workloads is that the states have been "the last to know" how much administrative funding will be available for any particular fiscal year.[58]

In short, it appears that the base/contingency funding process utilized by USDOL and its contribution to heavy reliance on temporary and seasonal workers is a serious problem. Apparently, the changes implemented by USDOL for FY 1987 contingency funding somewhat alleviated difficulties by increasing state flexibility in utilizing total administrative funding allocations, by simplifying the formula for determining the size of contingency allocations and by funding states for earned positions, even if they were not used.[59] Nonetheless, the exact impact of these changes on state operations cannot be determined at this time, and it is not yet known whether they will be continued in future years.

A closely related issue to the base/contingency impacts is the funding for administrative services, and technical support

---

56. Dunn and Griffin (1984: 12 and 5).
57. Corson et al. (1986: 93–95).
58. House Committee on Appropriations (1985: 23).
59. Jones (1986) and Balcer (1986).

(AS&T). Because USDOL has utilized a procedure for funding AS&T activities similar to the procedure for NPS costs discussed below, the adequacy of AS&T funding also has varied, depending on whether it has been attributed to base or contingency staffing. Apparently, USDOL assumes that less administrative/ technical support and training are required for a contingency than for a base staff position. This assumption has been challenged by the states. For example, Dunn and Griffin contend:

> The needs for training and supervision clearly are not less for temporary staff than they are for a permanent trained cadre.
> Any reasonable administrator—whether in the public sector or the private—knows that closer supervision and more training are required for overseeing the work of large numbers of people unfamiliar with normal operating and procedural requirements.[60]

The recent analysis by the House Committee on appropriations also emphasizes the serious implications for program quality of the heavy reliance of states on temporary employees, who cannot be adequately trained or retrained because of the nature of USDOL's contingency funding process.[61] USDOL's recent changes at least partially reduced these problems for FY 1987, since the states were given much more flexibility in determining how to allocate available funds among various spending categories (including NPS and AS&T costs).

Underfunding of Nonpersonal Services

The underfunding of nonpersonal services (NPS) also has impacted on the ability of states to effectively administer their programs. In recent years, various state agencies have attempted to cover their shortfalls in NPS funding levels in a number of ways, including the following: (1) the use of funding for staff positions and staff salary savings (the most common technique); (2) the use of penalty/interest funds assessed on delinquent employer tax accounts; (3) federal supplemental appropriations;

---

60. Dunn and Griffin (1984: 5).
61. House Committee on Appropriations (1985: 30–31).

(4) nonpayment for state-provided items (e.g., data processing services); and (5) the payment for NPS items with state, rather than federal, funds.[62] Although reliance on these methods for covering NPS shortfalls would not *necessarily* impact adversely on either payment accuracy or overall UC program quality, some of the methods might well have such impacts. In particular, the use of administrative funding that otherwise would be used for additional UC personnel clearly could reduce program quality and payment accuracy. Arizona, Florida and other states have contended that the high rates of payment errors found in USDOL's Random Audit program and the suggestions of declining program quality by USDOL's Quality Appraisal program clearly reflect NPS and staff funding shortages.[63]

The potential impacts of the conversion of staff dollars into NPS dollars have been summarized by Cheryl Templeman of the Interstate Conference of Employment Security Agencies, as follows:

> It has become a standard practice not to fill staff positions in order to use the salary and benefit dollars for NPS . . . The unfilled positions have to come from areas where the workload can be controlled, like tax audits and overpayment detection. Of course, this only hurts the program in the long run.[64]

Even more recently, the implications of NPS funding shortfalls for payment accuracy and overall UC program quality have been emphasized by state officials, including Arizona's UC program administrator.[65] State officials also have made the point that even supplemental budget appropriations for NPS shortfalls may not be an effective solution for this problem, because such funding is irregular and typically is received late in the fiscal year.[66]

---

62. For a summary of how individual states have covered NPS shortfalls, see House Committee on Appropriations (1985: 56–61).

63. House Committee on Appropriations (1985: 60–61).

64. Templeman (1984).

65. Vaughn (1985: 3).

66. House Committee on Appropriations (1985: 60).

Program Innovation Disincentives

It appears very likely that the funding process used by USDOL has encouraged inflexibility in state operations and has discouraged innovations. In part, this adverse feature of the funding system results from the uncertainty about how program changes might impact on future funding. If a state were to implement a new set of procedures to improve payment accuracy, for example, it would beeither very difficult or impossible to anticipate the resulting impact on the future administrative funding for the state. Consequently, such programmatic or procedural initiatives probably have been discouraged by the administrative funding process.

The problem of funding disincentives for program innovations also has been pointed out in other studies. For example, the National Governors' Association concluded, with respect to the funding procedures utilized prior to the most recent years, that:

> The current AS&T/NPS allocation methodology contains strong disincentives to reduce costs through reduction of manpower. . . . An individual state is better off to do nothing to reduce manpower requirements . . . than to actively pursue a program to cut costs while maintaining service delivery. Under certain circumstances, cost reductions will result in a greater proportionate reduction of resources allocated to the state. Simply stated, the SESA will be worse off financially for saving money.[67]

More recently, Corson, Hershey and Kerachky found, in a study of six states, that the funding process may well discourage particular types of innovations because:

> In the longer term, investing administrative resources in a tighter detection effort and a greater volume of determinations may raise a state's MPU and thus increase the rate at which the state's determinations are reimbursed. However, the increase in federal reimbursement might not match the increase in the resources

---

67. National Governors' Association (1983: 20).

devoted to tighter detection efforts by the state, since no assurance exists that state requests based on MPU studies will be accepted as submitted in the funding-decision process.[68]

An even more recent example of disincentives for states to seek innovative ways to improve their programs is provided by a bill considered by the State of Texas during 1985. The bill would have obtained outside funds for UC administrative purposes to supplement the administrative funds regularly provided by USDOL. Under the bill, "reimbursable" employers—those who currently do not pay for administrative costs of the UC program—would be required to contribute to cover UC administrative costs.[69] An unofficial opinion received from USDOL in April 1985 regarding the proposed bill and its likely effects was that its implementation (if in conformity with federal law) likely would: (1) not reduce the UC tax burden of other private taxpaying employers in Texas; (2) not increase the administrative funding for the UC program in Texas because USDOL probably would reduce its administrative funding allocation by an amount equal to any outside administrative funds provided by Texas itself; and (3) increase county/city/school taxes and hospital charges in Texas to pay for the contributions to UC administrative financing by these entities.[70]

Automation Disincentives
_____

A specific problem that is closely related to some of those already discussed—particularly the underfunding of NPS costs and innovation disincentives—is that USDOL's funding process apparently creates quite strong disincentives for the automation of state UC program operations. The historical concerns of states

68. Corson et al. (1986: 124).
69. Reimbursable employers include nonprofit organizations and state and local government units not subject to the FUTA tax. Since a portion of FUTA collections covers administrative costs, these entities pay only for the UC benefits paid to their former employees but not for the administrative costs associated with those benefits.
70. An official USDOL opinion on conformance with federal law would require an official request by a state agency. The unofficial opinion and the likely effects of implementing the proposed legislation were obtained by R.E. Harrington, Inc., a firm that specializes in handling UC related matters for private firms and public agencies.

about the effects of automation have been summarized by the National Governors' Association:

> Since personal services expenditures represent three quarters of a typical SESA's total expenditures, personal services reductions are the logical source of cost savings. Automation, the most common means of producing cost savings, usually reduces costs by reducing staff requirements. The number of positions required will have, through the action of the AS&T/NPS formula, a serious adverse effect upon the future financial well-being of the Agency. A prudent state administrator will not pursue a major cost reduction program of this type.[71]

State officials have provided a number of specific examples of automation disincentives, including the following: (1) USDOL has not developed comprehensive automation plans within which states could be assured of adequate funding if they were to automate their procedures; (2) states may not be able to meet USDOL's "payback" provisions in the form of reduced staffing allocations after automation, especially with the relatively short period allowed for such "paybacks;" (3) future NPS funding may not be adequate to cover the increased maintenance, equipment rental, communication, supply, software and eventual replacement costs associated with automation; (4) automation could result in unfair reductions in already inadequate MPU funding; (5) USDOL funding procedures may be arbitrarily altered in future years, with the result that automated states will be funding "losers;" (6) NPS allocations (which include computer allocations) are directly related to total staffing costs, which would be reduced by effective automation programs; (7) complex guidelines and excessive red tape are associated with obtaining special automation funding; and (8) too little funding is available for automation to justify the risk of losing staff funding as a result of automation.[72]

Available evidence does suggest that the disincentives for states to automate their programs apparently have been powerful.

---

71. National Governors' Association (1983: 21). For a discussion of the same issue, also see House Committee on Appropriations (1985: 33).
72. House Committee on Appropriations (1985: 66–71).

An April 1984 report prepared by the Interstate Conference of
Employment Security Agencies concluded that state systems are
"supported primarily with obsolete and inadequate computer
equipment and programs."[73] According to the findings of a
survey conducted by USDOL and released in July 1984: only 9
states were highly automated; 17 states were moderately automated; 17 states were partly automated; and 8 states were
automated only to a low degree.[74] It should be noted, however,
that USDOL has stated, in the process of determining FY 1985
appropriations, that it "believes that disincentives to automation
have been effectively removed."[75] Although USDOL in fact
changed its funding procedures (through a September 1983 Field
Memorandum) in recognition of the automation disincentives
that resulted from its previous procedures, state officials and the
Interstate Conference of Employment Security Agencies disagree with the USDOL belief that funding automation disincentives have been removed.[76]

Efficiency Disincentives

The lack of incentives for cost efficiency in state programs
obviously encompasses several of the funding impacts discussed
above. For example, base/contingency funding problems make it
difficult for states to effectively plan and implement changes that
could produce long-run savings. As another example, NPS
funding procedures and disincentives for both general innovations and automation contribute to cost inefficiencies. The
possibility that cost-saving changes in administrative procedures
could result in the full recapture of such savings by USDOL in
future years also could discourage states from emphasizing
efficient operations as strongly as they otherwise might.

The extent of these problems is further indicated by studies
prepared by the General Accounting Office (1984) and the House

73. Cited by House Committee on Appropriations (1985: 65).
74. House Committee on Appropriations (1985: 64–65).
75. House Committee on Appropriations (1985: 65).
76. House Committee on Appropriations (1985: 66–71).

Committee on Appropriations (1985).[77] Disincentives in the USDOL funding process documented by these studies and also by others include: (1) rewarding "inefficient" states and penalizing "efficient" states because efficiency savings in the form of reduced staff MPUs lead to future cuts—not just in staff funding, but also in NPS and AS&T funding levels (which are driven by MPU-based staff funding); (2) rewarding higher state salary rates in the funding process by higher funding allocations for both staff and related support services; (3) a focus on just costs, rather than a dual emphasis on costs and productivity (apart from arbitrary reductions in full funding for states with high MPUs), which does not appropriately encourage efficiency improvements; (4) discouraging efficient substitutions of automated operations for staff operations by relating total funding to staff costs; (5) providing no incentives to reduce costs below the level fully funded by USDOL; (6) an emphasis on short-run cost reductions at the possible expense of long-run productivity improvements; (7) a weak management-information system that does not allow USDOL to analyze or explain productivity differentials among the states (and thereby encourage improvements by less efficient states); (8) the absence of any efficiency or cost standards that could be utilized to encourage improvements in state operations or to assess state funding requests; and (9) a weak financial accounting system.[78]

Another aspect of USDOL's funding system is that it provides no positive incentives for reducing UC program complexity. In fact, a reasonable argument can be made that the procedures may well have induced at least some states to add to the complexity of their systems in attempting to increase their share of the total administrative funds available each year. Presumably, a state could increase its share of available funds by increasing the (measured) MPUs and salary levels for performing the tasks

77. See General Accounting Office (1984) and House Committee on Appropriations (1985: 31–33).

78. See General Accounting Office (1984); House Committee on Appropriations (1985: 31-35, 45-46, 52, 54 and 65); Dunn and Griffin (1984 and 1985); Interstate Conference of Employment Security Agencies and Macro Systems, Inc. (1979 and 1980); National Governors' Association (1983); Quality Control Subcommittee, Interstate Conference of Employment Security Agencies (1985); Templeman (1984); Thorne (1985a and 1985b); and Vaughn (1985).

required to operate its UC system. Such increases could be accomplished by increasing the complexities of the tasks required to process claims.

Although there is no proof that states may increase program complexity to obtain higher funding allocations, the wide variations among the states in both the MPUs required to perform essentially similar tasks and in average personnel costs certainly are consistent with this possibility.[79] This would be a tendency for those seeking to maximize either their budget levels or bureaucracy sizes (both of which have been suggested as motives for some public sector managers).[80] Since less than full funding typically is provided for those states with the highest MPUs (but evidently *not* for those with the highest salary levels) for a given claim processing function, it is not precisely clear what the final effects of such strategies on funding levels would be. However, a recent internal USDOL study concluded that:

> States with more complex (although not necessarily more efficient) laws and procedures may thereby receive a larger allocation of funds than a more efficient state. Again, this results in situations where State managerial decisions are made without regard to overall efficiency . . . .[81]

In short, although definitive evidence may not be available (or perhaps even obtainable) to prove that USDOL's funding procedures have tended to increase program complexity, it is clear that funding incentives neither directly encourage simplicity nor directly discourage complexity.

The view that USDOL's funding procedures have not encouraged administrative cost efficiency in state programs is not unanimously held. USDOL, for example, tends to attribute funding problems more to inefficient state management practices and operational procedures than to difficulties associated with

---

79. For evidence on differential state costs, see Interstate Conference of Employment Security Agencies and Macro Systems, Inc. (1979: III-9); National Governors' Association (1983: 6); House Committee on Appropriations (1985: 10-11); and Arizona Unemployment Insurance Administration (1985).

80. Niskanen (1971).

81. Cited in House Committee on Appropriations (1985: 74).

the funding process itself. They argue that not providing full funding for state MPUs (and particularly for the states with the highest MPUs) forces states to become more efficient.[82] Nevertheless, USDOL has not developed an objective basis for evaluating the causes of MPU differences among the states, and some differences clearly are due to factors outside of state management control (e.g., workload mix and the requirements contained in state law).[83]

Even without changes in USDOL's funding procedures and incentives, state operational efficiencies could probably be improved to some extent. For example, at least some states could improve their programs by: (1) developing more effective management control and financial accounting systems; (2) placing greater emphasis on efficiency and quality work in their employee reward systems; and (3) adopting the procedures for performing the same or similar tasks that are utilized in relatively efficient states.[84]

Lack of Payment Accuracy and Overpayment Detection/Recovery Incentives

The funding process utilized by USDOL also has failed to provide *direct* incentives for states to increase overpayment detection/recovery efforts. In fact, this deficiency and others in the administrative funding process have been noted in a recent position paper prepared by New York's former UC administrator, who explains that funding levels for benefit payment control activities are *not* related to the actual efforts or results of states in detecting and recovering overpayments.[85] Instead, such (general) funding levels depend on the total workloads processed in a state, regardless of its specific effort/result levels in benefit payment control activities. It appears that it would be appropriate for USDOL to consider including overpayment detection/recovery incentives in the administrative funding process.

---

82. House Committee on Appropriations (1985: 24–26).
83. House Committee on Appropriations (1985: 25–26).
84. See House Committee on Appropriations (1985: 11); Kingston, Burgess and St. Louis (1983: 49); and Kingston and Burgess (1981b: 54–58).
85. Dunn (1985).

There are, in fact, strong indications that USDOL has increased its emphasis on payment integrity, overpayment detection and recovery procedures, and other benefit payment control activities. As early as FY 1983, USDOL began to integrate such an emphasis into its "Program and Budget Planning" (PBP) process, perhaps partly in response to the K-B and B-K-S study findings discussed in chapter 2. More recently, USDOL has taken the additional step of adding "Measures of Achievement" to its PBP process to encourage the states to set explicit goals for enhancing efforts to prevent, detect and recover overpayments.[86] Furthermore, starting in FY 1985, states with problems indicated by Random Audit program findings were instructed to include corrective action plans in their PBP documents, with target dates for accomplishing certain goals.[87] Although these corrective action plans were suspended for FY 1986 (in anticipation of the implementation of the Quality Control program), some states continued to formulate and submit them. Hence, even though USDOL has not yet taken the additional step of backing its new emphasis on payment accuracy with substantive administrative funding incentives, it is clear that a much greater emphasis has been placed on prevention, detection and recovery of overpayments in recent years.

Possible Funding System Improvements

The above analysis clearly establishes the existence of some serious deficiencies in the USDOL system to fund the administrative operations of state UC programs. Unfortunately, identifying the adverse incentives is much simpler than it would be to eliminate them without creating other undesirable/unintended side effects. A number of possible reform approaches might be taken, but only some of the major possibilities are discussed in this section. Perhaps the most obvious approach would be to improve but maintain the essential features of the funding system

---

86. For the fiscal year 1985 and 1986 "Measures of Achievement," see U.S. Department of Labor (1984a and 1985b).

87. U.S. Department of Labor (1985b: Cover Memorandum).

by eliminating or at least substantially reducing many of its adverse features. Many other approaches also could be taken, however, including: (1) federal funding for ''model'' state UC systems, which would include cost standards; (2) a system of federal block grants to the states; and (3) ''devolution'' of administrative funding from the federal government to the states.[88]

In evaluating ways to improve the administrative funding process, it is extremely difficult and perhaps impossible to fully determine the benefits and costs of many specific proposals without substantial research and pilot testing. Administrative funding solutions that seem appealing should be carefully analyzed and evaluated prior to adoption for the UC system as a whole. Moreover, any attempt to substantively improve the administrative funding process also would benefit from a careful review of the findings of past attempts to improve the process.[89]

Pessimism about the likelihood that USDOL could rapidly respond to the problems analyzed in this chapter could be easily supported, based on the numerous other responsibilities already assigned to USDOL's relatively small Unemployment Insurance Service staff. Prior to the increase in staff for the recently implemented Quality Control program, the Unemployment Insurance Service staff had fallen to less than half of its peak of about 225 positions during the early 1970s. During the last few years, both Rubin and the National Commission on Unemployment Compensation have questioned whether the extremely small staff can ''perform even essential responsibilities competently.''[90] However, as noted above, USDOL already is in the process of addressing some of the adverse impacts analyzed in this chapter. Accordingly, the prospects of an improved administrative funding process appear to have increased considerably.

---

88. Another obvious possibility would be complete federalization of the UC system, but that approach is not considered because of the assumption made in this study that a federal-state UC system will continue to operate in the United States.

89. Ron Nairn, who is an administrative financing expert with the Oregon UC agency, has stressed that previous attempts to improve the administrative funding process provide a number of lessons for any future attempts in this area.

90. Rubin (1983: 30) and National Commission on Unemployment Compensation (1980: 129).

Maintaining But Improving the Funding System

The analysis in this chapter indicates that attempting to maintain but improve USDOL's administrative funding process would be a major undertaking because of the large number of adverse and interrelated impacts. The following issues would be relevant in determining how to improve that funding process: (1) the overall underfunding of state programs and the related issue of UC program complexity; (2) specific underfunding of NPS costs (including automation costs) and the need for more flexibility in allowing states to determine how to spend whatever total administrative funds they receive; (3) improved incentives for state innovations and automation; (4) incentives for states to minimize administrative costs, other things equal; (5) incentives for the detection/recovery of benefit overpayments; (6) incentives for states to achieve payment accuracy and other program quality criteria;[91] and (7) incentives for states to conduct the research and pilot tests necessary to evaluate various proposals for improving the existing UC system. The changes already implemented by USDOL for FY 1987 were noted above, and the apparent contribution of these changes to an improved system will be referenced in the following discussion of these seven issues.

Increase in Funding v. Program Simplification. The underfunding of state UC program operations is an issue that has been of great concern to state UC program administrators in recent years. The evidence offered to support this contention is that USDOL does not fully fund the MPUs resulting from its own Cost Model process. Certainly, recent federal budget decisions have forced USDOL to underfund state programs in the sense charged by state UC program administrators. In addition, the analysis offered earlier in this chapter suggests that an increase in administrative funding levels, given existing UC program complexity, likely would reduce payment errors (by an unknown amount). Increased (overall) administrative funding levels also

---

91. The importance of relating administrative funding to the quality of state UC program operations also was noted in a study by the Interstate Conference of Employment Security Agencies and Macro Systems, Inc. (1980: 607).

have been advocated by others, including the National Commission on Unemployment Compensation and Rubin.[92] Although not directly related to the issue of payment accuracy per se, the findings of Holen and Horwitz suggest that increased administrative funding may increase the rate of nonmonetary denials to (implicitly) ineligible claimants who would stop filing for benefits because of increased administrative scrutiny.[93] Corson, Hershey and Kerachsky also conclude that increased staff resources may be required to increase nonmonetary denial rates for ineligible claimants.[94] In short, a broad spectrum of informed opinion is available to support the contention that an overall increase in administrative funding might serve to improve the operation of the UC system.

There also is a strong basis for challenging the cost effectiveness of an increase in overall administrative funding as the major technique for correcting existing UC system deficiencies. The B-K-S study findings mentioned in chapter 2 (and discussed in further detail in chapter 7), for example, question the assumption that increased administrative funding actually would result in significantly improved administration of certain important aspects of the UC program. The investigators in that study required at least 50 times as much time as typically would be available in the operational UC system in attempting to *fully* verify the benefit eligibility of each claim. Clearly, neither legislators nor administrators would support such a large increase in funding for this purpose. Moreover, even with the extremely large resource commitment of the B-K-S study, it was found that nearly half or more of all reported worksearch contacts could *not* be verified as either acceptable or unacceptable in three of the five study states.[95] These findings suggest that marginal or even very large increases in administrative funding for enforcement of existing weekly UC eligibility criteria—especially in the absence of

---

92. National Commission on Unemployment Compensation (1980: 129–130) and Rubin (1983: 254–255).
93. Holen and Horwitz (1976: 426 and 428).
94. Corson et al. (1986: 124).
95. See chapter 7 and Kingston, Burgess and St. Louis (1986) for detailed analyses of worksearch verification and worksearch noncompliance problems.

many other changes advocated in this study—probably would be difficult to justify. The recent analysis of administrative funding by the House Committee on Appropriations also questions whether an overall increase in administrative funding would significantly improve the performance and quality of state programs.[96]

These considerations indicate that the underfunding issue raised by state administrators is just one aspect of a more basic social decision about how much UC program complexity is justified and should be funded. The current underfunding debate between USDOL and the states mainly misses this more fundamental point. Complexity issues need to be considered in the underfunding context. For example, should a federal-state funding system allow unlimited complexity in state programs that would be supported by administrative funds pooled from all UC jurisdictions? Suppose, for example, that some consensus could be reached on how much state program complexity would be accepted for federal-state administrative funding purposes. Once this decision was made, presumably no federal funding would be provided for complexity above that level. The requirement that states pay the administrative costs for any additional complexity probably would represent a strong incentive for simplification of state programs.

USDOL has persistently argued that achieving greater administrative and operational efficiencies would largely eliminate the "underfunding" that states perceive.[97] The analysis in this study certainly suggests that there is some validity to this contention. State UC program administrators—including several who support many other proposals included in this study—appear to be virtually unanimous in their opinion that their overall administrative funding levels are inadequate.[98] Nonetheless, the state position still does not appear to us to be a convincing one. Unless other very major changes were made in the UC system, it seems

---

96. House Committee on Appropriations (1985: 33).

97. For example, see House Committee on Appropriations (1985: 25).

98. For example, see Dunn and Griffin (1984 or 1985); House Committee on Appropriations (1985: 13-14, and 17-31); Quality Control Subcommittee (1985); Thorne (1985a); and Vaughn (1985).

doubtful that even a fairly substantial increase in (real) administrative funding levels alone would substantially improve the overall quality of the UC system.[99] In our view, it would be preferable to reduce complexity and improve efficiency in state operations rather than to increase administrative resources for the system as it currently operates.[100] However, a strong case can be made for correcting the underfunding of certain types of UC administrative costs, particularly the costs of automating state operations.

Increased Spending Flexibility and NPS Funding Levels. USDOL has made administrative funding allocations for specific workload items (e.g., initial claims and employer tax collections) and for specific types of costs (e.g., staff v. support services). The overall funding allocation for a state also has depended on the extent to which its workload has been funded with base or contingency positions. Besides adding to the overall complexity of the funding process, these distinctions and many others have resulted in a compartmentalized funding system.[101] Moreover, once such compartments were created, considerable restrictions limited the flexibility of states in reallocating their total funding among various cost categories.

Another issue that merits careful evaluation is whether basing NPS funding levels on historical cost data has perpetuated both interstate inequities and selected state inefficiencies through time.[102] It clearly is the case that the substantial interstate differences in NPS costs are difficult to explain, even accounting for "explainable differences" among the states in the costs of obtaining services.[103]

A much better general approach would be to give states more

---

99. The federal spending obligations for UC administrative purposes for fiscal years 1982-1984 ranged from $1.4-$1.7 billion. See National Foundation for Unemployment Compensation & Workers' Compensation (1985b).

100. Golding (1985: 3-4) also has stressed that the UC system would be better served by an analysis of how to more efficiently distribute existing resources than by an analysis of why the existing system is underfunded.

101. Some states even strongly contend that USDOL favoritism enters the funding process. See House Committee on Appropriations (1985: 14).

102. This possibility is suggested by Templeman (1984).

103. See Templeman (1984) for a brief discussion of these issues; see House Committee on Appropriations (1985: 36-62) for an extensive analysis of them.

flexibility in determining how to make detailed spending decisions (e.g., staff v. computers) to best utilize whatever level of administrative funding may be provided by USDOL. It is our view that each state can better determine the optimal allocation of resources for itself than can a (relatively small) federal bureaucracy with responsibility for that state and for 52 other UC jurisdictions. The recent changes implemented by USDOL for FY 1987 allocations appear to represent a major change in giving states just such flexibility.[104] This increased flexibility, which includes an increase in the period over which states are allowed to offset differences in "earned" v. "used" positions, also should contribute to easing the base v. contingency funding problems resulting from how USDOL has funded quarterly variations in workloads.[105]

Improving the current funding process by increasing its flexibility is supported by the following findings of a recent analysis of the House Committee on Appropriations:

> Some State officials indicated that NPS costs could be more effectively controlled with a better and more efficient allocation system and by removing certain Federal restrictions. For example, they stated that current Federal restrictions on the payment of interest on large capital acquisitions preclude States from using various long term financing options which could turn out to be more cost effective in the long run. They also cited restrictions on the funding of depreciation which preclude States from accumulating capital replacement funds to replace worn capital equipment. Moreover, they indicated that delays were often experienced in obtaining Federal approval for equipment acquisitions. They stated that such delays forced emergency upgrading of equipment needs, usually at a much greater cost.[106]

The recent emphasis of USDOL on increasing spending flexibility seems particularly important in the context of short-

---

104. Jones (1986).

105. For one proposal for revising existing base/contingency funding procedures, see Dunn and Griffin (1984: 3–4 and 9).

106. House Committee on Appropriations (1985: 55).

run reforms because such a change may well be the quickest and most effective way of eliminating or at least reducing several of the adverse features incorporated into the funding system through the years. Consistent with the overall approach advocated in this section, USDOL also indicates that it will focus its monitoring on State performance outcomes rather than on expenditure by cost category.[107]

The increased state flexibility indicated by these changes may reduce the adverse impacts of USDOL's past funding process and may be particularly important in reducing state concerns about underfunded NPS/ automation costs. However, it still is our view that past state concerns about underfunding for NPS/automation costs have been very legitimate ones, and that some increase in funding for such costs very likely could be justified on an overall cost/benefit basis. Certainly, the analysis provided earlier in this chapter supports the need for improved automation of the UC system, even as it presently operates. In addition, the analysis in chapter 3 strongly supports increased automation as a major feature of state efforts to reduce the complexity of their programs and to improve overall administrative efficiency. Subsequent analyses in chapters 6 and 7 suggest that states should increase the use of computers in routinely processing benefit claims in order to more effectively monitor claimant compliance with eligibility criteria. In sum, there is a strong basis for supporting increased UC system automation.

Innovation/Automation Incentives. Past funding procedures have contained fairly strong disincentives for general innovations and, particularly, for substituting automated operations for staff-based procedures. Our analysis suggests that these past funding procedures could be revised to: (1) provide positive incentives, rather than disincentives, for states to aggressively experiment with administrative, operational, or procedural changes that might contribute to reduced payment errors and increased program quality; (2) provide definitive guidelines to allow states to estimate in advance how potential changes (including automation) would affect future funding levels, other

---

107. Jones (1986).

things equal; (3) allow states to supplement administrative
funding allotments with "outside" funding, without reducing
federal funding to offset any such increases; (4) eliminate the
adverse NPS/automation funding impacts contained in the Cost
Model System because such funding is directly tied to overall
staff levels (including the specific disincentives for substituting
automated operations for staff-based procedures that result from
this practice); and (5) reduce the complexity, uncertainty and
severity of the payback provisions that relate to the relatively
small amount of special funding available for automation.
Implementing even some of the above suggestions could represent an important improvement over past procedures.

Incentives for Administrative Cost Minimization. Providing
incentives for states to emphasize administrative efficiency (for a
given level of program quality) would be another desirable
feature of a revised USDOL administrative funding system. This
goal could be partly accomplished by implementing the suggested funding improvements discussed above. In addition,
explicitly rewarding or penalizing states on the basis of the extent
to which they minimize administrative costs (other things equal)
also should be considered. The explicit incentive system could
be devised in a number of different ways,[108] but the suggestion
that states should be encouraged to emphasize administrative
efficiency is hardly a novel proposal. The need for such
incentives has been emphasized by the states themselves, the
National Governors' Association, the General Accounting Office, the House Committee on Appropriations and an internal
USDOL report.[109]

Some specific changes that might be considered in creating
specific incentives for states to minimize administrative costs

108. A particularly effective—although perhaps drastic—technique might be to vary the extent
to which a state's employers were allowed to receive an offset credit against the FUTA tax on the
basis of the administrative cost effectiveness of that state's UC system. This admittedly extreme
approach to "cost-rating" state UC systems presumably would induce both legislators and
employers to press for administrative simplicity and efficiency in state UC programs. Whether
this approach or some less drastic one were taken, however, cost-effective UC program
administration should be strongly encouraged by whatever revised funding system might result
from an intensive review of the present funding process.

109. See House Committee on Appropriations (1985: 31-33); General Accounting Office
(1984); National Governors' Association (1983); Thorne (1985a and 1985b); and Vaughn (1985).

and increase productivity could include: (1) altering the current policy whereby any short-run cost savings are fully recaptured by USDOL through future Cost Model studies; (2) changing the current policy of rewarding relatively inefficient states with relatively high staff levels or salary levels by *not* directly relating NPS funding to overall staffing costs; (3) providing incentives for states to reduce costs below the levels at which their staff MPUs are fully funded; (4) creating incentives to emphasize long-run cost reductions; and (5) providing incentives for reducing program complexity (which should result in reduced overall administrative costs). Specific changes such as these and others suggested in this chapter, together with a strong emphasis on administrative efficiency, would greatly improve USDOL's administrative funding process. However, USDOL evidently has rejected the possibility of encouraging states to minimize administrative costs through the adoption of federal cost standards (even though a USDOL-sponsored study concluded such an approach was feasible).[110]

Incentives for Payment Accuracy and for Overpayment Detection and Recovery. The administrative funding process also could be improved by providing explicit incentives that would encourage states to emphasize payment accuracy (in terms of both underpayments and overpayments) and also the detection and recovery of UC benefit overpayments.[111] At least some portion of the administrative funding received by a state should be directly related to the *results* of such activities. Given an accurate payment error measurement system, it would be possible to evaluate the payment error detection procedures used routinely by state agencies. Alternatively, or in combination

---

110. House Committee on Appropriations (1985: 74–75).
111. The raw data available for this study only relate to UC benefit overpayments (and, to a more limited extent, underpayments) to claimants, not UC tax underpayments (or overpayments) by employers. However, the frequent misreporting of wages by employers (for benefit determination purposes) found in the B-K-S study suggests that employer errors in paying taxes also may be a common problem. In any case, the current administrative funding system does not directly encourage the detection/collection of UC tax underpayments. Consequently, incentives similar to those that would encourage benefit payment accuracy and benefit overpayment detection/recovery efforts could be utilized to encourage UC tax underpayment prevention/detection/collection efforts. Nonetheless, only benefit payment issues are discussed in the text.

with an emphasis on *results*, agency *efforts* in these areas could be encouraged by direct funding, instead of basing funding on overall claim load activity. Funding incentives to encourage state overpayment detection/recovery efforts have been strongly advocated by several state agencies, including those in Arizona, Florida, New York and Oregon.[112] Furthermore, Dunn has provided a careful analysis of the adverse incentives contained in USDOL's past administrative funding process for overpayment detection/recovery efforts, and also has formulated a specific proposal for altering the administrative funding process.[113] Another approach for enhancing benefit overpayment recovery efforts would be to allow states to make the recovery of (nonadministrative) benefit overpayments separate "profit centers" in which resources could be spent on recovering benefit overpayments as long as (marginal) recovery costs were less than or equal to (marginal) overpayments recovered.[114]

Incentives for Payment Accuracy and Overall Program Quality. Emphasizing compliance with payment accuracy and other quality criteria through the administrative funding process would force states to directly confront the underlying causes of any problems they had in meeting such criteria. One possible paradox of utilizing funding incentives to enforce compliance with quality criteria is that states with programs of lower quality would receive less administrative funding (other things equal) than states with programs of higher quality. It could be argued, however, that the former states actually would need more administrative funds to correct their problems. Even though this paradox might represent a problem in the initial stages of implementing a revised funding system, it also must be recognized that the financial rewards and penalties provided by the

---

112. See Vaughn (1985); Burnett and Pendleton (1985); Dunn (1985); and Thorne (1985a).

113. See Dunn (1985). In particular, among other deficiencies in USDOL's funding system, Dunn points out that the real workload involved in controlling fraud is the actual number of fraud cases they process, not total weeks claimed (which has been USDOL's basis for funding state "benefit payment control" activities). Dunn proposes that funding for benefit payment control activities instead be directly related to state efforts in detecting, establishing and prosecuting overpayments.

114. This approach would be consistent with a position taken by Arizona's UC program administrator that direct incentives should be provided to state agencies for detecting/recovering overpayments. See Vaughn (1985).

administrative funding system probably would be among the strongest incentives that realistically could be provided for complying with quality criteria. In the longer run, such an approach presumably would induce states to revise their UC systems in order to comply with quality criteria. However, it might be appropriate to provide for an initial grace period, prior to applying financial sanctions, to allow states to make the changes required to comply with such criteria.

Incentives for Research/Pilot Studies. Several suggestions for improving the existing administrative funding system have been provided above. Taken together, these recommendations would eliminate many of the adverse incentives which characterize the current funding system and would provide a number of positive inducements for states to reduce the complexity of their programs and to enhance the integrity of their payment systems. Once again, however, the importance of conducting research and demonstration projects to evaluate these proposals should be emphasized. The interactions that characterize the UC system are very complicated ones, and seemingly desirable changes in administrative funding policies or procedures could produce unanticipated and undesirable side effects. Consequently, another important feature of a revised administrative funding system would be appropriate incentives to encourage state UC agencies to participate in such research and demonstration projects. Alternatively, USDOL could directly fund such research and demonstration projects.

Administrative Funding for "Model" State Programs

Another approach to revising current administrative funding procedures would be for USDOL to fund each state only for performing the tasks contained in a "model" UC system that included cost standards to reflect efficient administrative procedures and operations. Under this approach, a consensus view of an "ideal" or "acceptable" UC system would have to be developed. The development of any (reasonable) "model" system for funding purposes obviously would be an extremely difficult task, requiring substantial state input and a considerable research effort. In developing a "model" system, it also would be necessary to account for the adverse features of USDOL's funding system (and suggested improvements) discussed above. As one example, any revised funding system could provide strong incentives for a reasonable level of payment accuracy and for the detection/recovery of benefit overpayments. Rather than discussing aspects such as these, however, a few comments on certain broad issues that would be involved in developing a "model" UC program for funding purposes are provided below.

Simply specifying the elements of a "model" UC system for administrative funding purposes would involve a number of difficult decisions, given the large degree of diversity currently found among state UC systems. A few of these issues are raised for illustrative purposes. One set of decisions involved in specifying a "model" system would relate to what eligibility criteria should be included for funding purposes. Relevant questions would include the following. What would the monetary eligibility criteria be and would these include a weeks-of-work requirement? What would the job separation criteria be and would these criteria allow for distinguishing a few, many or no extenuating circumstances? What would the weekly eligibility criteria be and would these include an active search requirement? How long would maximum weekly support last? Should dependents' allowances be allowed? Many other specific and difficult issues also would be involved in determining the content of a "model" UC system, but the above questions indicate the nature of the task.

Once the basic content of a "model" UC program were identified, it then would be necessary to deal with a number of other issues to determine the funding required in each state to administer the program. How much funding variation would be allowed for serving claimants in different areas (e.g., a claimant in rural Alaska v. one in Phoenix)? Would somewhat different funding levels per unit of activity be justified for smaller than for larger states?[115] How much funding variation would be allowed for processing claims in different ways, such as filing for

---

115. For example, the Florida UC agency has suggested that different funding models might be appropriate for small, medium and large states. See Burnett and Pendleton (1985).

benefits in person v. by mail? The above questions are not exhaustive, but rather indicate the nature of the issues that would have to be resolved.

Such issues, in addition to questions of administrative and operational efficiency, would have to be carefully evaluated in order to develop cost standards that could be utilized in determining the actual funding allowed for particular state programs. Under this approach, it would be possible to emphasize administrative cost minimization by use of cost standards to define the maximum funding levels allowed for particular processes or activities. USDOL has attempted to improve state administrative efficiency in a number of ways through the years, so the idea of cost or efficiency standards would not be a novel one. Previous experience seems to suggest, however, that in the absence of effective incentives, at least some states are reluctant to replace less efficient with more efficient (and proven) operational techniques already utilized in other states. It was found in the "Operational Improvement and Cost Equalization" project jointly conducted by the states and USDOL in 1977 that many states failed to implement suggested improvements.[116] Accordingly, the development and implementation of cost standards probably would be a difficult process. A report prepared for USDOL in June 1984 concluded it would be feasible to incorporate cost standards into USDOL's funding process.[117] However, the concept of cost standards evidently was not accepted or further explored by USDOL (perhaps partly because of the recent emphasis of the Reagan administration on "devolvement," discussed later in this chapter, and on increasing state spending flexibility, discussed earlier in this chapter).

If a "model" UC system could be developed, it then could be used as the basis for funding state programs. States choosing to administer programs that were more costly than the "model" would have to fund the extra costs, since the federal-state funding system would provide funds only for the operation of a "model" system in each state. That is, states would be respon-

---

116. House Committee on Appropriations (1985: 10–11).
117. House Committee on Appropriations (1985: 74–75).

sible for their own administrative funding to cover the additional costs for: more complexity; less efficient techniques; extra monitoring of claimant compliance with eligibility criteria; and any other choices that resulted in a more costly program than that indicated by the "model" program.

The development of a "model" UC system for administrative funding purposes would be extremely difficult. Assuming that such a complex task could be accomplished, however, the end result could be a simpler funding system with fewer of the adverse features contained in the present funding system. This approach probably will not be a strong contender as a replacement for the existing administrative funding process, however, because it likely would be perceived by many as an attempt to impose federal standards on state programs.

Federal Block Grants for State Programs

One defect in USDOL's past funding process has been its lack of spending flexibility for the states. As noted above, the changes implemented by USDOL for FY 1987 allocations have greatly increased the flexibility states how have. If this concept were further extended, it could provide states administrative funds through block grants, which could be allocated among various cost categories at the discretion of each state. If such a system were combined with other improvements in the USDOL's funding system suggested in this chapter, the result could be a very substantial improvement over USDOL's past funding system. A recent study by the House Committee on Appropriations also has concluded that the block-grant approach could simplify the existing funding system and "improve both the quality and efficiency of the UI program."[118] An issue that would arise under such an approach is the provision for contingency funding for the administrative costs of dealing with the sudden workload

---

118. See House Committee on Appropriations (1985: 75-76) for a discussion of federal block grants, including further details on how such an approach could be utilized in place of USDOL's current funding system.

increases due to the need to process in a timely fashion the claims of all persons who file for benefits.[119]

Devolution of Administrative Funding Responsibility to States

The final possibility discussed in this chapter for improving the funding process would place the main or sole responsibility/authority for funding administrative operations on each state. In effect, such a change would carry the block-grant approach even further by essentially eliminating the federal role in administrative funding. The possibility of such "devolution" of administrative funding to the states has been discussed for some time among state and federal UC program administrators. In fact, at least one such proposal was advanced as early as 1955.[120] The recent discussion on this topic has been generated by the fact that the existing funding process creates net "winners" and "losers" among the states in terms of the portion of FUTA taxes paid by a state's employers that is returned in the form of administrative funds.[121] Not surprisingly, many of the net losers tend to question the equity of the existing funding process.

A strong rationale for devolution proposals is that they could correct several of the adverse incentives in USDOL's administrative funding process discussed earlier in this chapter. Making each state responsible for its own administrative funding might result in greater incentives for administrative efficiency, automation and innovations than have been contained in USDOL's funding system.[122] In addition, such a change would effectively

---

119. Both the Arizona and Oregon UC agencies have stressed the importance of providing some mechanism for a contingency funding process in any administrative financing system. For example, see Vaughn (1985).

120. J. Eldred Hill, Jr. of UBA, Inc. pointed out that this early proposal included a provision for allowing state employers to take up to a 95 percent offset of their federal FUTA UC tax liability against state taxes paid. For the details of the proposal, see Study Committee on Unemployment Compensation and Employment Service (1955).

121. Any other federal funding system also would create net winners and losers, unless the federal government simply were to serve as a collection agent for each state (in which case the funding system would be controlled by the states, not by the federal government).

122. Improved state administrative efficiency also is cited as a major rationale in the Reagan administration's May 1985 draft proposal for devolution. See National Foundation for Unemployment Compensation & Workers' Compensation (1985a).

eliminate the inflexibility of USDOL in recognizing state diversity, which has been a common complaint among the states.[123] It very well may be that devolution also would encourage states to reduce the complexity of their UC systems, as suggested by the Oregon agency.[124]

Another rationale for the devolution of administrative funding to the states is simply to make the funding of administrative costs (the smaller part of total UC program costs) comparable to the funding of benefit costs (the larger part). Since there is no comparable pooling and redistribution of UC tax collections to fund benefit payments for regular claims among state programs, one clearly could question how a federal pooling and redistribution system can be justified for administrative funds. One could marshal at least as strong an argument for federal funding of benefit payments (which may reflect unemployment resulting from national economic policy) as for federal funding of administrative costs (which are more directly within the control of state officials); in fact, such reasoning was used to justify the federal share of extended benefits (EB) paid when unemployment rates exceed certain threshold levels.

Many other considerations not addressed above also would be relevant in evaluating various devolvement proposals. The overall desirability of such a step also depends on value judgments that reflect political and economic philosophy. For example, devolution might weaken the concept of a national UC system, which currently has certain broad guidelines for some uniformity in terms of coverage and benefit entitlement requirements. Also, because of the existing cross-subsidization of administrative costs in some states by employer taxes collected in other states, devolution obviously would have major practical ramifications, including immediate administrative funding surpluses and deficits (relative to current operating levels) among various states. Another issue, as several state agencies have emphasized, is the need for a contingency funding process to allow states to serve all claimants in a timely manner, even though claims may vary

---

123. For example, see Dunn and Griffin (1984: 9); Ward (1985: 3); and House Committee on Appropriations (1985: 55).
124. Thorne (1985a).

sharply from quarter to quarter.[125] Some of the legal/administrative issues that would arise in implementing devolvement proposals have been addressed in a specific proposal advanced by three state governors.[126]

The devolution of administrative funding to the states has received some support from the Reagan administration.[127] In the February 4, 1985 USDOL news release on its FY 1986 budget, Ford stated:

Also included in this year's budget submission is a recommendation that Congress transfer administration and financing of the State Unemployment Service and Employment Service from the Federal government to state governments beginning in 1988.[128]

In May 1985, Deborah Steelman, special assistant to the President, Office of Intergovernmental Affairs, released a draft proposal for giving states full control over UC program administrative funding.[129] Further details on the administration's devolvement proposal subsequently were provided by Cogan.[130] Although this preliminary proposal lacks many of the specifics that would be required to implement such a change, it demonstrates that the Reagan administration has seriously considered such a change. Consistent with one of the main themes of this study, a major rationale given by the administration to support its proposal is the need to increase the administrative efficiency of state UC programs.[131]

With the devolution of administrative funding to the states, many adverse features of the current federal-state funding process would still be issues for individual states in determining how to allocate funds in their own UC programs. Accordingly,

---

125. For example, see Vaughn (1985).

126. See Evans, Atyieh and Robb (n.d.).

127. Long-run reforms have not yet been announced by USDOL. It still is possible that devolution could represent such a long-run change, although it now appears to the authors that devolution is less likely than fundamental changes in the existing funding process.

128. Ford (1985: 3).

129. This proposal was presented during the national meeting of the National Foundation for Unemployment Compensation and Workers' Compensation. See National Foundation for Unemployment Compensation & Workers' Compensation (1985a).

130. Cogan (1985).

131. National Foundation for Unemployment Compensation & Workers' Compensation (1985a).

much of the earlier discussion of adverse funding impacts and suggested funding improvements could still be relevant at the state level.

Conclusions

The analysis in this chapter demonstrates that a number of USDOL's funding procedures have adversely affected payment accuracy and overall program quality in state UC programs. Although a number of these adverse consequences probably were not anticipated by those who designed the federal-state administrative funding system, the consequences must be recognized by both UC program administrators and policymakers. Moreover, there appears to be little doubt that the adverse funding impacts are so serious that major reform of USDOL's funding system would be required to correct them. A number of different approaches to improving that system could be taken. The discussion of possible solutions in this chapter indicates that correcting all the deficiencies would be an extremely complex undertaking, even given the best of intentions by those involved in the process. Nonetheless, it must be noted that the short-run administrative funding changes implemented by USDOL for FY 1987 allocations appear to represent an important start toward potentially significant changes.

5
Federal Criteria for
State Agency Performance

While the administrative funding process discussed in chapter 4 probably represents the most important of a number of federal impacts on state UC program operations, there are many other ways in which federal policies and procedures affect state programs. For example, the Congress has established a number of standards and requirements to be administered by USDOL. Title III of the Social Security Act (which, along with Title IX, established the federal-state UC system) includes a requirement that state laws must contain provisions to ensure that UC benefits are paid *when due*, and Section 3304 of the Internal Revenue Code contains essentially the same requirement.[1] Subsequently, the Secretary of Labor determined that each UC jurisdiction's employment security law must contain provisions for the detection, prevention and recovery of overpayments.[2] In addition, USDOL has the statutory responsibility for ensuring that states operate "effective and efficient" UC programs. These requirements and others, combined with control of the administrative funding process, give USDOL substantial power to regulate state UC programs, and this power has been upheld in a number of court decisions. In fact, Rubin contends that USDOL's power over state administrative matters "is sufficiently broad to permit

---

1. U.S. Department of Labor (1979: 1). The Federal Unemployment Tax Act transferred Title IX of the Social Security Act to Chapter 23 of the Internal Revenue Code, of which Section 3304 is a part.
2. U.S. Department of Labor (1979: 1).

131

virtually any federal control over administration the DOL sees fit
to impose."[3]

A number of federal standards and performance criteria have
been established since 1935 relating to USDOL's responsibility
for ensuring that state UC programs are effectively operated and
that claimants are paid benefits when due.[4] The number of such
standards and other (less stringent) performance criteria have
greatly increased since the early 1970s.[5] It appears that the
escalation of federal standards and performance criteria during
the 1970s can be traced partly to changes in federal law and, to
a greater degree, to some major court cases that affected the UC
system in that decade. Perhaps two of the most significant
judicial decisions were the Supreme Court's unanimous opinion
in the 1971 *Java* case and the 1975 ruling of a federal district
court in Illinois in the *Burtton* case. In the *Java* case, the
Supreme Court unanimously ruled that the administrative appeal
procedures at issue failed to insure the payment of benefits
"when due."[6] According to the Court, the Social Security Act
requires that benefits be paid at the earliest date that is "administratively feasible." In direct response to the *Java* ruling,
USDOL issued a promptness standard for appeals in 1972 to
ensure that claimants receive the prompt hearings required by
federal law.[7] In the *Burtton* case, the federal district court was
"appalled" by a state agency's delays in paying benefits, and
concluded the agency was violating the Social Security Act's
requirement to pay benefits "when due."[8] Largely in response to
this latter case, USDOL issued a benefit payment promptness
standard in 1976, which was revised in 1978.[9] It is clear that
USDOL's initial development of a strong emphasis on prompt-

---

3. Rubin (1983: 42).
4. For an extensive discussion of federal standards, see Rubin (1983: Ch. 3).
5. For example, a revised standard for claim filing issued in 1970 describes in great detail the circumstances that states must adhere to in processing claims, including detailed requirements about the services that must be provided to different categories of claimants. For a detailed discussion of this standard and the escalation of other criteria since the early 1970s, see Rubin (1983: 11-33 and 41-64).
6. *Java v. California Department of Human Resources Development*, 402 U.S. 1 21 (1971).
7. Rubin (1983: 43).
8. Rubin (1983: 224).
9. U.S. Department of Labor (1984g: 4) and Rubin (1983: 225).

ness was the direct result of the above (and other) court decisions.[10] In fact, Carolyn Golding, director of USDOL's Unemployment Insurance Service, recently underscored the importance of these judicial decisions in causing USDOL to publish promptness standards.[11]

The above background provides a context for the analysis of USDOL performance criteria and quality measures undertaken in this chapter. The focus is a fairly narrow one emphasizing: selected performance criteria and quality measures utilized by USDOL to evaluate state programs; some adverse incentives created by these measures, including the possibility that payment errors may have resulted in at least some states from attempts to comply with certain criteria; and some possible improvements in these performance measures.[12] The chapter is organized as follows. First, several dimensions of USDOL's system for more broadly measuring state program quality—the UI Quality Appraisal system—are considered. Then, the implications of the relative emphasis placed by USDOL on the quantity v. the quality of UC "production" are considered, particularly how this emphasis may have contributed to the payment error problems discussed in chapter 2. Finally, a brief discussion of possible improvements in USDOL performance criteria is provided.[13]

Quality Appraisal System

A task force of federal and state staff was established by USDOL in 1975 to determine how USDOL should assess the

10. For a discussion of promptness standards for appeals, including the role of judicial decisions in leading to those standards, see Owen and Wood (1980) and Rubin (1980).

11. Golding (1985: 2–3).

12. Other important federal performance criteria include those contained in the pay/performance rating system that applies to USDOL employees. If the incentive system to which federal employees respond contained adverse features, such adverse features might contribute to some of the quality problems discussed in this and other chapters. Because the authors have no substantive basis for analyzing this issue, it is not considered in this chapter. However, the possibility that the federal bureaucracy may adversely affect the UC system has been discussed in a different context by Rubin (1983: 31-33).

13. A much briefer discussion of many of the adverse impacts and some of the responses discussed in this chapter may be found in a 1983 report prepared for USDOL. See Kingston, Burgess and St. Louis (1983).

quality of state operations, consistent with its responsibility to ensure that states operate "effective and efficient" programs. According to USDOL, the basic approach taken was to restrict the performance levels developed to reflect only the requirements included in federal law.[14] The result was a Performance Appraisal Package which was utilized in all states in fiscal years 1976 and 1977.[15] Following this initial effort, "desired levels of achievement" (DLAs) were established for several aspects of state program operations starting in FY 1978.[16] In FY 1979, the Performance Appraisal Package was further revised and retitled the UI Quality Appraisal program. Subsequently, annual revisions have been made in the program, but the basic DLAs have remained quite similar since its inception.

DLAs and State Performance

The desired levels of achievement established by USDOL may be illustrated by those included in the FY 1984 Quality Appraisal program (see table 5-1). The 24 DLAs include 17 distinct criteria for the payment and processing of benefit claims, four for tax collection and processing activities, and three for state trust fund management activities.[17] Twelve of the DLAs for the payment or processing of UC benefit payments relate to promptness or timeliness, and only five relate to the quality of performance achieved in these activities.[18]

If the Quality Appraisal results for benefit payment or processing activities during the early years of this program could be accepted as good indicators of state UC program quality, then a case could be made that the states generally were more deficient in meeting promptness than quality criteria. For example, many

14. Golding (1985: 2).
15. U.S. Department of Labor (1984g: 3).
16. U.S. Department of Labor (1984g: 3).
17. A total of 20 criteria are listed in part I of table 5-1 for benefit payment/processing. However, six of the DLAs for initial claim promptness actually represent only three distinct criteria because separately stated criteria are included for states with v. without waiting weeks.
18. This mix is fairly similar to that in earlier years. For example, the mix for FY 1980 also was 12 promptness and 5 quality criteria, as reported in chapter 2 (see table 2-1). Also, the FY 1982 mix included 11 promptness and 4 quality criteria, as reported in U.S. Department of Labor (1982c: 6).

TABLE 5-1
USDOL Desired Levels of Achievement
FY 1984

Part I. Benefit Payment/Processing

Initial Claims Performance
— A maximum of three confirmed issues per 100 cases

Initial Claims Promptness—Intrastate
— In Waiting Week States: A minimum of 87 percent of first payments made within 14 days of first compensable week ending date
— In Nonwaiting Week States: A minimum of 87 percent of first payments made within 21 days of first compensable week ending date
— A mimimum of 93 percent of first payments made within 35 days of the first compensable week ending date

Initial Class Promptness—Interstate
— In Waiting Week States: A mimimum of 70 percent of first payments made within 14 days of first compensable week ending date
— In Nonwaiting Week States: A mimimum of 70 percent of first payments made within 21 days of first compensable week ending date
— A minimum of 78 percent of first payments made within 35 days of the first compensable week ending date

Initial Claims Promptness—UCFE
— In Waiting Week States: A mimimum of 70 percent of first payments made within 14 days of first compensable weeke ending date
— In Nonwaiting Week States: A minimum of 70 percent of first payments made within 21 days of first compensable week ending date
— A minimum of 78 percent of first payments made within 35 days of the first compensable week ending date

Weeks Claimed Performance
— A maximum of 7 percent of total weeks claimed affected by confirmed weeks claimed issues

Nonmonetary Determinations Performance—Intrastate
— For Separation Cases: A minimum of 75 percent of cases acceptable
— For Nonseparation Cases: A minimum of 80 percent of cases acceptable

Nonmonetary Determination Promptness—Intrastate
— A minimum of 80 percent of determinations timely

Combined Wage Claims
— A minimum of 75 percent of wage transfers made timely

Appeals Performance
— A minimum of 80 percent of cases scoring 80 percent or more

TABLE 5–1
(continued)

Part I. Benefit Payment/Processing

Appeals Promptness—Lower Authority
— A minimum of 60 percent of appeal decisions made within 30 days
— A minimum of 80 percent of appeal decisions made within 45 days

Appeals Promptness—Higher Authority
— A minimum of 40 percent of appeal decisions made within 45 days
— A minimum of 80 percent of appeal decisions made within 75 days

Part II. Tax Collection/Processing and Fund Management

Status Determination Promptness
— A minimum of 80 percent of determinations of employer liability made within 180 days of the liability date

Field Audits
— A minimum of 4 percent penetration

Report Delinquency
— A minimum of 90 percent of employers filing reports by end of quarter

Collections
— A minimum of 75 percent of delinquent accounts with some monies obtained within 150 days from the end of the quarter

Fund Management
— A minimum of 90 percent of collected taxes deposited within 3 days of receipt
— A maximum of 2 days for which funds are on deposit in the Clearing Account before being transferred to the Trust Fund
— A maximum of one day for withdrawal of money from the Trust Fund before paying benefits

Source: USDOL (1984g: Figure I–2).

more states failed to meet the promptness than the quality-of-performance criteria in FY 1980; similarly, more states failed to meet the promptness than the quality criteria in the FY 1982 Quality Appraisal.[19] Such results could have been used as a basis

19. See U.S. Department of Labor (1980: 9–53) and U.S. Department of Labor (1982c: 9–24).

for an increased emphasis by USDOL on promptness in processing and paying claims.

More recent Quality Appraisals, however, yield a different
pattern of results. For FY 1984, for example, the findings
indicate that the percentage of states deficient in meeting
promptness criteria and quality criteria generally does not differ
sharply. Between 10 and 59 percent of the participating states
failed to meet the five quality criteria listed in table 5-1, with a
simple average of about 30 percent failing to achieve these
DLAs,[20] while between 2 and 54 percent failed to meet the 12
promptness DLAs, with a simple average of about 25 percent
failing to satisfy these criteria.[21] One possible explanation for the
change in the extent to which states have satisfied the promptness
v. quality DLAs over the past several years could be that
USDOL increased its emphasis on the promptness criteria in
those years. Such pressures, in turn, could have led to increased
overpayments and reduced program quality, as discussed in more
detail in a subsequent section of this chapter.

Selected Limitations of the Quality Appraisal System

The Quality Appraisal system does not constitute a comprehensive or valid system for measuring the *overall* quality of state
UC program administration. The purpose here, however, is not
to provide an in-depth evaluation of this system, or even of that
portion related to benefit processing and payment activities.
Rather, a few important limitations of the benefits component of
the Quality Appraisal program are identified, including: (1) an
overemphasis on the promptness v. the quality of claim processing and payments; (2) sampling and statistical issues; (3) the
review process; and (4) certain other limitations. These are noted
as background for a discussion of their effects on the problem of
payment errors and its control.

Promptness v. Quality. A major limitation of the Quality
Appraisal system is that prompt processing has been emphasized
much more heavily than the quality with which claims are

20. U.S. Department of Labor (1984g: 8–32).
21. U.S. Department of Labor (1984g: 8–32).

processed and paid. This is indicated in part by the mix of DLAs in the system, with nearly two-thirds of the DLAs concerned specifically with processing and payment promptness. The imbalance of emphasis is even more clearly illustrated by the fact that an explicit DLA related to either overpayments or underpayments has not been included in the Quality Appraisal program.[22] Combined with the historical emphasis which has been placed on processing and payment promptness, the absence of any DLA related to payment accuracy is, in our view, a particularly serious limitation of the Quality Appraisal program.[23]

It should be noted, however, that just as the earlier USDOL emphasis may have led to improved state promptness, additional emphasis on quality could lead to improved state performance in this area as well. As noted in chapter 4, USDOL already has begun to move in the direction of encouraging the states to improve their performance with respect to the control of overpayments. As early as FY 1983, USDOL began to add an emphasis on payment integrity and overpayment detection and recovery procedures to its Program and Budget Planning (PBP) process.[24] More recently, USDOL has added Measures of Achievement in its PBP process to encourage state UC agencies to set explicit goals for improving procedures to prevent, detect and recover overpayments.[25] In fact, beginning in FY 1985, states with overpayment problems (documented through Random Audit program results) were expected to formulate and submit

---

22. The desired levels of achievement for fiscal year 1985, for example, included no DLAs for overpayment prevention or detection. See U.S. Department of Labor (1984a: 29-31). Furthermore, no DLAs were added for overpayment prevention or detection for FY 1986; see U.S. Department of Labor (1985b).

23. The findings of the 1980 K-B study discussed in chapter 2 indicate that most overpayments are *not* detected by routine state UC agency procedures; even if USDOL had wanted to monitor state performance in detecting overpayments, an accurate measure of such performance could not have been obtained from operational data in past years in any case. However, it also should be noted that either the Random Audit system implemented in 46 states by 1984 or the recently introduced Quality Control Program could provide the basis for more accurately determining actual overpayment rates and for measuring state UC agency performance in detecting (but not in preventing or recovering) overpayments.

24. U.S. Department of Labor (1984a and 1985b).

25. For the Measures of Achievement included in the planning process for fiscal years 1985-86, see U.S. Department of Labor (1984a and 1985b).

corrective action plans (including specific dates by which certain goals were to be achieved) as a part of the budgeting and planning process.[26] While it appears that USDOL is moving to correct the historical imbalance in its emphasis on promptness v. payment accuracy, such measures and the necessity for them do not imply that the prompt payment of UC benefits is unimportant or unnecessary. Undue delay in the payment of benefits can cause considerable hardships for claimants and their families. Furthermore, given that the pressures for the prompt payment of benefits have originated primarily from judicial decisions that cannot be ignored, the timely payment of benefits will continue to be among the priority goals of UC program administrators. Nonetheless, it still remains our judgment that the past imbalance between speed and quality has not been sufficiently corrected. It will be important to ensure that the information provided by the Random Audit program and the recently initiated Quality Control program is *effectively* utilized to enhance program quality. The formulation of Measures of Achievement for various payment control activities in the PBP process constitutes an important first step but will not, of itself, be sufficient to overcome the overemphasis on the promptness criteria.

Sampling and Statistical Issues. Another major limitation of the Quality Appraisal system is related to a number of technical limitations in the guidelines provided by USDOL for selecting samples for measuring state performance in terms of initial claims, weeks claimed, nonmonetary determinations and appeals (reported above in table 5-1).[27] One of these limitations is that the sampling methodology does not provide for the selection of samples from the annual population of claims in a state. Instead, the samples are selected during a very short interval of a few weeks, and the results obtained from examining these samples

26. According to the PBP guidelines for FY 1986, corrective action plans were suspended during FY 1985 in anticipation of the implementation of USDOL's new Quality Control program, but some states evidently continued to emphasize such corrective action plans. See U.S. Department of Labor (1985b: Cover Memorandum).
27. For the sampling methodology developed by USDOL, see U.S. Department of Labor (n.d.). For a summary of the sample selection procedures for FY 1984, see U.S. Department of Labor (1984g: 46-47).

are presumed to be indicative of the operations of a state's UC program over an entire year.

A second limitation related to sampling procedures is the practice of selecting only a few local offices from which information on UC claims or claimants is obtained for the appraisals. Even though the findings generally are interpreted as reflecting statewide performance, no statistical tests are conducted to ascertain the extent to which the samples are representative (in terms of sex, age, industry, etc.) of the statewide population of claims.[28] In fact, it is quite possible that the samples selected are not even representative of the small subsets of statewide populations from which they are selected, particularly because the samples specified in USDOL guidelines are extremely small ones.[29] Another sampling limitation is that the guidelines for selecting samples within each local office also are deficient; they refer to ''random samples'' but do not provide specific rules for identifying the exact population to be sampled and the exact sampling procedures to be utilized to obtain a random sample (that could be replicated) from a well-identified population.[30]

Unfortunately, these and other sampling deficiencies in the Quality Appraisal system make it impossible to statistically generalize the findings to meaningful and identifiable statewide populations of claims or claimants.[31] The sampling guidelines thus make it impossible to obtain statistically sound estimates of

---

28. For a brief discussion of why representative samples (not just randomly selected samples) are an important consideration, see Burgess, Kingston and St. Louis (1982: 86-89).

29. U.S. Department of Labor (1984g: 46–47).

30. As one example, USDOL guidelines for selecting samples of active claimants within particular local offices for evaluating initial claims and weeks claimed in the Quality Appraisal indicate that at least 50 percent more claimants than required should be scheduled for interviews; this overscheduling is intended to compensate for the fact that some claimants probably will not appear at the designated times and places. These guidelines further suggest that in the event that too few claimants appear for such interviews, additional persons should be selected from among the claimants found in those local offices on the days the interviews are scheduled. Even if the sampling methodology for the selection of claimants were otherwise appropriate, no provisions are made in USDOL guidelines to identify or correct the serious sample biases that may result from these procedures.

31. A discussion of making inferences about populations on the basis of sample evidence may be found in introductory texts on sampling theory. For example, see Scheaffer, Mendenhall and Ott (1979) and Winer (1971).

statewide population characteristics on the basis of the sample evidence obtained.[32]

It is important to emphasize that the above sampling deficiencies are *not* relevant for USDOL's established DLAs for payment promptness. In contrast with procedures used in the Quality Appraisal program to assess state compliance with quality criteria, the procedures involved in measuring state compliance with the payment promptness criteria avoid all of the statistical and sampling problems described above. These latter procedures involve a census rather than the selection of samples, so that sampling errors are irrelevant for the DLAs for payment promptness. Moreover, information on payment promptness is gathered by USDOL every month of the year, rather than during a few weeks of each year.[33] These differences in the quality of information sought by USDOL about state compliance with the promptness criteria again suggest the extent of imbalance in the relative emphasis placed on compliance with the two types of criteria.

Review Process. Another limitation of the Quality Appraisal system has been the process utilized to review the potential issues detected for initial claims and weeks claimed. Periodically, teams of out-of-state adjudication experts, selected by USDOL, review the performance of each state's own personnel in processing cases. These review teams make site visits to local offices or mail claim centers to conduct detailed reviews of the

---

32. USDOL strongly disagrees with our assessment. In fact, Golding (1985: 3) recently stated that:

> . . . in the development of the quality appraisal system, there was extensive input in developing the statistical sampling component of the program from a private contractor who specializes in that area and from another contractor to validate the process. We also drew substantially upon our own staff capabilities.

Note that our criticisms of the statistical sampling plans used in the Quality Appraisal program do not relate to the techniques used to measure the promptness with which claims are processed and paid. No sampling is required for these measures because the time lapse performance measures used by USDOL are based on a *monthly census* of claims. The criticisms discussed in the text relate primarily to the sampling plans used to measure other dimensions of program quality. The weaknesses associated with these plans are sufficient, in our view, to seriously impair the usefulness of the statistics produced, either for individual local UC offices or for statewide UC programs.

33. These monthly reports are regularly published by USDOL and have been required since at least 1980. For a typical monthly report, see U.S. Department of Labor (1983).

quality and correctness of the decisions made in processing initial claims and weeks claimed for sampled cases. However, each state's eligibility rules are quite complex, and it is probable that only experts from a particular state could appreciate all the subtleties that might arise in specific cases for that state. This is apparently the rationale for allowing each state to appoint a policy committee of its own personnel to review the preliminary findings of the out-of-state experts. These state policy committees evaluate the findings of the performance appraisals conducted by the out-of-state review teams and either accept (confirm) or reject each potential issue.[34]

Although the rationale for the review process can be easily understood, the practical effect of using state policy committees often may be quite different from the intended effect. Because the desired levels of achievement established by USDOL for Quality Appraisal results relate to confirmed issues, a strong incentive exists for state policy committees to confirm only a certain number of potential issues to ensure that their states at least meet the desired levels of achievement established by USDOL. Indeed, a review of published Quality Appraisal results, which include both potential and confirmed issues, indicates that the discrepancy between the two is very large in some states.[35] Although many states may not respond to the incentive to confirm only an acceptable number of potential issues, the incentive obviously exists and it would not be unreasonable to assume that some states respond to that incentive. Potential incentives of this type should be carefully considered in structuring whatever review process might be established for payment accuracy (and other quality) indicators in either the Quality Appraisal system or the Quality Control program.

Other Limitations. Other limitations of the Quality Appraisal system include: (1) comprehensive measures of program quality, particularly for payment accuracy, are lacking; (2) much of the

---

34. For a discussion of these Quality Appraisal procedures, see U.S. Department of Labor (n.d.). It should be noted that, where Random Audit program results were available, USDOL substituted these results for the weeks-claimed and initial-claim portions of the Quality Appraisal program.

35. For example, see U.S. Department of Labor (1982c and 1984g).

review procedure relies on a simple review of the information originally used to process the case, and thus largely ignores the major issue of whether other information (that could have been but was not obtained) would have produced a different decision; (3) much of the review procedure does not require that original source documentation be obtained or verified; (4) the results are available only on an annual basis, rather than more frequently; and (5) perhaps partly because of the limitations discussed above, the Quality Appraisal system is not effectively utilized to improve program quality, at least in the view of UC program personnel in some states.[36] In summary, it appears that the Quality Appraisal system would require substantial modification to become an effective system for comprehensively measuring and evaluating many aspects of statewide UC program quality beyond the promptness criteria that are currently emphasized.

Effects of Overemphasis on Promptness

The prompt processing and payment of benefit claims obviously is one important aspect of overall UC program quality, consistent with the requirements of the Social Security Act. When promptness is emphasized so heavily as to virtually exclude concern about other factors, however, undesirable and unintended side effects are likely to occur. These impacts merit careful consideration. The expected impact of USDOL's emphasis on payment promptness, for example, may be appropriately compared to the effects of dropping the penalty for errors in a timed typing test. Just as typists would type much faster if there were no penalties for errors, UC program personnel would be expected to process or pay claims much more rapidly with no "deductions" for processing or payment errors. In fact, at least during the 1979-1982 interval when both the K-B and B-K-S studies were being conducted (and apparently also since that time), at least some UC jurisdictions evidently have participated

---

36. For example, approximately three-fourths of the respondents to a survey of state UC program personnel conducted as part of the 1979-80 K-B study disagreed or strongly disagreed that Quality Appraisal results were effectively utilized to improve efforts by local office personnel in their states to prevent overpayments. See Kingston and Burgess (1981b: 55).

in a nationwide "contest" in terms of the percentages of first payments that were promptly made.[37] The unbalanced emphasis USDOL places on prompt payments appears to adversely impact state UC program operations, as would be expected. For example, the state UC agency personnel who participated in the 1979-80 K-B study were of the opinion that the USDOL promptness standards reduced the emphasis on payment accuracy in state programs, as indicated by the following composite opinion:

Unfortunately, the work environment and the "incentives/ reward" system for local office employees do not effectively encourage the prevention of overpayments. Even though the UI cost model provides minutes per unit (MPUs) for the prevention of overpayments by local office personnel, the primary emphasis within the local office is on "production" and not on preventing overpayments. Local office employees do not believe they are given sufficient time to effectively conduct the activities described above and, beyond the cost-model time credited for issuing a nonmonetary determination, local office personnel believe that they receive no positive encouragement to prevent overpayments.

Employees with the least experience oftentimes are placed on the new claims line and, because they lack training and experience, they are unable to detect a number of potential issues that should be referred for adjudication. Moreover, once potential issues are referred for adjudication, the local office deputies typically are under great pressure to issue nonmonetary determinations within a relatively short period of time. Personnel performance evaluations for these local office deputies often place a great weight on the number of determinations issued per day or per week . . . . local office employees are encouraged to achieve

---

37. For example, Tennessee often ranks as the first-payment promptness "winner." In fact, the Tennessee UC agency hailed its first place finish for the year ending March 1980 in its agency newspaper during the K-B study. See the May 1980 issue of *Searchlight News*, published by the Tennessee Department of Employment Security.

relatively high rankings for their local offices, as measured by the monthly reports of first pay timeliness performance.[38]

The above summary view makes it clear that efforts to achieve USDOL performance criteria for first payments may have important effects on the overall incentive and reward structure used to evaluate employee performance in local UC offices. Such effects clearly would be expected to adversely impact on overall state UC program quality, particularly given limited administrative funding and the absence of any payment accuracy criteria. Moreover, the summary statement is not an isolated or outdated perception by state UC program personnel. For example, despite the recent steps taken by USDOL to add an emphasis on quality, the Interstate Conference of Employment Security Agencies, Inc. has raised the issue of how to balance this new emphasis with USDOL's long-standing emphasis on prompt processing:

> We need a definite understanding of the desired balance between the emphasis on quality which now appears to be in vogue as opposed to the emphasis on quantity and promptness which has been stressed for the last 10-12 years. Are we now to assume both tasks with the understanding that they are to require equal emphasis? Will additional dollars be provided to implement quality standards? It is one thing to develop and implement data collection but quite another to implement and carry out corrective action.[39]

The adverse incentives of emphasizing promptness have been stressed recently by several state UC agencies. For example, in commenting on an earlier version of this chapter, Oregon's Employment Division director, Raymond Thorne, wrote:

---

38. Kingston and Burgess (1981: J-1 and J-2). Respondents to the K-B study survey were the personnel who worked on that project in their respective states. Because the respondents were *not* chosen randomly, their views cannot be considered to statistically represent the views of the larger populations of other UC agency personnel in the study states. Also, the questionnaire was *not* distributed to state UC program directors, regional/district supervisors or local office managers. It is possible that the views of these groups might not coincide with the views summarized in the text. For further details on the survey, see Kingston and Burgess (1981b: 49-60 and Appendix J).

39. Heartwell, Jr. (1985: Attached Briefing Paper, 3).

I agree with your statements that incentives to parties involved with UI are lacking. Essentially, DOL expects speedy completion of all benefit payment procedures and penalizes those that cannot meet [the]. . . timeliness [criteria]. It puts our field staff into a "survival mode" of simply processing the claims within the underfunded time allocation. It caused us to cut our own management information system in favor of putting additional staff out on the "front lines." We have seen quality deteriorate in Oregon dramatically in the last two years, resulting in the errors that Random Audit is beginning to find.[40]

This same theme of the pressure of time lapse performance criteria, combined with limited administrative funding, has been emphasized by New York's former UC program administrator, Gerald Dunn.[41] The adverse impacts of USDOL timeliness criteria on state operations also have been stressed recently by James Hanna of the Nevada UC agency and Thurman Burnett and James Pendleton of the Florida UC agency.[42]

Some critics have contended that the evidence produced by the K-B and B-K-S studies fails to support the above contentions. They argue that, if federal timeliness requirements were responsible for many overpayments, the principal causes of the overpayments detected in those studies should reflect incorrect decisions when first payments are made. Because the most frequent overpayments in both the K-B and B-K-S studies were those due to violations of worksearch requirements, these critics have argued that federal promptness criteria apparently have little impact on UC overpayments.[43]

The first weakness in the reasoning of the critics is that federal promptness criteria are imposed for issuing nonmonetary determinations, not just for processing initial claims and making first

---

40. Thorne (1985b: 2).
41. Dunn and Griffin (1984: 12).
42. Hanna (1985) and Burnett and Pendleton (1985: 7).
43. Although only a small proportion of the total UC benefits paid statewide in the B-K-S study were overpaid because of errors in original monetary determinations, a relatively large percentage of all sampled cases involved errors in initial monetary determinations that affected either weekly or maximum benefit awards. To some extent, these errors in monetary determinations may reflect time-lapse pressures, as well as the absence of strong incentives for accurately obtaining wages by UC agency personnel or for accurately reporting wages by employers, and perhaps undue complexity in reporting requirements or reporting forms.

payments. These nonmonetary determinations relate specifically to eligibility criteria—including the ability, availability and, in most states, the active search requirements—that must be monitored for claimants on a weekly basis by UC agencies. Hence, to the extent that federal time lapse criteria relate to the nonmonetary eligibility criteria, the findings of both the K-B and B-K-S studies would be consistent with the potential for conflict between speed and quality in processing UC claims.

A second response to the argument is that the emphasis placed on rapid processing would be expected to set the overall tone and affect the incentive environment within which many other local office functions would be conducted. Great pressure on local office personnel to emphasize production speed probably results in reduced emphasis on payment accuracy. However, as noted in chapter 2, there was little substantive evidence prior to 1980 to support the belief that the timeliness criteria may have contributed to the problem of payment errors.

Since these payment error problems have been documented in the K-B and B-K-S studies and confirmed by USDOL's expanded Random Audit program, there has been an increase in emphasis on payment accuracy by USDOL. Particularly in light of the lead time required for a large bureaucracy to effectively respond to politically sensitive issues, USDOL's recent movement towards a more balanced emphasis that includes payment accuracy in evaluating the performance of state programs is certainly an encouraging development.

Some Possible Improvements in USDOL Performance Criteria

The overall implication of the analysis in the prior two sections is that USDOL performance criteria may have contributed both to increased overpayments and to other quality problems in state UC programs. It also appears likely that these problems may be important ones for some, and perhaps many, state UC agencies. Accordingly, a number of issues related to the improvement of the performance criteria by which USDOL evaluates state UC programs are discussed in this section.[44] In considering possible policy responses, however, it is important to reemphasize a major theme of this study. High overpayment rates are not the only problem; they also very likely are symptomatic of even more important problems, including: undue program complexity (chapter 3); adverse incentives (chapters 4, 5 and 6); and the severe problems state UC agencies confront in attempting to monitor claimant compliance with the continuing UC eligibility criteria (chapter 7). Federal and state responses to perceived overpayment problems should be formulated in light of these broader considerations, rather than being myopically targeted just on reducing payment errors.

Payment Accuracy Criteria

One basis for emphasizing benefit payment accuracy is the Social Security Act's requirement that benefits be paid "when due," assuming this requirement also implies that such payments should be made *only* when due. In fact, USDOL has explicitly argued that this interpretation of the "when due" clause is appropriate in a recent conformity hearing before an administrative law judge (even though USDOL never has adopted any payment accuracy performance criteria). In this case, USDOL contended that it "has consistently construed" the Social Security Act

> . . . to require state laws to insure full payment of unemployment compensation when due and also to prevent payment when not due. Each state agency is under an obligation to protect the financial integrity of its unemployment insurance fund by avoiding unjustified payments.[45]

Significantly, the administrative law judge in this case agreed with the USDOL position in a February 1985 decision in which the "when

---

44. A few of the ideas contained in this section have been briefly discussed by the authors in earlier work. Some possible improvements suggested by an analysis of the K-B study are provided in Kingston and Burgess (1981b: 51-56) and in Kingston, Burgess and St. Louis (1981). Some possible improvements suggested by an analysis of both the K-B and B-K-S study data are contained in Kingston, Burgess and St. Louis (1983).

45. Commerce Clearing House (1985: Para. 21, 749, 3999-69).

due'' clause was interpreted as not referring solely to the timeliness of payments to claimants.[46] A logical and direct extension of the position USDOL has taken in the above case obviously would be to develop payment accuracy criteria for state programs.

Payment accuracy criteria would, of course, most appropriately encompass underpayments as well as overpayments.[47] As noted in chapter 2, however, until very recently USDOL had no accurate basis for measuring compliance with any payment accuracy criteria that might have been developed for either overpayment or underpayment errors. Nonetheless, the Random Audit program (which was operating in 46 states by 1984) did provide a conceptually sound basis for measuring payment error rates in statewide UC programs. In anticipation of implementing a new Quality Control program, however, the Random Audit system was discontinued as of March 1985. At that time, Secretary of Labor Brock suspended the implementation of the proposed Quality Control program, pending a review of its purposes and design.[48] The core component of the Quality Control program was implemented in April 1986; it provides for the estimation of both overpayment and underpayment errors. The program has limitations, however, which will result in an underestimation of underpayment errors, as explained in the appendix to chapter 2.

One problem likely to be encountered in defining ''acceptable levels'' of state performance with respect to payment accuracy (and other quality) criteria arises from the diversity among different state UC systems. States with a worksearch requirement, for example, are much more likely to have high overpayment rates than states without this requirement (as explained in detail in chapter 7). As another example, states with more

---

46. Commerce Clearing House (1985: Para. 21, 749, 3999–67 and 3999–71).

47. Underpayments represent a relatively small percentage of benefit *payments actually made* in error, so the main payment accuracy issue would be overpayments. The main issue in terms of broadly defined underpayments presumably revolves around claimants who are incorrectly denied any payment, not claimants who incorrectly receive a smaller payment than that to which they are entitled. However, no reliable evidence yet is available on broadly defined underpayments.

48. For the announcement of the decision to review the design of Quality Control after its recent suspension, see *Federal Register* (1985: 31787-31792).

complex eligibility requirements are likely to experience higher
payment error rates than otherwise similar states with simpler
requirements.[49] In developing payment accuracy or other quality
criteria, policymakers will have to determine whether to impose
the same or different criteria on all states because of the
widespread differences that characterize state programs. Overall,
it is our view that the state diversity argument does not constitute
a valid basis for preventing or discouraging the development of
payment accuracy (and other quality) criteria, although state
diversity will make the development of such criteria a much
more difficult task than would be the case in a system that had no
state differences.

Other Program Quality Criteria

Many factors other than the prompt or accurate payment of
benefits could be included in a full set of UC program quality
criteria. Several possibilities for developing some of these other
criteria are briefly set out in this section. It should be strongly
emphasized at the outset that the discussion is merely suggestive
of some of the issues that may merit consideration. The experts
in this area would be the federal and especially the state UC
program administrators and operational personnel, who have a
detailed working knowledge of the UC system. Any quality
criteria developed should rely heavily both on the input of these
experts and on the informed opinions of the claimants and
employers served by the system. Given that qualification, the
following types of UC program interactions might be relevant for
consideration. The aspects of UC program quality discussed
relate to UC agency/claimant interactions, UC agency/employer
interactions and internal UC agency operations.

Claimant Interactions. Many UC agency/claimant interactions
would be relevant in evaluating overall UC program quality. First,
despite its limitations discussed earlier in this chapter, the existing

---

49. The Florida UC agency has made the point that state UC administrators must decide what
will be emphasized in their states. Burnett and Pendleton argue that, given fixed administrative
funding, more complexity in state law/policy implies more aspects of that law/policy must be
ignored, and this results in more payment errors. See Burnett and Pendleton (1985: 8).

Quality Appraisal system does include the following quality-of-performance criteria for such interactions (see table 5-1 above): (1) state performance in processing initial claims (focused narrowly on confirmed issues); (2) state performance in processing continued claims (focused narrowly on weeks claimed which are affected by confirmed issues); (3) state performance in terms of the completeness and correctness of nonmonetary determinations; and (4) the quality of appeal hearings and decisions rendered. Given an appropriate sampling framework, these items (or similar ones) could be included as part of a comprehensive system for evaluating overall UC program quality.

Other quality dimensions that might be considered for evaluating UC agency/claimant interactions could include the following: (1) accurate estimates of errors in incorrect denials of payments to eligible claimants (as discussed in the appendix to chapter 2); (2) an evaluation of the monetary determination process, including monetary determination errors that affect weekly benefit amounts or maximum benefit awards; (3) the extent of horizontal equity achieved in the nonmonetary eligibility determination process, including determinations that are or are not made; (4) the extent to which routine benefit payment control functions actually detect payment errors that occur; (5) evaluation of the overpayment collection process, probably including some emphasis on the volume (but not the percentage alone) of overpayments recovered; and (6) additional criteria for appeals, including the accuracy and horizontal equity involved in the decisions made.

Employer Interactions. Employer/UC agency interactions also are important in evaluating overall program quality. The existing Quality Appraisal system already includes the following quality-of-performance criteria for such interactions (see table 5-1 above): (1) a field audit penetration criterion for employer accounts; (2) an employer reporting delinquency criterion; and (3) a criterion for collecting funds due from delinquent employer accounts. Some other relevant employer/UC agency interactions to consider in developing quality criteria might include: (1) wage reporting errors (even if they do not result in underpayments or overpayments); (2) errors in benefit charges to employer accounts; (3) the overall tax collection process, including errors in tax rate determinations and payments; (4) employer interactions in the overall nonmonetary determination process, especially in terms of separation issues; (5) the overall process of identifying and acting on job refusals; (6) the overall process of identifying and acting on unreported earnings in covered employment; (7) the overall process of identifying employers who do not voluntarily report their existence; and (8) employer participation in the appeal process, including the accuracy and horizontal equity of the decisions made.

Internal Agency Operations. Other aspects of overall UC program quality relate more directly to factors involved with internal agency operations. The Quality Appraisal system already includes three technical criteria for the deposit, management and withdrawal of funds in UC trust fund accounts. Additional quality criteria for internal UC agency operations that relate more nearly to the focus of the present study might include factors such as: (1) measures of program complexity; (2) the effectiveness of agency personnel performance and compensation criteria in encouraging effective employee performance (*including* the minimization of payment errors) and in fostering other dimensions of program quality; (3) whether state law/policy conforms to federal law; (4) whether UC agency administrative policies and procedures are consistent with federal and state law; (5) the level of knowledge of UC agency personnel about existing provisions of state law, policy and procedures; (6) the overall quality of agency training and retraining policies and procedures; (7) the flow of pertinent information within the agency, including the effectiveness of communicating new policies/procedures and whether payment/processing errors are effectively brought to the attention of those responsible for the errors; and (8) measures of the effectiveness with which agency personnel prevent potential overpayments and detect actual overpayments.

Some Issues in Developing Performance Criteria

A number of factors should be considered in developing either the above suggestions or other proposals for evaluating state UC program quality. These include: (1) the use of a benefit/cost framework; (2) the importance of state UC agency input; (3) public perceptions; (4) timing delays; and (5) inducing state compliance. Each is briefly discussed below.

Benefit/Cost Framework. The appropriateness of any performance criteria for state UC programs depends on the costs as well as the benefits of imposing and assessing compliance with such criteria. Even though the benefits of introducing additional quality indicators appear obvious, indicators would have to be developed that could be implemented and administered in a cost-effective manner. Compliance by state UC agencies might be difficult to determine in many instances, especially given the limited staff available to USDOL for such purposes.

Other potential costs of quality criteria would include any unintended and undesirable side effects that might result from the imposition of particular criteria. This possibility is illustrated by the discussion earlier in this chapter of the likelihood that USDOL's promptness criteria have (unintentionally) resulted in some decrease in payment accuracy in the UC system. As another example, several years ago USDOL established a desired level of achievement for state performance that related to the percentage—but not the volume—of overpayments that were recovered; one unintended side effect of this criterion was an inducement for states to establish only (or primarily) those detected overpayments that were likely to be recovered.[50] These considerations suggest that a substantial amount of research and pilot-testing would be required to develop an effective and comprehensive set of UC program quality criteria free of such unintended and negative side effects.

---

50. During FY 1982, USDOL included a DLA that required state agencies to recover at least 55 percent of established overpayments. Such a DLA could produce undesirable side effects, including the possibility that states actually would reduce their emphasis on establishing overpayments (or at least difficult-to-recover overpayments) to ensure the recovery of a high percentage of established overpayments. Possibly in recognition of these adverse side effects, USDOL removed this recoupment criterion from the list of DLAs for the FY 1983 Quality Appraisal Program. Nonetheless, a similar overpayment recovery criterion was again included in fiscal years 1985 and 1986 (see U.S. Department of Labor, 1984a: 30 and 1985). The possibility that such a criterion may produce undesirable side effects also has been noted by a number of UC program administrators. For example, Dunn provides a particularly good discussion of the possible consequences (see Dunn, 1985: 2 and 4).

State UC Agency Input. Given the diversity among state UC programs, it is strongly recommended that state UC program personnel be involved in a very major way in the development of state performance criteria. Although the state diversity issue does not, in our view, lessen the need for or the desirability of performance criteria, it does merit full consideration in the development of the criteria to be imposed on most or all state UC systems. Because state UC program personnel are most likely to be sensitive to the state diversity issue, they should be heavily involved in any effort to develop performance criteria for state programs.

Public Perceptions. Another issue likely to arise in the formulation of additional performance criteria is that realistic desired levels of achievement might not necessarily be acceptable to the general public. For example, a reasonable overpayment rate criterion (defined as one that realistically could be achieved by most states) initially might have to be set as high as 10 percent (or even higher) of total benefit payments. Although the public might well question such a high overpayment rate criterion,[51] both USDOL and the states would know that the relatively low overpayment rates acceptable to the public at-large would likely be unattainable by the great majority of state UC programs. Despite the discomfort this problem may cause UC program administrators, this public acceptance issue is one that we believe should not (and probably cannot) be avoided.

Timing Delays. The development of appropriate criteria for evaluating the quality of claim processing and payment activities in state UC programs is likely to be a very time consuming process. Until such criteria have been developed and implemented, the imbalance between the promptness and quality criteria is likely to continue to contribute to overpayment and related quality problems. An interim approach that may merit consideration would provide for a reduction in USDOL's strong emphasis on the promptness criteria until additional quality

---

51. It may be the case that public acceptance of overpayments varies with the type of overpayment. Burnett and Pendleton (1985: 8) argue the public probably would not tolerate even a small percentage of overpayments due to unreported earnings, whereas much larger overpayment percentages might be tolerated for errors in applying eligibility criteria.

criteria have been implemented. The extent to which USDOL may relax its promptness criteria—pending the implementation of an offsetting emphasis on payment accuracy—is not entirely clear. In surveying the history of conformity issues and related court cases, Rubin states:

> A Federal District Court in Illinois, appalled by the long time lapse of that state, concluded that the state agency did not adhere to the requirements of Section 303(a)(1) of the Social Security Act. Although it did not determine that DOL had improperly certified the state for granted funds, it did determine that the state was not making payments "when due." The court concluded that the "when due" requirement meant that the state agency must mail checks out within 14 days from the end of the first compensable week of unemployment in all cases in which the claimant has provided all necessary information, and external factors beyond the agency's control do not intervene. . . .
>
> It became obvious that unless DOL developed a promptness standard (rather than merely guidelines) the courts would do so. And different courts may well develop different standards. On March 5, 1976, a proposed standard for Benefit Payments Promptness was published in the Federal Register.[52]

Under these circumstances, it may not be possible for USDOL to reduce the 14 or 21 day limits currently included in the promptness criteria. It may, however, be possible to establish desired levels of achievement with respect to percentages processed within these time limits that are lower than those currently in place (e.g., the 87 percent criterion for the 14/21 day time limit for initial, intrastate claim processing might be reduced).

Another approach that might, at least in some states, have an effect similar to reducing the percentage requirements for the existing timeliness criteria would be to discourage the states from engaging in any sort of national "contest" with respect to time-lapse performance. When a criterion is set that requires 87 percent of first payments to be made within the current 14/21 day time limits, it is at least worthwhile to question how or why

---

52. Rubin (1983: 224–5).

states endeavor to substantially exceed that criterion. For example, during FY 1984, 4 states were able to pay in excess of 95 percent of intrastate initial claims in a timely manner and 12 states were able to pay more than 93 percent of such claims within the 14/21 day time limit.[53] Just as there currently is special attention given to those states that do not meet the time-lapse performance criteria, perhaps there also should be a careful review in those instances in which the criteria are substantially exceeded. If such performance resulted from especially efficient procedures, then other states would undoubtedly be interested in determining whether they could adopt the same or similar procedures. In contrast, if rapid processing were obtained only or primarily at the expense of reduced payment accuracy or other reductions in overall program quality, questions about such adverse effects would be appropriate.

Inducing State Compliance. In addition to developing and implementing performance criteria for UC program quality, the issue of effectively inducing state compliance with the criteria also arises. One approach would be to periodically release to the public the results for any quality indicators utilized, on the assumption that public pressure would induce appropriate state responses. This apparently is the approach USDOL plans to use with respect to the payment error findings by the Quality Control program.[54] However, an effective emphasis on quality may well require stronger incentives for inducing state compliance with whatever performance criteria are developed.

One way to induce state compliance with USDOL performance criteria would be to formulate these criteria in terms of formal standards established by the Secretary of Labor. States found to be out of compliance with such administrative standards would confront the possible loss of the administrative funds allocated by USDOL to the states. However, because such a challenge is a drastic step, it is a response that has been used very

---

53. U.S. Department of Labor (1984g: Figure I-5).

54. USDOL established a technical workgroup and an advisory roundtable group to assist in the design and implementation of the Quality Control program. Both groups have considered the format of a proposed national report on QC program results, but the final design had not been announced by April 1987.

infrequently by USDOL. Moreover, compliance challenges may invite expensive legal responses that may take years to resolve. For these and other reasons, including the potential strain on the "partnership" concept, such challenges do not appear to be the most desirable approach for encouraging states to comply with performance criteria. Other approaches to link administrative funding allocations to various measures of state UC program quality would appear to be potentially more useful to achieve desired qualitative changes in state programs.[55] More discussion and perhaps considerable innovation might be fruitful in terms of developing a more flexible set of tools for inducing state compliance with an appropriate set of performance criteria.

Conclusions

The potentially adverse impacts of existing USDOL performance criteria on payment accuracy are indicated by the analysis in this chapter. It seems particularly clear that the strong emphasis placed on the prompt processing and payment of benefits, in the absence of an offsetting and effective emphasis on payment accuracy, very likely has resulted in increased UC payment errors. The likelihood of such a result is, of course, increased by the existing level of program complexity discussed in chapter 3, combined with the relatively limited administrative funding and the adverse impacts of USDOL's administrative funding procedures discussed in chapter 4. Perhaps the analysis in this chapter will serve to clarify the nature of the potentially adverse impacts of existing USDOL performance criteria and thereby stimulate the further work required to devise an improved set of criteria. It is clear that developing an effective and comprehensive set of performance criteria would be a much larger undertaking than identifying the deficiencies in the exist-

---

55. Such an approach also would be consistent with one of the recommendations made by the National Commission on Unemployment Compensation. The Commission made the argument in its final report that less drastic sanctions than conformity challenges presumably would be more effective in achieving compliance with broad federal guidelines, simply because such sanctions would be more frequently utilized than conformity challenges. See National Commission (1980: 144-48).

ing performance criteria and providing the general suggestions for improvements contained in this chapter. Although such an undertaking would be a major one, it could contribute to an improved UC system in general and to payment accuracy in particular.

6

Adverse Incentives in State UC Programs

Federal impacts on state UC programs were emphasized in the prior two chapters. At the state level, it also is the case that program participants—claimants, covered employers and state UC agency personnel—respond to the incentives provided by those who legislate and administer UC law/policy in each state. Over a decade ago, in fact, Martin Feldstein drew widespread attention to the "adverse incentives" and "distributional anomalies" that characterized some aspects of state systems.[1] Since that time, a large number of academic papers on the incentive effects of the UC program on the behavior of individual UC program participants have emerged. Initially, most attention was given to the impact of UC support on various dimensions of the labor market experiences of UC claimants, including the duration of unemployment, the frequency of unemployment spells, reemployment earnings, job search intensity, and, more recently, the misreporting of job search activity in order to collect UC benefits.[2] In recent years, considerable emphasis also has been placed on analyzing how the experience rating provisions of the UC system impact on the behavior of employers; these studies have emphasized how deviations from "perfect" experience rating have increased the likelihood of temporary layoff

---

1. Feldstein (1973 and (1974).
2. See, for example Ehrenberg and Oaxaca (1976); Burgess and Kingston (1976 and 1981); Kingston and Burgess (1977); Barron and Mellow (1979); Black and Carr (1980); and St. Louis, Burgess and Kingston (1986).

unemployment and, consequently, the overall rate of unemployment.[3]

The focus of this chapter is on how the incentives confronted by state UC program participants relate to the problems of payment errors and other quality problems in the UC system. An understanding of these incentives should prove useful in formulating effective proposals to reduce overpayments, promote horizontal equity and enhance the general quality of state UC systems. Many of the adverse incentives analyzed in this chapter may have resulted in part from the federal/state interactions discussed in the prior two chapters. Nonetheless, the incentives provided within state programs are largely shaped by the states themselves. In keeping with the overall limitations of the study discussed in chapter 1, it should be noted again that the analysis in this chapter is a generalization for state UC systems taken as a group; particular aspects of the discussion do not necessarily apply to particular states. Also, although the focus is on incentive problems within individual state systems, effective resolution of these problems would be facilitated by appropriate support from the federal partner.

The analysis in this chapter fits well within the framework developed more than a decade ago by Alchian and Demsetz for analyzing behavior within a business firm.[4] They explained that incentives to "shirk" on contractual obligations are significantly related to the benefits and costs of monitoring compliance with such obligations. From the perspective of noncompliance with UC eligibility criteria, the Alchian/Demsetz analysis suggests that frequent "shirking" in the UC system—as documented by high overpayment rates—may be related to the benefits and costs of monitoring compliance with the criteria. Hence, the factors that influence these benefits and costs are emphasized in the following discussion.

The chapter is organized in the following manner. First, consideration is given to how state UC program procedures and

---

3. See Feldstein (1973); Brechling (1979); Becker (1981); Topel and Welch (1980); and Topel (1983, 1984 and 1986).
4. Alchian and Demsetz (1972).

policies impact on the incentives confronted by claimants, covered employers and state agency personnel.[5] In each section, existing incentives are evaluated and possible responses are discussed. A brief conclusion completes the chapter.

UC Claimants

UC benefit claims that are overpaid may be the result of either deliberate noncompliance or they may occur by accident. Given the complexities of the program and the limited funds available for program administration, accidental payment errors might occur frequently. In fact, however, there is evidence to suggest that deliberate noncompliance with UC eligibility criteria also may be a relatively common occurrence. It should be emphasized from the outset that such evidence does not imply that UC claimants are less honest than labor force participants as a whole. Rather, such evidence suggests that UC recipients respond to the incentives that they confront in the UC system. In this context, the existence of adverse incentives would be expected to encourage claimant behavior that, from society's viewpoint, may be considered undesirable. In the discussion below, the reasons for expecting deliberate noncompliance within the UC system are first briefly explained. Thereafter, some possible responses that would alter the adverse incentives currently provided to UC claimants are considered.

Claimant Incentives for Deliberate Noncompliance

UC claimants may choose to knowingly accept UC benefits to which they are not entitled if they estimate that the expected monetary benefits of such actions exceed the expected monetary costs.[6] The monetary benefits are, of course, determined by the

---

5. A brief analysis of the incentives confronted by UC program participants is contained in a 1983 report prepared for USDOL. See Kingston, Burgess and St. Louis (1983). For a more recent discussion, see Kingston, Burgess and St. Louis (1986).

6. Other factors, however, obviously are involved. The time and psychic costs (or benefits) of filing for and receiving UC support to which they are not entitled also would be expected to influence the behavior of claimants. These additional factors are ignored in the text discussion.

size of the weekly benefit payment. The expected monetary costs of receiving benefits to which they are not entitled depend on claimants' perceptions of the extent to which stated program eligibility criteria are actually enforced. Many claimants no doubt are aware of the complexities that characterize the existing UC system and they may correctly perceive the limited extent to which stated program requirements are enforced. Given that both the time and other costs associated with filing claims for UC support generally may be quite low for many claimants (and hence are ignored in the discussion which follows), these circumstances may explain why ineligible claimants are encouraged to file for benefits. In fact, for any given weekly benefit payment, the expected net monetary gain associated with deliberate action to obtain an overpayment depends on the expected cost of such a decision. These costs of receiving UC benefits as an ineligible claimant, in turn, are dependent on claimant estimates of: (1) the likelihood of noncompliance with UC eligibility criteria being detected; (2) the likelihood that an overpayment would be established (i.e., formally processed by the state UC agency) in instances of detected noncompliance; (3) the nominal penalties associated with established overpayments; and (4) the extent to which nominal penalties are effectively enforced. It appears that these cost factors typically are quite low in the UC system.

Likelihood of Detecting Noncompliance. Strong evidence that many instances of noncompliance occur but are not detected by routine claim processing and benefit payment control procedures is available from both the K-B and B-K-S studies. For example, as shown in table 2-2 of chapter 2, the rates of overpayments detected by the special investigative procedures utilized in six metropolitan areas were: at least double the rates detected by routine state procedures in all six of the cities; at least four times the rates detected by routine procedures in five cities; and 42 times the rate detected by routine procedures in one city.[7] The estimated dollar amount of overpayments uncovered by the special procedures used in the B-K-S study for just five states (of

$392 million) exceeded by 60 percent the total overpayments actually detected/ established/reported by all 53 UC jurisdictions combined for a comparable one-year period.[8] In light of the fact that these studies tended to produce low-side estimates of actual overpayment rates (including the absence of postaudit procedures in the B-K-S study), these findings provide substantive documentation that many overpayments are not detected by conventional UC program procedures.

Other evidence of deliberate noncompliance has been provided by Black and Carr, who analyzed unreported earning violations among UC recipients in the Seattle and Denver Income Maintenance Experiments. Although the samples analyzed by Black and Carr—claimants from relatively low-income families— cannot be viewed as representative of UC claimants generally, the findings for unreported earnings support the implications of the K-B and B-K-S studies that noncompliance with UC eligibility criteria often is undetected. Black and Carr found that:

> The empirical findings for the samples of Seattle and Denver UI recipients quite consistently reveal that undetected underreporting of earnings and, by implication, overpayments, is a major problem. On the average, underreporting over the 3-year period occurred in 7.6 and 13.6 percent of the person-weeks in Seattle and Denver, respectively. Furthermore, the average weekly dollar amounts of underreported earnings are quite large for the subset of misreporters. . . . When extrapolated to the statewide claimant population, these estimates imply large aggregate amounts of overpayments.[9]

In addition to the above direct findings on UC overpayments, it also should be noted that economic activity "off the books" apparently has been increasing over the past decade, and this trend may further increase the difficulty of detecting unreported earnings in the UC system. For example, one study found that the size of the underground economy has been increasing since the mid-1960s and estimated that it may have accounted for as

---

8. Kingston, Burgess and St. Louis (1983: 16).
9. Black and Carr (1980: 554).

much as 6 percent of GNP in 1980.[10] More recently, some estimates indicate that the size of the underground economy may have nearly tripled between 1975 and 1982, and could have amounted to as much as 14 percent of GNP in 1982.[11] If such estimates are at all accurate, it appears that it may become increasingly difficult to detect claimants who simultaneously work in the underground economy and collect UC benefits.

Violations of the weekly UC eligibility criteria other than unreported earnings—especially those for refusals of suitable work and inadequate job search—also are very difficult to detect. However, because the problems of monitoring compliance with the worksearch requirement are considered in more detail in chapter 7, the final illustration provided here relates to detecting claimant refusals of suitable work. Unless it is the case that very few UC claimants in fact refuse suitable work, available evidence strongly suggests that it is virtually impossible to detect such violations. For example, notwithstanding the resource-intensive nature of the B-K-S study (involving 8-13 hours of investigative time for a single week of unemployment), not a single overpayment was established for refusal of suitable work in that study in any one of the five pilot test states over a one-year period.[12] Furthermore, USDOL data on actual nonmonetary determinations issued in all 53 UC jurisdictions combined for FY 1983 indicate that only about 3 percent of all nonmonetary determinations for nonseparation issues were for refusals of suitable work, and that less than 30 percent of these determinations led to a denial of benefits.[13] In fact, for the nationwide system as a whole during FY 1983, only about two per 10,000 of all weeks claimed were denied for refusal of suitable work.[14]

It is perhaps worth exploring for illustrative purposes some of the problems involved in attempting to detect instances of suitable work refusals. Although the rationale for this eligibility criterion is obvious, several factors interact to reduce the

---

10. Tanzi (1983: 302).
11. Porter and Bayer (1984: 178–179).
12. Kingston, Burgess and St. Louis (1983: 33).
13. U.S. Department of Labor (1984b).
14. Computed from data in U.S. Department of Labor (1984b and 1984c).

likelihood that such violations can be detected. First, it is extremely difficult to determine precisely what constitutes an offer of suitable work, as summarized by Felder:

> These (eligibility) criteria include the health and safety of the worker, the moral hazard of the job; the job requirements as they relate to the claimant's educational background, experience, and physical fitness to do the work; the wages, hours and length of potential employment in that position; the relationship of the employment to the customary occupation of the claimant; and the distance of the job from the claimant's home. Federal statutes forbid any state law's definition of suitable work to include as suitable any job that is vacant due to a labor dispute, that has less favorable conditions of work than those prevailing in the local economy, that requires the joining of a company union, or that requires resigning from a bonafide labor organization.[15]

Other factors that could impact on the concept of suitable work include: how long an individual is unemployed; whether the claimant previously had voluntarily left a similar position or had previously refused a similar position; the reputation of the business offering the work (if it could be shown that the claimant's moral standards could be injured); and whether the claimant is satisfactorily pursuing an approved training program.[16] As a result, determining whether a refusal of suitable work has occurred almost necessarily becomes an *ad hoc* process in which even well-trained UC program personnel might render quite different judgments for any given set of facts surrounding a particular case.

A second reason why it is so difficult for state UC agencies to detect refusals of suitable work is that, in the absence of active employer cooperation, there is virtually no way that UC program personnel ever would be aware of such violations. It would be neither cost effective nor feasible to have UC agency personnel routinely contact all employers to determine if suitable job offers had been refused. Also, it oftentimes is the case that an

15. Felder (1979: 12).
16. Arizona Department of Economic Security (n.d.: Section 533330).

individual employer would not find it worthwhile to report such an occurrence.

A third reason why so few refusals of suitable work are detected is that UC claimants can, by their own behavior, avoid job offers they do not wish to accept. How claimants respond during personal interviews and how well they perform on any on-site tests that might be conducted both could impact on the likelihood that job offers would be extended. Thus, it would be quite easy for a claimant who would not accept an offer of suitable employment to avoid receiving such a job offer.

The above discussion indicates that many violations of UC eligibility criteria may not be detected, especially by the routine procedures typically employed by state agencies for benefit payment control purposes. Because of these relatively low detection likelihoods for selected types of noncompliance, many claimants might be encouraged to obtain UC benefits to which they are not entitled. In any case, relatively low detection likelihoods certainly do not effectively discourage deliberate noncompliance with eligibility criteria.

Likelihood of Establishing Overpayments. Detected instances of noncompliance with UC eligibility criteria often do not result in the establishment of overpayments. Several examples serve to illustrate this point. In the K-B study, there was substantial resistance by UC agency officials in one project city to "retro-actively" establish overpayments for certain violations of the weekly eligibility criteria.[17] In three of the five B-K-S study states, overpayments for violations of the active worksearch requirement could not be established (either for the entire study period or for a portion of it) unless the claimant had previously received a written warning that his/her job-seeking activities were deficient.[18] Also, the existence of certain "finality rules" in state employment security laws or policies often prohibit, after the expiration of some definite period, the establishment of an overpayment for an issue that has been considered previously, even if it subsequently were determined that the original decision

---

17. Kingston and Burgess (1981b: 35–36).
18. Kingston, Burgess and St. Louis (1983: 25).

was erroneous.[19] As a final example, it may be noted that, despite the intensive efforts to verify job search contacts in the B-K-S study states, nearly half or more of all job contacts reported by UC claimants could not be verified as either acceptable or unacceptable contacts in three of the five states; nevertheless, no overpayments were established for this lack of verifiable job contacts alone in any of these states.[20]

The example of unverifiable job contacts merits additional comment because it illustrates the basic "burden of proof" presumption that characterizes many state programs. The basic issue involved is whether the "burden of proof" rests with the UC claimant (to demonstrate eligibility) or the state UC agency (to demonstrate ineligibility). At the time claims are filed and prior to the payment of benefits for particular weeks, the burden of proof typically is shared, with perhaps a somewhat greater responsibility placed on claimants to provide whatever information is routinely requested for the processing of continued claims. Once the decision has been made to pay benefits for a particular week, however, this burden of proof shifts markedly towards the UC agency in most states. That is, establishing an overpayment for a previous payment (or disallowing a previous payment) typically requires that the state UC agency convincingly demonstrate that an error has been made. In the event that such compelling and substantive evidence cannot be obtained, an overpayment typically would not be established or, if established, likely would be reversed on appeal. Because of the difficulties involved in obtaining the documentation required to satisfy this burden of proof, especially for suspected violations of the weekly eligibility criteria (e.g., refusals of suitable work, worksearch violations, etc.), state UC program personnel are not likely to establish many actual overpayments.

Nominal Overpayment Penalties. The nominal penalties asso-

---

19. Typically, in order for an overpayment to be established in such circumstances, compelling new evidence not originally considered must be found. See Burgess, Kingston and St. Louis (1982: 23).

20. Kingston, Burgess and St. Louis (1983: 28–29). Also see chapter 7 and Kingston, Burgess and St. Louis (1986) for further analysis of worksearch verification difficulties and for estimated "worksearch noncompliance" rates for the five B-K-S study states.

ciated with overpayments established for most types of noncompliance with UC eligibility criteria tend to be quite low. This is the case primarily because, at least in most UC jurisdictions, the great majority of detected violations are established as nonfraud overpayments.[21] During FY 1984, about 75 percent of all overpayment cases established nationwide were processed as nonfraud overpayments.[22] These circumstances result from the fact that most state employment security laws require that "willful intent" must be proven before a fraud overpayment is established or upheld on appeal. Given the difficulties involved in ex-post efforts to verify a claimant's eligibility for UC support, including the "burden of proof" issue noted above, it becomes extremely difficult in most instances to prove such intent on the part of the claimant.

In contrast with fraudulent overpayment penalties, which may even include fines and imprisonment, the typical (nominal) penalty imposed for a nonfraud overpayment is the repayment of the benefits erroneously received by the claimant. Consequently, assuming fraud may be ignored, an ineligible claimant who was evaluating the expected benefits and costs of receiving a UC payment would compare the virtual certainty of receiving the weekly UC payment with the less certain prospect that the payment would have to be refunded to the state UC agency; under these circumstances and on purely monetary grounds, the claimant probably would be willing to risk having to repay the UC benefits and would accept monies to which s/he was not entitled.

Enforcement of Nominal Penalties. Effective penalties for violations of UC eligibility criteria typically are considerably smaller than the nominal penalties imposed for such violations. For example, cash repayment is not required for overpayments established in some states; rather, the overpayments are "offset"

---

21. See Kingston and Burgess (1981b: 34) and Burgess, Kingston and St. Louis (1982: 53). The State of Louisiana represents at least one exception to this generalization, however. In the B-K-S study, 37 percent of the dollars overpaid in Louisiana were set up as fraud overpayments. In contrast, the simple average of the percentages of dollars overpaid that were established as fraud cases in the other four states amounted to only 10.5 percent. See Burgess, Kingston and St. Louis (1982: 53).

22. U.S. Department of Labor (1985f: 3).

against the benefits that the claimant otherwise would receive during a subsequent claim period. Some states limit the percentage of presently due benefits that may be utilized as an offset for the repayment of prior overpayments. Some states "waive" the repayment of outstanding overpayment balances after a certain period of time. Also, some states do not charge interest on outstanding overpayments, so that an implicit subsidy is provided to overpayment recipients even if repayment ultimately occurs. In fact, however, repayment oftentimes does not occur. An Assistant Inspector General for Audit in USDOL reported in 1983 that:

In summary, SESAs [state employment security agencies] are neither effectively nor efficiently detecting and collecting benefit overpayments. Because of the size of the UI benefit payment program—more than 15 billion in calendar year 1981—and the program's susceptibility to both fraudulent and non-fraudulent overpayments, changes in laws, procedures and practices must be made immediately.[23]

For many years, effective enforcement of nominal penalties also was limited because federal law prohibited the "offsetting" of benefits paid under most federal programs to repay amounts overpaid under state programs. This federal restriction was not removed until 1986.[24] Consequently, only very recently have the states had the opportunity to obtain repayment for overpayments in state programs through offsets of benefits paid under federal programs.

Other evidence also indicates that overpayment recoupment rates are quite low. For example, the results of the FY 1982 Quality Appraisal indicated that only 22 state UC agencies met the desired level of achievement of recouping at least 55 percent

---

23. Peterson (1983: 1).

24. For a discussion of this issue from the perspective of the Oregon UC agency, see Richey (1985). Section 12401 of Public Law 99–272 signed into law April 7, 1986 amended Section 303(a)(5) of the Social Security Act and Sections 3304 (a)(4) and 3306(f) of the Federal Unemployment Tax Act to permit states to recover overpayments made under any federal or state UC law through cross program and interstate offset from any unemployment benefits payable to the overpaid individual.

of overpayments subject to recovery.[25] For all UC jurisdictions combined, overpayment recoveries during FY 1982 amounted to about 53 percent of all overpayments subject to recovery during that year.[26] Similar information was not released by USDOL for FY 1983, but the comparable overpayment recovery percentage for FY 1984 for the UC system as a whole was 55.6 percent.[27]

Even if overpayments were detected, established and recouped, however, it also should be noted that many states "restore" the amounts overpaid to claimants' maximum benefit awards. This tends to further reduce the severity of nominal penalties imposed, since the same funds originally overpaid may be paid again to the claimant at a later point in his/her benefit year. The impact of restoring overpaid amounts in this manner would be greatest, of course, for those who exhaust their entitlements to benefits; for these individuals, the establishment and even recoupment of an overpayment simply would delay the second payment of the same benefits during the benefit year.

Conclusions. Most types of deliberate noncompliance with UC eligibility criteria—especially those in which fraud cannot be established—are only weakly discouraged in the existing UC program. Available evidence indicates that detection likelihoods for deliberate noncompliance are low and that even a detected instance of noncompliance often may not be established as an overpayment because of the difficulties involved in assembling the required compelling evidence and documentation. Furthermore, nominal penalties for established overpayments tend to be quite small and the ineffective application of nominal penalties further reduces their deterrent effect.

Not all UC overpayments occur because of deliberate calculations by claimants, however. Some claimants receive benefits to which they are not entitled simply because they are not aware of certain eligibility rules or because they incorrectly interpret those rules they do know. The complexity of UC eligibility criteria contributes to each of these problems. It should be noted,

25. U.S. Department of Labor (1982b: 26).
26. U.S. Department of Labor (1982a: 3).
27. U.S. Department of Labor (1985f: 3).

however, that claimants also lack appropriate incentives to become knowledgeable about UC eligibility rules.

Responses to Encourage Claimant Compliance

Claimant compliance with UC eligibility criteria could be increased by either reducing the expected benefits or increasing the expected costs associated with the receipt of an overpayment. The expected benefits of noncompliance are determined primarily by the size of the weekly benefit amount. Although it would be possible to lower these benefits by reducing the amount of weekly UC program support, such an approach would lower the weekly benefit amount for eligible as well as ineligible claimants.[28] Consequently, it would seem most appropriate to increase claimant compliance with UC eligibility criteria by raising the expected costs to claimants of accepting UC benefits to which they are not entitled. The approaches for increasing such costs, discussed below, include: (1) making claimants more aware of eligibility criteria and enforcement provisions; (2) increasing noncompliance detection likelihoods; (3) increasing the rate at which overpayments are established for instances of detected noncompliance; (4) increasing nominal penalties for established overpayments; and (5) more effectively applying any nominal penalties assessed.

Increasing Claimant Awareness. Some overpayments no doubt occur simply because claimants do not fully understand UC eligibility criteria and what must be done to satisfy these requirements. Thus, it would seem appropriate to more completely inform claimants about UC eligibility criteria, what actions are required to demonstrate compliance with these

---

28. The incentive effects of supplementing the weekly benefit amount with cash bonuses for reemployment have been emphasized in a recent paper by Spiegelman and Woodbury. This research is relevant in the present context because it provides an additional illustration of how the behavior of UC claimants may be influenced by changing the benefits associated with certain aspects of their labor market behavior. See Spiegelman and Woodbury (1986). Even more recently, the U.S. Department of Labor and the New Jersey Department of Labor approved the experimental design for the New Jersey Unemployment Insurance Reemployment Demonstration Project. Among other features, this design provides for the payment of reemployment bonuses for structurally unemployed workers. For details, see U.S. Department of Labor (1986a). This experiment also is further discussed in chapter 7.

requirements, and the penalties for noncompliance with these criteria. Providing additional information about claimant responsibilities presumably would tend to reduce overpayments that do not result from deliberate claimant actions, whereas providing more information about existing penalties for noncompliance might increase claimant perceptions of the expected costs of deliberate noncompliance. Moreover, if increased (nominal) noncompliance penalties and more effective application of such penalties were implemented, it would be especially important that claimants understand UC eligibility criteria and the associated penalties for noncompliance.

Increasing Noncompliance Detection Likelihoods. The typical approach to monitoring claimant compliance with UC eligibility criteria in most state programs is to treat nearly all claimants identically. Most claimants pass through a relatively superficial verification process before benefits are paid to them. As a result, most claimants with experience in the UC system undoubtedly perceive that the likelihood of detecting any overpayment they might receive is very low.

Possibilities for increasing noncompliance detection likelihoods could include any or all of the following: (1) an increase in the administrative funds available for monitoring claimant compliance with UC eligibility criteria; (2) implementing more specific criteria that may be more easily or effectively monitored with existing administrative resources; (3) eliminating some eligibility criteria that cannot be effectively administered with either presently available or even increased administrative funding, so that increased monitoring could be directed at enforcing compliance with the remaining criteria; or (4) reallocating any given level of administrative resources to more effectively detect overpayments that do occur.

As discussed in chapter 4, significant increases in administrative funding for monitoring claimant compliance with UC eligibility criteria (option (1) above) are not likely. Possibilities (2) and (3) are not discussed further in this chapter because they are discussed in more detail in chapter 7 as those options relate to the active worksearch requirement. Consequently, the discussion below focuses on the more effective use of existing

administrative resources and specifically on the use of computerized screening profiles to more effectively detect overpayments
that occur (option (4)).

Currently, most state UC agencies attempt to verify eligibility
for nearly all claimants in a virtually uniform manner before
payments are made, and postaudits constitute the primary overpayment detection device for payments already made. Under a
revised approach, discussed in more detail elsewhere,[29] most
claims would be processed routinely each week without any
attempts at even superficial verification (as long as claimants
certified that they had met the eligibility requirements). Then, a
relatively small group of "high-risk" claimants, who would be
selected on the basis of computerized screening profiles, would
be given in-depth benefit eligibility reviews to determine if
overpayments had occurred. The intended effect of this approach—combined with sufficient publicity—would be to con-
vince the claimant population as a whole that there was some
reasonable chance that any overpayment they might receive
would be detected by these intensive audits. As a result, more
claimant self-compliance with UC eligibility criteria could be
encouraged.

An important issue in determining the feasibility of this
approach is whether the limited administrative resources devoted
to this effort could be effectively targeted on groups of claimants
who tend to have above-average overpayment rates. Although
very little work has been done along these lines, the available
evidence suggests that it may be possible to identify groups with
higher than average overpayment propensities on the basis of
personal, labor market and UC program characteristics. Burgess,
Kingston, St. Louis and De Pippo explored the feasibility of
developing "high-risk" profiles for violations of worksearch/

---

29. See Kingston and Burgess (1986) and St. Louis, Burgess and Kingston (1986). The
computerized screening profiles relate to identifying violations of the weekly eligibility criteria
other than those due to unreported earnings by those who also are receiving UC support. This
approach is taken because effective techniques for detecting overpayments due to unreported
earnings in covered employment already exist (if states choose to utilize them), and those
techniques previously have been analyzed by Porterfield, St. Louis, Burgess and Kingston
(1980).

availability requirements in the five Random Audit program pilot test states, and concluded that:

> The results presented in the Summary Table strongly indicate that the prediction profiles developed in this study are more accurate in identifying "high risk" claimants than a random selection of claimants. . . . The results, however, must be cautiously interpreted since the same data were used to build and test the models. . . . Hence, although the results indicate potential, further work is required before any state should attempt to implement such a procedure in an operational setting.[30]

Although the conclusions were cautiously stated, the findings in this study and the further analysis of the same data set by Kingston and Burgess have clearly established the potential usefulness of conducting further work on the screening profile approach.[31] Furthermore, a subsequent analysis of data for the same five states by St. Louis, Burgess and Kingston indicated that the propensity of UC claimants to over-report the number of job contacts they made was strongly related to a number of labor market and demographic variables, including the size of the weekly UC benefit payment, usual weekly earnings in the preunemployment period, union status, sex, age and the duration of the current unemployment spell.[32] In short, it may be feasible to design effective screening profiles to detect UC claimants who have above-average likelihoods of receiving worksearch/availability overpayments. Whether or to what extent similar profiles could be developed to detect deliberate noncompliance with other aspects of UC eligibility criteria remains an open question, but further research in this area certainly appears to be warranted.

Development of statistical profiles essentially involves the use of *group* characteristics to select *individual* claimants for comprehensive audits. Such a procedure is, in a technical sense, a "discriminating" one because personal, labor market and UC-related characteristics are used to estimate the probabilities that overpayments have been received by particular individuals. A fundamental question to be

---

30. Burgess, Kingston, St. Louis and DePippo (1983: vii).
31. Kingston and Burgess (1986).
32. St. Louis, Burgess and Kingston (1986: 109).

addressed is whether the development of high-risk profiles from the analysis of *randomly selected* samples of claimants would unfairly discriminate against certain groups of claimants.[33] A random selection of claimants may well result in the conclusion that variables such as sex, age or ethnic status would be important ones in identifying high-risk claimants. Consequently, the political/legal feasibility of using screening profiles in the operational UC system obviously must be evaluated before a major effort is undertaken to explore the technical feasibility of developing such profiles.

An argument for the development of high-risk screening profiles—regardless of the particular characteristics that might be important in identifying high-risk claimants—is that the UC program would unfairly discriminate against those claimants who do *not* accept overpayments if existing administrative resources could be, but were not, targeted on those who have the highest propensities to be overpaid. Also, because it would be necessary to periodically update such screening profiles to account for changes in the characteristics of high-risk v. low-risk claimants through time, adaptive behavior by particular types of claimant groups originally found to have above-average over-payment propensities could subsequently remove them from the high-risk target groups identified by such screening profiles. Overall, it probably is the case that the efficient allocation of any given amount of administrative funds would be enhanced through the use of screening profile techniques.

Establishing Overpayments for Detected Noncompliance. A complementary approach to increasing the likelihood of detecting noncompliance would involve increasing the chances that detected instances of noncompliance result in the establishment

---

33. The development of accurate screening profiles requires data sets that accurately classify claimants as overpaid v. properly paid. Routine operational data in the UC system do not contain accurate classifications of claimants into these two groups because many claimants with overpayments are not detected in the routine system. The only data sets available (prior to those that will result from the Quality Control program) that are reasonably accurate in classifying claimants into these two groups are the Random Audit program data sets that have been classified on the basis of intensive eligibility verifications. Because these data sets represent *random* samples of payments made in each participating state, utilizing them would result in the development of high-risk profiles on the basis of a random selection of claimants. For a discussion of this issue, see Burgess, Kingston, St. Louis and DePippo (1983: 7-8) and Kingston and Burgess (1986).

of overpayments. State UC agencies could, of course, review their employment security laws and policies to identify those provisions that limit the establishment of overpayments in instances of detected noncompliance (e.g., formal warning requirements). Whether specific changes should be made obviously is a subjective decision that would depend on the perceived benefits and costs of such changes in particular states. For the most part, these decisions presumably are best left to individual state policymakers and administrators who are most knowledgeable about both the intended and actual consequences of such provisions in their states.

Attempts to increase the likelihood of establishing overpayments for detected instances of noncompliance also will confront the "burden of proof" issue discussed previously. For several reasons, this issue must be approached both cautiously and realistically. Caution is warranted because of possible unintended and undesirable side effects that could result from fundamental changes in current requirements. Placing the burden of proof on the claimant to demonstrate his/her eligibility could, at some point, involve undue hardships for and horizontal inequities among claimants, in addition to costly reporting requirements for employers to provide the types of documentation needed by claimants. Issues related to the type of documentation required, the length of time that such evidence would have to be retained, and similar matters would have to be resolved if claimants were to bear significantly increased responsibilities in this regard. Care must be taken that, because of varying circumstances among claimants, inequities do not arise as a result of imposing uniform reporting or record-keeping requirements.

Realistic expectations of what might be gained by altering the burden of proof also are required. For example, it would be impossible for a claimant to provide evidence (beyond a certification) that he/she did *not* participate in certain types of disqualifying behavior (e.g., a refusal of suitable work or the receipt of disqualifying earnings). If changes were made to increase the claimant's responsibility for demonstrating eligibility for UC program support, such measures should be carefully developed and most probably should be carefully pilot-tested to determine whether they should be operationally implemented. Furthermore, it should be recognized that, in the absence of other changes (e.g., the simplification or removal of certain eligibility criteria), the benefits of altering the burden of proof might not exceed the costs, given the possible problems that such actions could impose on all system participants.[34]

Despite the above cautions, placing the burden of proof more on individual claimants and less on state agencies still appears to merit serious consideration. The main benefits of increasing the burden of proof for individual claimants include both increased self-compliance and increased effectiveness of state UC agency efforts to monitor and verify claimant eligibility. To the extent to which claimants were expected to assume greater responsibility for documenting their eligibility for UC support, administering compliance with stated UC eligibility criteria would be similar to the procedures utilized by the Internal Revenue Service in processing and auditing individual tax returns. For example, the receipt by the IRS of a tax return does not constitute acceptance by the IRS of the contents of that return; the individual taxpayer still remains subject to audit, and the burden of proof remains squarely on the taxpayer to provide appropriate documentation, if required. Similarly, under a revised approach in the UC system, timely payments could be made on the basis of only a cursory review of certification forms, but the payment of benefits would not preclude more comprehensive audits of benefit eligibility at later dates. At any such subsequent review, the main burden of proof could be placed on claimants.

Some recent events have indicated that some changes may be forthcoming with respect to the burden of proof issue. For example, the Michigan Employment Security Act of 1984 requires, among other things, that a claimant must provide "tangible evidence to the commission that he or she has engaged in a systematic and sustained worksearch effort during that week."[35] Similarly, an administrative law judge in the District

---

34. For a more complete discussion of the problems associated with this "burden of proof" issue, see Broden (1962: 311-324).
35. State of Michigan (1984: 69).

of Columbia recently recommended that the District be found out of conformity with federal law because its appeal procedures—specifically the presumption of eligibility for claimants charged with disqualifying misconduct—failed to protect the financial integrity of the District's UC trust fund; the judge argued that state laws must not only insure the payment of UC benefits "when due," but also must prevent the payment of benefits when they are not due.[36] These developments suggest that shifting the burden of eligibility proof to claimants may be a viable possibility for increasing claimant compliance with UC eligibility criteria.

Increasing Nominal Penalties. Another facet of increasing the expected costs to claimants of receiving overpayments would involve increasing nominal overpayment penalties. Nominal penalties for violations that now carry no penalty—other than the repayment of the benefits to which the claimant was not originally entitled—could be increased in a number of different ways which (depending on the type of violation) could include: (1) imposing either definite or indefinite disqualification periods (which already are imposed for certain types of violations); (2) reducing claimant maximum benefit awards by the amount (or some multiple) of any overpayment established;[37] (3) imposing monetary penalties in addition to requiring repayment of over-paid amounts; and (4) assessing interest charges on outstanding overpayment balances. However, a possible problem that may arise in attempting to impose stricter nominal penalties should be noted. State agency personnel exercise considerable administrative discretion in establishing the overpayments that result in the imposition of whatever nominal penalties may be contained in state laws/policies. One study of UC eligibility enforcement procedures concluded that increased nominal penalties may lead some agency personnel to ignore some violations that they detect because they believe the penalties for such violations are

---

36. Commerce Clearing House (1985: 4).

37. In this regard, however, the National Commission on Unemployment Compensation recommended that state laws be prohibited from reducing a claimant's entitlement to benefits, except in the case of fraud in the receipt of disqualifying income. See National Commission on Unemployment Compensation (1980: 48).

unreasonably severe.[38] Thus, as also would be the case with many other changes that might be made, the potential for unintended side effects must be considered and accounted for in evaluating how to effectively increase nominal penalties for established overpayments.

Effective Application of Nominal Penalties. For any given set of nominal penalties, increasing their effective application also would increase claimant self-compliance because of the resulting increase in the costs of noncompliance. Although some states already may have considered or adopted such measures, some possibilities that may merit consideration in many states could include: (1) removing legal or administrative provisions that allow for only a portion of a current benefit payment to be offset against prior overpayments; (2) not waiving outstanding overpayment balances; (3) fully computerizing the overpayment accounting and collection process; (4) adopting more effective collection techniques, such as the collection of outstanding balances through the state income tax collection process, telephone inquiries or by turning difficult recoupment cases over to private firms that specialize in such collections;[39] and (5) simply increasing administrative resources devoted to overpayment recovery efforts (within the limits justified by resulting benefit/cost ratios). The appropriateness of these (or other) changes obviously varies among the states, but they are suggestive of the types of changes that may merit consideration.

Covered Employers

One characteristic of the UC program in the United States that distinguishes it from similar programs in other countries is the

38. As explained by Corson et al., increased nominal penalties may have two quite different effects: (1) claimant self-compliance may increase because claimants may be less willing to accept overpayments due to increased penalties, but (2) state UC agency personnel—who exercise considerable administrative discretion—may become less willing to hold claimants ineligible for benefits because of the increased penalties. See Corson, Hershey and Kerachsky (1986: 127-128).

39. As noted in chapter 3, for example, three of the states that participated in the Quality Unemployment Insurance Project (Illinois, North Dakota and Pennsylvania) during 1985–1986 have determined how to improve their overpayment collection activities.

manner in which benefit payments are financed. In this section, some background on the purposes and extent of the experience rating method of financing the UC program in the United States is first provided. Then, the effects of these financing provisions on the incentives of covered employers to monitor both claimant compliance with eligibility criteria and the general efficiency of UC program operations are discussed. Finally, the impact of improved experience rating on such incentives is briefly considered.

Experience Rating Background

Many other countries obtain funds to pay UC benefits from employers, employees and from general government revenues. Typically, other countries also tax employers at a uniform rate.[40] In contrast, the UC system in the United States is financed by taxes levied only on employers in almost all states,[41] and tax rates are supposed to vary according to the individual employer's "experience" with unemployment. This is usually accomplished by assessing higher tax rates on firms whose employees experience a considerable amount of insured unemployment than on firms that rarely lay off their employees.

Experience rated UC tax rates are intended to stabilize employment by forcing employers faced with declining or variable sales to weigh the UC tax costs of laying off current employees against the wage (and other) costs of smoothing their employment level fluctuations. "Perfect" experience rating would cause all of a firm's UC benefit costs to be reflected in its tax rate so that the costs of laying off workers would be paid by the individual firms responsible for the layoffs. Consequently, in addition to its impact on layoff decisions made by firms, effective experience rating of UC taxes also provides incentives for covered employers to participate in the administration of the

---

40. See Blaustein and Craig (1977) for an excellent comparison of the features of UC systems in the United States and 21 other countries.

41. As of January 1985, both employers and employees contributed to finance the payment of UC benefits in Alabama, Alaska, New Jersey and Pennsylvania. See National Foundation for Unemployment Compensation & Workers' Compensation (1985b: 29).

UC program to control the amount of benefits paid to former employees.

Effective experience rating was strongly encouraged by the original federal interpretation of one of the major provisions of the Federal Unemployment Tax Act; this provision stipulated that a state could not give employers reduced tax rates except on the basis of their individual "experiences" with unemployment or other factors related to the risk of unemployment.[42] This provision originally was interpreted by federal officials to imply that all benefits paid to former employees must be charged to individual employer reserve accounts. In 1944, however, this interpretation was altered by federal officials so that states were required to charge only those benefits that assured a tax structure reflecting a "reasonable measure" of the experience of individual employers with respect to unemployment risk.[43] This revised 1944 position was partly justified on the basis that individual employers should not be held liable for the continued unemployment of claimants following a period of disqualification from UC support due to voluntary quits or other factors deemed to be outside the control of employers. Also, since labor market conditions (rather than individual employers) were deemed responsible for extended periods of unemployment, it was believed that some deviations from "full" experience rating should be permitted.

Even though only one UC jurisdiction currently does not use some form of experience rating, the *extent* of experience rating varies dramatically among jurisdictions.[44] Existing research indicates that deviations from "perfect" experience rating occur primarily because of two features of UC program financing: the *noncharging* of benefits and the *ineffective charging* of benefits.[45] Noncharging occurs when the cost of the benefits paid to a former employee of a given firm are not charged to that

---

42. UBA, Inc. (1981: 1).
43. UBA, Inc. (1981: 2).
44. Only Puerto Rico had no experience rating in its law as of January 1986. See National Foundation for Unemployment Compensation & Workers' Compensation (1987: 13-14).
45. See Becker (1981: 79–86) and U.S. Department of Labor, Office of Inspector General (1985d).

particular employer's reserve account, but rather are "socialized" and charged to all employers. All state laws permit some noncharging, particularly in those instances in which it is considered inappropriate to hold the individual employer responsible for a worker's unemployment, but the details of these provisions vary considerably among the states. The most frequent noncharging provisions are for benefits paid following a period of disqualification for voluntary quits, discharges for misconduct or refusals of suitable work.[46] Noncharged benefits represent a significant percentage of UC benefits paid in many states. For example, according to a study undertaken by Joseph Becker, noncharged benefits in 1978 amounted to at least 10 percent of UC benefit payments in 32 states, at least 20 percent of benefit payments in 21 states and at least 25 percent of benefit payments in 13 states.[47]

The second major deviation from "perfect" experience rating—ineffective charging—occurs when benefits are charged to the reserve accounts of employers whose UC tax rates already have reached the maximum rates established by law because their reserve accounts have been exhausted by prior benefit charges. In such cases, charging additional benefits to employer accounts neither draws on reserves accumulated from past tax collections nor increases such employers' tax rates. Experience rating becomes essentially irrelevant to such employers, at least if it also is the case that no reasonable attempts to reduce (expected) future benefit charges would result in expected reductions in tax rates. Becker has argued that the ineffective charging of benefits is, for most states, the most important factor in explaining the reduction in experience rating that has occurred in the UC program.[48] A more recent study by Becker indicates that the percentage of total benefits ineffectively charged exceeded 20 percent in many states between 1971 and 1978.[49]

Additional information on the extent of experience rating in

46. National Foundation for Unemployment Compensation & Workers' Compensation (1985b: 23–24).
47. Becker (1981: 81).
48. Becker (1972: 109).
49. Becker (1981: 85).

the UC program recently has become available from a study conducted by USDOL's Office of the Inspector General.[50] The study was conducted in 12 states, which jointly paid about 35 percent of total UC benefits for the nation as a whole in 1983. Among the findings of this study were the following: (1) the percentage of benefits charged to active employers with positive reserve balances fell from 51 percent in 1970 to 36 percent in 1983; (2) nearly one-half of the $6.3 billion in benefits that were paid in 1983 represented "socialized" costs that were not charged to individual employers; (3) the degree of effective charges ranged from a low of 35 percent to a high of 75 percent among the 12 states studied; and (4) on the average, the UC systems in these 12 states were about 50 percent experience rated.[51] Among the principal causes of the low (and declining) extent of experience rating in these states, the following were identified: (1) low maximum tax rates, which accounted for about 39 percent of socialized costs; (2) noncharging, which accounted for about 17 percent of socialized costs; (3) writing off past benefit charges from the benefit payment histories used to set employer tax rates; (4) utilizing alternative tax schedules, which often assign the largest tax increases to employers with the most favorable employment histories; and (5) using fixed taxable wage bases that do not increase as benefit levels increase.[52]

The effects of less than "perfect" experience rating have received a great deal of attention from economists in recent years. For example, a study by Brechling revealed that industrial layoff rates among the states during the 1962-1977 period were significantly correlated with minimum and maximum UC tax rates.[53] More recently, Topel estimated that the typical experience rated employer pays only about 75 cents per dollar of UC benefits drawn by that employer's former workers and that a one-third reduction in the extent of this implicit employer cross-subsidy would reduce the layoff unemployment rate in the

50. U.S. Department of Labor, (1985d).
51. U.S. Department of Labor, (1985d: iii.).
52. U.S. Department of Labor, (1985d: v-vi.).
53. See Brechling (1979) and Wandner and Crosslin (1980: 274).

sample he analyzed by a "nontrivial" amount.[54] These studies illustrate the basic point that most of the recent academic attention given to experience rating in the UC system has emphasized its effects on temporary layoff unemployment. The particular interest in experience rating within the context of the present study, however, is in terms of its implications for employer monitoring of both UC agency administrative efficiencies and the compliance of former employees with UC eligibility criteria.

Experience Rating and Employer Monitoring Incentives

In considering experience rating and employer incentives, it is useful to distinguish between what might be referred to as "macro" and "micro" employer interests in the UC system. From a macro viewpoint, employers as a group have strong incentives to seek relatively strict eligibility criteria for claimants as a whole in order to constrain UC benefit payments. For similar reasons, employers as a group have strong interests in encouraging effective UC agency administrative operations in order to minimize administrative costs for any level of service. In effect, employers have a strong interest in advocating measures that minimize UC program costs because of the expected UC tax savings that may result. Thus, one would expect to find strong lobbying efforts by employers at both the federal and state levels to attempt to constrain UC program costs. Such activities also probably occur to some extent as a defensive device to check the activities of organized labor or other groups that may seek to expand program coverage and the amount or duration of program benefits. Similarly, it would be expected that employers would actively participate in advisory groups that stress administrative efficiencies in both USDOL and state UC agency operations. It should be noted, however, that the incentives for employers, as a group, to engage in the above types of activities arise because

---

54. Topel (1984: 88). More recently, Topel has concluded that in a typical year as much as 20 percent of unemployment among covered workers can be attributed to the operation of the UC program. See Topel (1986: 28).

UC taxes are levied on employers as a whole, regardless of the experience rating of individual employers.[55]

The motivation of individual employers to engage in micro monitoring to control charges to their individual reserve accounts are quite different from the macro monitoring incentives discussed above. In particular, micro monitoring incentives for employers vary directly with the extent to which employer tax rates are effectively experience rated and inversely with the costs incurred by firms in monitoring the compliance of their former employees with UC eligibility criteria. As a result, it is likely that the trend towards reduced experience rating in the UC program has contributed to an overall weakening of employer incentives to engage in micro monitoring activities. Evidence available from the recent study undertaken by USDOL's Office of Inspector General supports this view. The frequency with which employers filed appeals (and hence participated in the enforcement of UC eligibility criteria) was found to be greater for those whose tax rates could increase with a rise in benefit charges, compared with employers whose tax rates were already at the maximum rate.[56]

Even in a world of "perfect" experience rating, individual employer incentives for monitoring many types of issues might be extremely limited because of either low payoffs or high costs. For example, an employer would have no direct financial incentive to report a refusal of suitable work if the person involved was not a former employee who was collecting UC benefits that would be charged to the employer's reserve account. Similarly, an employer probably would not find it cost effective to monitor and evaluate the job search activities of former employees because of the high costs involved; recall, for example, that several hours per case were devoted to attempting to verify job search contacts reported by claimants for a single week of unemployment in the K-B and B-K-S studies, often with inconclusive results. In fact, most employers would have little

---

55. This assumes that employers are unable to fully shift UC taxes either forward to consumers in the form of higher prices or backward to workers in the form of lower wages. For analysis of this issue, see McLure, Jr. (1977).

56. U.S. Department of Labor, (1985d: iv.).

direct and continuing contact with their former employees that
would allow them to determine if such employees continued to
meet all UC eligibility criteria throughout their compensated
unemployment spells.[57]

Even though improved (or even perfect) experience rating
probably would have only a modest impact on employer incentives to monitor claimant compliance with eligibility criteria, the
extent of experience rating in the UC program is an important
matter. In fact, the extent of experience rating has an important
impact on employer layoff decisions and consequently on the
temporary layoff rate of unemployment. Hence, the trend towards a decline in experience rating in the UC system continues
to merit careful study and appropriate policy action.

The basic conclusion of this section is that employer participation in the UC system is likely to focus primarily on macro
efforts to constrain UC program costs. With the exception of
monitoring separation issues and the monetary eligibility of
former employees, employer incentives for independently engaging in micro efforts to monitor claimant compliance with the
weekly eligibility criteria are likely to remain fairly weak. As a
result, in the absence of additional measures to increase self-
compliance by UC claimants, the primary burden of enforcing
the weekly eligibility criteria will remain with state UC agency
personnel. The incentives confronted by this group are considered in the following section.

State UC Agency Personnel

The employees of state UC agencies also confront incentives
that affect both payment accuracy and overall UC program
quality. Little direct evidence is available, however, to assess the

---

57. It is interesting to note that some indirect evidence from the B-K-S study suggests that
individual employers may even have relatively weak incentives to monitor the monetary
eligibility of their claimants. As one aspect of each case reviewed in the B-K-S study, the
qualifying wage credits reported for the claimant's base period were verified. Incorrect base
period wages were found for more than 70 percent of the sample cases in one state, and for more
than one-fourth of the sample cases in two other states [Burgess, Kingston and St. Louis (1982:
50)]. A substantial number of these base period wage errors were due to misreporting of base
period wages by employers.

impact of these incentives on the efforts of state UC program personnel to prevent or detect overpayments. Consequently, the discussion in this section tends to be quite general and the evidence presented to support the conclusions tends to be less direct than that presented in most other sections.

Incentive Problems

It certainly is not possible to prove that state UC agency personnel typically operate in an environment characterized by inappropriate incentives. Somewhat less directly, however, it is possible to deduce from known operating characteristics of state UC programs a number of fundamental issues and problems related to payment errors and overall program quality. The complexity of UC program eligibility criteria interacts with limited administrative financing of the program so that it simply is not possible to ascertain with any reasonable degree of precision whether the great majority of UC claimants satisfy UC eligibility criteria. Federal time lapse standards even further tend to frustrate serious attempts by state UC agency personnel to ensure that benefits are paid only to eligible claimants. Also, the effectiveness of monitoring efforts by state UC program personnel depends to a large degree on the motivations of employers and claimants to cooperate in such efforts. However, as explained earlier in this chapter, incentives for both claimant self-compliance and for employer assistance in terms of micro monitoring are quite limited. Also, substantial administrative discretion necessarily is exercised by UC agency personnel who process UC claims. In light of the minimal emphasis that has been placed on preventing or detecting overpayments prior to very recent years, the existence of frequent overpayments and other quality problems perhaps should not be unexpected.

Some limited evidence that supports the above views was obtained during the K-B study. Although unscientific in nature (because the survey respondents were not randomly selected to represent all state UC program personnel), this evidence is summarized and discussed here because each of the respondents was well qualified to express an informed view about the issues considered in this section. Also, it should be emphasized that even though this evidence reflects only the views of those who participated in the K-B study, the strong opinions expressed by the great majority of those surveyed have not been contradicted in our subsequent (direct) interactions with state UC program personnel in at least the first 15 of the states to participate in the Random Audit program.

The survey was conducted among all of the project supervisors and field investigators assigned to the K-B study in each of the six metropolitan areas. Nearly all of these individuals had substantial UC program experience, either as adjudication deputies in UC local offices or as investigators in fraud/investigation units. The following summary is based on excerpts taken from the composite responses that were developed to reflect the consensus views of the individual respondents:

Unfortunately, the work environment and the "incentives/ reward" system for local office employees do not effectively encourage the prevention of overpayments. Even though the UI cost model provides minutes per unit (MPUs) for the prevention of overpayments by local office personnel, the primary emphasis within the local office is on "production" and not on preventing overpayments. Local office employees do not believe they are given sufficient time to effectively conduct the activities described above and, beyond the cost-model time credited for issuing a nonmonetary determination, local office personnel believe that they receive no positive encouragement to prevent overpayments. Employees with the least experience oftentimes are placed on the new claims line and, because they lack training and experience, they are unable to detect a number of potential issues that should be referred for adjudication. Moreover, once potential issues are referred for adjudication, the local office deputies are under great pressure to issue nonmonetary determinations within a relatively short period of time. Personnel performance evaluations for these local office deputies often place a great weight on the number of determinations issued per day or per week. . . .

Local office personnel also are not encourged to prevent overpayments because there is no system in place to measure, let alone reward, local office personnel for preventing overpayments. In the absence of any means by which this dimension of performance could be assessed, it is not surprising that relatively little emphasis is placed on the types of activities that would tend to prevent overpayments. Rather, local office employees are encouraged to achieve relatively high rankings for their local offices, as measured by the monthly reports of first pay timeliness performance.[58]

This summary includes a brief comment on the impact of the federal time lapse criteria. If an increased emphasis on either payment accuracy or overall program quality conflicts with these criteria, state agency personnel could be under heavy pressure to trade off those factors for increased production speed. This indeed appears to be the case, based on the responses to a number of questions included in the K-B study survey (see table 6-1). These findings indicate that 76 percent of the respondents either disagreed or strongly disagreed with the idea that federal time lapse criteria for first payments had little or no effect on efforts to prevent overpayments in local UC offices (Line 1). In contrast, more than two-thirds of the respondents indicated that the first-payment time lapse criteria greatly reduced local office efforts to prevent overpayments (Line 2). It also is interesting to note that only 16 percent of the respondents believed that local office personnel understood that these time lapse criteria supposedly include a quality, as well as a quantity, dimension. These findings also reveal that three-fifths of the respondents either disagreed or strongly disagreed that the timeliness criteria for nonmonetary determinations had little or no effect on efforts to prevent overpayments in local offices (Line 4). In fact, nearly two-thirds of the respondents agreed or strongly agreed that these criteria had greatly reduced local office efforts to prevent overpayments (Line 5). In addition, four-fifths of the respondents believed that the nonmonetary determination time lapse criteria were not commonly understood to include a quality, as well as a quantity, dimension (Line 6). The following composite

---

58. Kingston and Burgess (1981b: J-1 and J-2).

TABLE 6–1
Kingston-Burgess Study Survey Results on
Federal Time Lapse Performance Criteria Impacts

Statement	Don't Know or Blank	Strongly Agree	Agree	Neither Agree Nor Disagree	Disagree	Strongly Disagree
1. Federal timeliness requirements for FIRST PAYS have had *little or no* effect on efforts to *prevent* overpayments in local offices.	0%	12%	12%	0%	36%	40%
2. Federal timeliness requirements for FIRST PAYS have *greatly reduced* efforts to *prevent* overpayments in local offices.	0%	36%	32%	4%	20%	8%
3. The federal timeliness criteria for FIRST PAYS are commonly understood by local office personnel to include a *quality* as well as a *quantity* standard.	4%	0%	16%	4%	48%	28%
4. Federal timeliness requirements for NON-MONETARY DETERMINATIONS have had *little or no* effect on efforts to *prevent* overpayments in local offices.	4%	12%	24%	0%	36%	24%
5. Federal timeliness requirements for NON-MONETARY DETERMINATIONS have *greatly reduced* efforts to *prevent* overpayments in local offices.	4%	24%	40%	8%	20%	4%
6. The federal timeliness criteria for NONMONE-TARY DETERMINATIONS are commonly understood by local office personnel to include a *quality* as well as a *quantity* standard.	4%	0%	16%	0%	56%	24%

Response Distribution spans the Strongly Agree, Agree, Neither Agree Nor Disagree, Disagree, and Strongly Disagree columns.

Source: Kingston and Burgess (1981: 52).

response was prepared to summarize respondent views on the time lapse performance criteria:

Federally mandated timeliness requirements for making first payments and issuing nonmonetary determinations, and competition among local office managers to exceed these time lapse standards, are perceived to be the basis of the pressure to emphasize the rapid payment of benefits over the accurate payment of benefits.[59]

The composite response suggests that federal time lapse criteria have adversely affected the overall incentive environment faced by local office workers who represent the "first line of defense" for payment accuracy and overall UC program quality. It appears that state agency personnel typically receive few positive incentives to encourage either payment accuracy or overall UC program quality.

Improving Incentives for UC Agency Personnel

Implementing major improvements in the incentive environment confronted by state UC agency personnel would be extremely difficult unless at least some of the improvements in USDOL procedures or policies discussed in chapters 4 and 5 were implemented. These included: (1) improvements in the process of providing administrative funds to state UC agencies; (2) development of additional measures of program quality; and (3) a more balanced emphasis on the accuracy and speed with which payments are made. In addition, reduced program complexity and measures to encourage additional self-compliance with UC eligibility criteria by claimants would be particularly important steps in obtaining more effective administration of program requirements by state agency personnel. If these improvements occurred, some specific changes in the incentive environment for state agency personnel could have a major impact. The fundamental change required to improve the incentives of state UC program personnel is an effective emphasis on

---

59. Kingston and Burgess (1981b: J-2).

both payment accuracy and overall program quality. Once useful quality indicators for state UC program performance have been developed, their use in both performance and merit pay evaluations for state agency personnel should be carefully considered.[60]

Conclusions

The incentives confronted by state UC program participants—claimants, employers and state agency personnel—obviously have an important impact on the interactions of these participants with the UC system. The analysis in this chapter indicates that the incentives in many state systems fail to encourage and may even discourage a strong emphasis by these participants on either payment accuracy or more broadly defined program quality. Employers as a group have strong macro incentives to advocate measures restraining UC program costs and tax rates. However, current incentives for individual employers to engage in micro monitoring of claimant compliance with the weekly eligibility criteria typically are quite weak, and these incentives would be very limited even in a system with substantially increased experience rating.

The above conclusion suggests that efforts to improve claimant compliance with stated UC eligibility criteria almost necessarily must be directed at state agency personnel and at claimants themselves. In this context, the main change that appears to be necessary in the typical incentive system for state agency personnel is to implement an effective emphasis on payment accuracy. Nonetheless, the most effective technique for increasing claimant compliance with UC eligibility criteria probably would be to induce claimants themselves to increase their self-compliance. Claimant self-compliance with many aspects of

---

60. More open communication among the various divisions of at least some state UC agencies probably would be desirable. For example, in at least some state UC agencies, the local office personnel who approve claims for payment are not routinely informed about which of those claims result in overpayments. Similarly, benefit payment control/investigation units often have information or insights that could be very useful to local office personnel in the prevention of overpayments, but opportunities for such interactions apparently do not routinely occur in at least some state UC agencies.

stated eligibility criteria is likely quite low in the existing UC system simply because the expected costs of noncompliance (relative to the weekly benefits that can be obtained) are extremely low. However, claimant self-compliance could be increased by: (1) increasing the likelihood of detecting noncompliance with eligibility criteria (perhaps by utilizing computerized screening profiles to identify "high-risk" claimants); (2) increasing the rate at which overpayments are established for detected instances of noncompliance; (3) increasing the nominal penalties for nonfraud overpayments; and (4) more effectively applying whatever nominal penalties are assessed for established overpayments.

Needless to say, the overall effectiveness of the approaches discussed in this chapter would depend somewhat on the extent to which the changes discussed in other chapters also were implemented. Nonetheless, it appears that improved incentives for state program participants—particularly claimants and also state agency personnel—could contribute to an improved UC system. Moreover, it appears that some progress along these lines could be initiated by individual states, even in the absence of the improvements in USDOL incentives for state programs discussed in the previous two chapters.

7
Administering Weekly UC Eligibility Criteria

State UC program personnel face major difficulties in attempting to effectively monitor claimant compliance with the eligibility criteria that must be satisfied on a weekly basis. Such criteria include provisions that claimants must not have earnings (or days of work) that exceed specified amounts, must not refuse suitable work and must be able/available for work. Most UC jurisdictions also require active job search as an additional test of a claimant's availability for work.

The difficulties involved in enforcing the active worksearch requirement are the focus of this chapter. This emphasis was selected for several reasons. First, as noted in chapter 2, available evidence indicates that the most frequent cause of detectable overpayments is noncompliance with the worksearch requirement. Second, the worksearch requirement actually appears to be more specific and conducive to enforcement than at least several of the other weekly criteria. Accordingly, analysis of the problems involved in attempting to enforce the worksearch requirement provides insights about similar, but perhaps even more severe, problems involved in attempting to enforce claimant compliance with general availability requirements. Third, as information on statewide overpayments becomes more widely understood, noncompliance with worksearch requirements presumably will become a major policy issue that must be confronted by the UC system. The problems discussed in this chapter, however, generally would be relevant to enforcement of the broader availability-for-work (and other) requirements included in all state law/policies.

Although all states require that claimants be available for work, forty states, as of 1985, imposed a separate statutory requirement that claimants demonstrate their availability for work by actively seeking work. There tends to be considerable variation among the states, however, in precisely what actions claimants must take to satisfy the worksearch criterion, as illustrated by the five states participating in the B-K-S study. In one state, the worksearch criterion was satisfied if the claimant had made one job search contact during the key week that could be verified by state agency personnel. In another state, three worksearch contacts per week were required, although apparently not all of them had to be verifiable. In the remaining three states, the actions that would satisfy the worksearch requirement tended to be much less uniform or specific, but were generally supposed to be consistent with actions of a "reasonable" person who was seeking work in similar circumstances.

Worksearch requirements may be specified in a state's employment security law but also may be found in policy rules used to implement state employment security statutes. As one example, the Arizona Benefit Policy Rules manual, upon which the claimant eligibility flowchart presented in chapter 3 is based, contains the following language with respect to the worksearch requirement:

In order to maintain continuing eligibility for unemployment insurance a claimant shall be required to show that, in addition to registering for work, he has followed a course of action which is reasonably designed to result in his prompt reemployment in suitable work. Consideration shall be given to the customary methods of obtaining work in his usual occupation or for which he is reasonably suited, and the current condition of the labor market. Subject to the foregoing, the following actions by a claimant either singular or in combination may be considered a reasonable effort to seek work.

a. Registering and continuing active checking with the claimant's union hiring or placement facility.

b. Registering with a placement facility of the claimant's professional organization.

c. Applying for employment with former employers.

d. Making application with employers who may reasonably be expected to have openings suitable to the claimant.

e. Registering with a placement facility of a school, college, or university if one is available to the claimant in his occupation or profession.

f. Making application or taking examination for openings in civil service of a governmental unit.

g. Registering for suitable work with a private employment agency or an employer's placement facility.

h. Responding to appropriate "want ads" for work which appear suitable to the claimant.

i. Any other action found to constitute an effective means of seeking work suitable to the claimant.[1]

In addition, Arizona claimants would be found in violation of the worksearch requirement if they willfully acted to discourage prospective employers from offering suitable work.[2] However, if the prospects of obtaining suitable work through sources other than the Job Service are so remote that an active search would be "fruitless" to the claimant and "burdensome" to employers, then registration with the Job Service is deemed sufficient to satisfy the worksearch requirement.[3]

This overview of state worksearch requirements, though certainly not exhaustive, is sufficient to indicate the type of language typically found in state employment security law and policy related to the worksearch requirement. Evidence to document the problems involved in enforcing the worksearch/availability criteria is provided in the next section. Then, some possible strategies or responses to deal with worksearch noncompliance are considered. A brief conclusion completes the chapter.

---

1. Arizona Department of Economic Security (n.d.: Section R6–3–52160).
2. Arizona Department of Economic Security (n.d.: Section R6–3–52160).
3. Arizona Department of Economic Security (n.d.: Section R6–3–52160).

Evidence on Worksearch/Availability Overpayments

Evidence on the frequency of worksearch/availability overpayments is available from a number of sources, including: (1) overpayment studies; (2) studies of nonsearch by UC claimants; and (3) USDOL and state reports. Each of these is discussed below, followed by a summary of the monitoring implications of this evidence.

Overpayment Studies

Violations of the active worksearch requirement were detected in both the K-B and B-K-S studies on the basis of extremely intensive eligibility verification procedures. At the time each case was randomly selected for audit in these studies, it was assumed that the claimant had met the worksearch as well as other UC eligibility requirements. Only in those instances in which sufficiently strong evidence of noncompliance was found was the decision made to establish a worksearch (or other) overpayment. As noted earlier, these investigations generally required between 8–13 hours per case, with much of this time devoted to efforts to verify the job-seeking activities of claimants.

One of the principal findings of the 1980 K-B study was that the most common type of noncompliance detected was the failure of claimants to actively seek work.[4] Additional evidence subsequently provided by the 1982 B-K-S study of the Random Audit program pilot tests also indicated that the single most frequent cause of UC overpayments was noncompliance with active worksearch requirements.[5] In fact, the B-K-S study findings indicated that nearly half or more of the dollars overpaid in each of the five study states, and more than seven-tenths of the dollars overpaid in two states, were due to worksearch violations.[6] Even in states with a worksearch requirement, however,

---

4. This was the case even though only five of the six cities actually had active search requirements. See Kingston and Burgess (1981b: 43).
5. Burgess, Kingston and St. Louis (1982: 58).
6. Burgess, Kingston and St. Louis (1982: 53–58).

not all claimants were required to search for work; further analysis of the B-K-S data revealed that the rate of noncompliance among just those who were required to search for work was even more pronounced than indicated by the estimated overpayment rates alone. For example, of the claimants who were required to actively search for work in the five study states, over 25 percent failed to do so in one state and over 20 percent failed to do so in another; the simple average of these worksearch noncompliance rates for the five states was 14.2 percent.[7]

Another B-K-S study finding also is indicative of the difficulties involved in monitoring compliance with the active worksearch requirement. Even though the intensive eligibility verifications required an average of 8-13 hours of investigative time per week of compensated unemployment, it was found that nearly half or more of claimant-reported job contacts could not be verified as either acceptable or unacceptable in three of the five states, and at least one-fourth of these reported contacts could not be verified as acceptable or unacceptable in all five states.[8] Such reported worksearch contacts were classified as "unverifiable" but were not used as a basis to establish overpayments.

Nonsearch Studies

In a study conducted for the National Commission on Unemployment Compensation, Black and Carr analyzed data collected in conjunction with the Seattle and Denver Income Maintenance Experiments to determine the extent to which low-income UC recipients actually searched for work. The Black-Carr findings for the 1971-1973 period in Seattle indicate that: (1) about one-third of the "person-weeks" of unemployment analyzed involved the payment of benefits to individuals who were not searching for work; and (2) about one-fifth of the "person-weeks" analyzed involved individuals who were neither searching for work nor available for work.[9] The results reported by

---

7. See Kingston, Burgess and St. Louis (1986: 329).
8. Kingston, Burgess and St. Louis (1986: 330).
9. Black and Carr (1980: 529–530, 539). In this study, UC claimants were assumed to have

Black and Carr for Denver for the 1972-1974 period were nearly identical to the above results for Seattle.[10] Even though the low-income UC recipients analyzed by Black and Carr obviously were not typical of all UC recipients, the findings nonetheless suggest very substantial noncompliance with worksearch requirements, at least among the low-income UC recipients analyzed.

Although the Black and Carr findings might be appropriately discounted because they applied only to a fairly atypical group of (low-income) UC recipients, additional analysis of the B-K-S study data suggests that the tendency to conduct no search (as opposed to insufficient search to satisfy active search requirements) also is a major problem among the general population of UC recipients. This further analysis revealed that an estimated 18.7 percent of all claimants who were required to search for work actually made no job search contacts during single weeks for which benefits were claimed and paid.[11] Moreover, this tendency to make no job search contacts was not randomly distributed among the sample analyzed, but rather tended to vary systematically with various personal and labor market characteristics. St. Louis, Burgess and Kingston found that the subgroups with the largest proportions of persons who had zero job search contacts were: women (23.4 percent); young persons (26.0 percent); those with unemployment durations of at least 20 weeks (27.4 percent); those not laid off from their prior jobs (29.3 percent); and nonunion workers (22.4 percent).[12] In addition to providing additional documentation of the problems

---

engaged in job search if they looked for work at any time during the same month that included a given week of UC-compensated unemployment. This procedure tends to overstate the job-seeking activities of the UC recipients included in the SIME-DIME samples. For individuals who did not search for work, as defined above, their reported reason for nonsearch was examined. Persons who reported that they did not look for work because of personal or family reasons, labor disputes, illness or disability, school enrollment or because they simply "didn't want to work" were classified as unavailable for work.

10. Black and Carr (1980: 530).
11. St. Louis, Burgess and Kingston (1986: 98). This percentage is based on the 1074 claimants who were required to seek work and who had at least one job search contact verified as acceptable or unacceptable.
12. St. Louis, Burgess and Kingston (1986: 98). These percentages also were calculated for the 1074 claimants who were required to seek work and who had at least one job contact verified as acceptable or unacceptable.

associated with administering the worksearch requirement in the UC program, these results also provide some insight into possible causes for higher *reported* unemployment rates among certain labor force groups.[13]

USDOL/State Reports

The evidence presented above indicates that there are substantial difficulties involved in attempting to detect worksearch violations, once *payments have been made* to UC recipients. It would be useful, however, to also examine the impact of the worksearch requirement in terms of screening UC claims *before* they actually are paid. Unfortunately, no separate USDOL/state statistics are available on the number of weeks claimed that were denied payment because claimants had not conducted an adequate search for work. Instead, the available evidence combines nonmonetary determinations issued both to prevent and to establish overpayments.

For FY 1983, a total of 2.5 million nonmonetary determinations were issued for potential violations of able/available (including worksearch) requirements in state UC programs, and these determinations accounted for about one-half of all those issued for nonseparation reasons.[14] This total of 2.5 million determinations for able/available/worksearch issues amounted to slightly more than one determination per 100 weeks claimed during FY 1983, and about two-fifths of these determinations resulted in the disqualification of claimants from benefits for one or more weeks.[15] In an earlier study, the National Commission on Unemployment Compensation (NCUC) reported that about 1.3 million claims for calendar year 1979—representing about 0.7 percent of the total 194.5 million claimant contacts for the year—were denied or postponed because of violations of the

---

13. Official unemployment rates are computed by the Bureau of Labor Statistics on the basis of responses to the Current Population Survey. Individuals who satisfy other criteria and report that they have looked for work in a recent period are included among the unemployed. Because these unemployment rates are based on *reported* rather than *actual* job-seeking efforts, it is quite possible that high measured unemployment rates for some groups could be due at least in part to a tendency to overreport job search efforts.

14. U.S. Department of Labor (1984b and 1984c).

15. U.S. Department of Labor (1984b and 1984c).

able/available requirement.[16] In an even earlier study conducted in Arizona, it was found that 82,000 nonmonetary determinations were issued for approximately 60,000 Arizona claimants who established benefit years during the first three quarters of FY 1976; nearly 25,000 of these determinations were for availability issues, and inadequate job search was the most frequent basis for these determinations.[17] Approximately one-half of the Arizona determinations issued for inadequate worksearch resulted in the disqualification of claimants from benefits.[18]

The above evidence from USDOL, NCUC and state-agency sources is consistent with the possibility that some screening of claims to prevent payments (and thus overpayments) to ineligible claimants does occur because of the existence of the able/available and active worksearch requirements in state UC programs. The existence of such an effect is an important consideration in evaluating the merits of these eligibility criteria. More specifically, even if the existence of the worksearch requirement does result in many overpayments (because of the difficulty of monitoring claimant compliance), the worksearch requirement may constitute an effective screen in preventing at least some payments to claimants who are not actually available for or seeking work. Additional evidence on this point would be very useful in evaluating the overall impact of the worksearch requirement.

Summary of Monitoring Problems

In discussing the problems of administering the able/available eligibility criteria (including the worksearch requirement), Roche concluded that:

If the issues about ability and willingness to work and availability are hard to resolve, the decisions on them are even harder to document in a way that meets the requirements of due process of

16. National Commission on Unemployment Compensation (1980: 46).
17. Green et al. (1978: 14–16).
18. Green et al. (1978: 16).

law. Nonetheless, it is in them that the unemployment insurance program most directly comes face to face with the realities of the labor market. . . . The confrontation has been very painful, and the wisdom of Solomon would barely be adequate to cope with it. Trying to summarize or to characterize the various outcomes of claimstaking and appeals appears to be next to impossible and would not be very informative. Every outcome is imbedded in the particular labor market situation of an individual claimant as seen by a claims examiner, referee, or appeals board and is, in a sense, unique. Many of these outcomes have been made into precedent cases . . . but the unique features of the precedent case and its factual matrix are not always clearly described so that the "rule" in the case is often hard to figure out. . . .

It should be noted, finally, that the frustrations engendered by inability to handle some kinds of availability issues have routinely led to the use of more tangible ways to disqualify suspect claimants (e.g., on an issue of refusal of suitable work) or to legislation of the kind discussed in the following chapter which denies insured status to some group about which an availability issue frequently is raised (e.g., by provisions about those quitting for domestic reasons).[19]

What was written by Roche more than a decade ago continues to be an apt description of the problems associated with monitoring claimant compliance with the weekly eligibility criteria. In fact, given the pressures placed on the UC system during the 14 years since Roche's study, it is quite likely that the administrative problems he discusses have increased. In any case, the findings strongly suggest that effective monitoring of any substantive worksearch requirement for all UC claimants simply is not feasible within the UC system as it currently operates. Furthermore, if the worksearch requirement is actually more objectively defined and easily monitored than the broader availability criteria, then effective monitoring would be even more difficult for these other requirements. Despite these problems, however, it must be recognized that the worksearch requirement also may serve a screening function in preventing some payments to ineligible claimants.

---

19. Roche (1973: 82).

Responses to Worksearch/Availability Monitoring Problems

The discussion below focuses narrowly on responses that might be considered because of the difficulties of monitoring the worksearch requirement, although some of the issues discussed also would be relevant for other features of the weekly eligibility criteria. The possibility of responding to the problem by greatly increasing the administrative funds provided to states for monitoring worksearch compliance is not considered in this chapter because, as noted earlier, such additional funding is likely to be neither available nor (in the absence of other fundamental changes) effective. The responses discussed include: (1) elimination of the worksearch requirement, with no compensating changes in other criteria; (2) elimination of the worksearch requirement, with compensating changes in other criteria; (3) imposition of stricter requirements; (4) improved administration of existing (or altered) requirements; and (5) use of direct reemployment incentives.

It should be emphasized from the outset, however, that none of the approaches discussed constitutes an entirely satisfactory response to the worksearch problem. Claimants differ markedly in their job-seeking skills, in their motivations to work and to seek work, in their preparation for employment and in the job market circumstances they confront. To subject all claimants to the same job search requirements, whether more or less strict than those presently imposed, will no doubt cause hardships for some or benefit others. To subject different claimants to different job-seeking requirements may create uncertainties as to what requirements apply and confusion about how they are to be satisfied, with the result that equity in the application of eligibility criteria will not be achieved. Nearly all of the approaches described will either increase or decrease claims filing by both those with strong and weak attachments to the labor force, and they will also influence the frequency with which overpayments occur. Consequently, each of the four approaches examined represents, at best, a starting point from which a more careful examination may begin.

Elimination of the Worksearch Requirement
Without Compensating Changes[20]

One response to the difficulties encountered in attempting to monitor claimant compliance with the worksearch requirement would be to eliminate this criterion. In fact, 13 UC jurisdictions did not have such a statutory requirement as of 1985; some of these jurisdictions used as principal tests of availability for work the actions of claimants in registering with the Job Service or their reactions to offers of suitable work.[21] In its 1980 report, the National Commission on Unemployment Compensation recommended that all states eliminate specific "actively seeking work" requirements.[22]

One obvious result of eliminating the worksearch requirement would be an immediate reduction in the rate of detected overpayments. This conclusion is based on the fact that the single most frequent cause of the overpayments detected in both the K-B and B-K-S studies was noncompliance with state worksearch requirements. However, a number of other issues would be important in evaluating the desirability of eliminating the worksearch requirement, including the effects of such a change on: (1) the overall volume of UC claims filed; (2) the proportion of claims filed that would be paid; and (3) the overall volume of UC benefits paid.[23] Each of these effects is briefly summarized below.

Elimination of the worksearch requirement would be expected to increase the overall volume of UC claims *filed* (for any given level of aggregate demand). Because such a change would reduce the costs of filing, some otherwise eligible claimants who previously did not file because of the worksearch requirement would be expected to file for benefits. The worksearch require-

20. For a much more detailed analysis of the issues raised in this section, see Kingston and Burgess (1986).

21. U.S. Department of Labor (1985a: Table 400). The states without a statutory worksearch requirement were Alaska, Arizona, Florida, Massachusetts, Mississippi, Nebraska, Nevada, New York, Pennsylvania, Puerto Rico, South Dakota, Tennessee and Texas. Some of these states (e.g., Arizona) did have a worksearch requirement in their Benefit Policy Rules.

22. National Commission on Unemployment Compensation (1980: 49).

23. For a detailed discussion of these and other effects of eliminating the worksearch requirement, see Kingston and Burgess (1986).

ment undoubtedly discourages some persons—who actually are not unemployed for UC purposes because they are not interested in immediately finding suitable employment—from filing for benefits because they are not willing to certify that they are actively seeking work. Removal of the worksearch requirement would be expected to induce some of these persons to file for benefits.

Elimination of the worksearch requirement also would be expected to result in an increase in the proportion of claims *paid* out of any given number filed. Existing worksearch requirements prevent payments to some claimants who file for benefits because UC personnel are able to detect that they actually are not actively seeking work, despite certifications signed by such claimants to the contrary. Furthermore, worksearch requirements probably increase the extent to which UC agency personnel can effectively enforce general availability criteria and job refusal provisions. Accordingly, elimination of the worksearch requirement would eliminate its associated screening effects and, consequently, would be expected to increase the proportion of filed claims that would be paid, other things equal.

The above two effects—increases in claims filed and in the proportion of filed claims paid—would result in an increase in the overall volume of UC benefit payments (for any given level of aggregate demand). Employer tax rates also would be expected to increase in order to finance the resulting increase in benefit payments.

Elimination of the Worksearch Requirement
With Compensating Changes

One basis for requiring that claimants actively seek work is to prevent payments to those who have weak or no intentions of finding immediate reemployment. Since it is extremely difficult for UC personnel to evaluate claimant job-search activities, a possible response would be to replace the worksearch requirement with other criteria that could be more easily measured and enforced. A number of such replacements might be considered. For example, a claimant's past work attachment in terms of covered earnings or employment can be measured much more objectively, consistently and less expensively than can search activities or intentions to return to work. Moreover, all states already impose monetary eligibility criteria which claimants must meet in order to obtain benefits, so that changing such criteria would be relatively simple from an administrative viewpoint.

The approach discussed in this section focuses on imposing additional or stricter measures of past work attachment to replace the active worksearch requirement.[24] One possibility would be to substitute stricter earnings and/or weeks-of-work requirements for the worksearch requirement. Such an approach merits at least some consideration to the extent that: (1) UC system support is intended to ''insure'' the loss of past wages; (2) objectively measurable and easily monitored criteria are considered superior to vague and difficult-to-monitor criteria; and (3) enforcing claimant compliance with stated eligibility criteria at relatively low administrative cost is considered desirable.

The attractiveness of this approach would be enhanced if those who could not satisfy stricter criteria related to *past* work attachment also tended to be the same individuals who do not comply with current availability/active search requirements. There is a strong conceptual basis for linking past work attachment to present intentions to actively seek work. The logic underlying this expected relationship is that (currently) foregone earnings due to unemployment presumably are larger for claimants who have higher prior wages and more stable prior employment. Such individuals would have greater incentives to return to work (and hence to seek work) than otherwise similar individuals with lower prior wages and less stable prior employment. The limited evidence currently available on this topic suggests that the relationship between past work attachment and current worksearch noncompliance may indeed be a valid one. This evidence, based on an analysis of the B-K-S study data, indicates that claimants with weaker past work attachments—proxied by lower past wage and employment stability levels—were more

---

24. This approach also is discussed in Kingston and Burgess (1986).

likely to overreport job search contacts.[25] Nonetheless, considerably more research is required before any systematic and stable
relationship may be presumed between past work attachment and
current worksearch noncompliance.

If measures of past work attachment were substituted for the
active worksearch requirement, an important issue would be
exactly how to measure past work attachment, and whether that
attachment should be measured over a period of more than one
year. Although apparently little consideration has been given to
the possibility of utilizing base periods that encompass more than
one year, it would be possible to lengthen UC base periods.
Another way of increasing the emphasis on past work attachment
would be to add weeks-of-work requirements in those states that
do not have such requirements. Weeks-of-work requirements
could be utilized as an alternative to or in combination with
longer UC base periods.

While such changes merit consideration,[26] it should be noted
that, depending on the types of requirements imposed, the
overall volume of UC claims filed and paid could rise, fall or
remain unchanged. If more stringent monetary eligibility and
weeks-of-work requirements were substituted for the worksearch
requirement, implementation should be carefully monitored to
identify impacts on the size and composition of UC claim filing
so that any unintended and undesirable side effects could be
identified and evaluated. It is quite clear, for example, that more
stringent monetary (including weeks-of-work) requirements

---

25. St. Louis, Burgess and Kingston (1986).
26. Presently, four different measures of prior work attachment are used by state UC
agencies: weeks of work; multiples of weekly benefit amounts; multiples of high quarter earnings;
and flat earnings minimums. A major study was conducted a number of years ago to investigate
the desirability of using these measures as indicators of past work attachment [see Pleatsikas,
Bailis and Dernburg (1978)]. For details on the monetary eligibility criteria, including weeks of
work requirements, used by state UC agencies as of January, 1985, see National Foundation for
Unemployment Compensation and Workers' Compensation (1985c: 37–39). A number of studies
have recommended that states without weeks-of-work requirements should be encouraged to
adopt them for evaluating the extent of past work attachment by claimants. See, for example,
Haber and Murray (1966: 43); Hamermesh (1977: 95); W.E. Upjohn Institute Unemployment
Insurance Research Advisory Committee (1975: 17); and National Commission on Unemploy-
ment Compensation (1980: 37). For additional analysis of the weeks-of-work requirement, see
Munts (1980).

would reduce the number of labor market entrants or reentrants who would be eligible for UC program support.

Stricter Worksearch Requirements

The possible responses discussed in the previous two sections involved the elimination or replacement of the worksearch requirement. However, it also would be possible to implement stricter worksearch requirements than those currently imposed. This approach is illustrated by the introduction of relatively strict worksearch (and suitable work) provisions in the federal-state Extended Benefits (EB) program. Under the original 1970 legislation which authorized the EB program, worksearch (and suitable work) requirements were the same as those for benefits paid under regular state programs. Stiffer suitable work provisions were first introduced in the Federal Supplemental Benefits (FSB) program in 1977 (Public Law 95-19) and subsequently in the EB program in 1980 and 1981. However, the provisions of particular interest in the context of this section are the stricter worksearch criteria contained in Public Law 96-799. Under these provisions, which became effective as of April 1981, EB claimants were required to provide tangible evidence that they were actively seeking work. To implement these new requirements, USDOL issued the following directions to state UC agencies:

An EB claimant is expected to make a more diligent and active search for work than would normally be required of an individual receiving UI benefits. To meet EB eligibility requirements, the claimant's search for work must be "systematic and sustained." A "sustained" effort to obtain work is a continual effort maintained at length throughout each week. Under the requirement to actively seek work, passive availability for work is not sufficient. A "systematic" effort to obtain work is a work-search conducted with thoroughness and with a plan or methods to produce results.[27]

---

27. U.S. Department of Labor (1981a: 8).

Furthermore, no exceptions to this policy were supposed to be permitted (as otherwise would be allowed in most states) for illness, jury duty and other factors.

Other provisions of the stricter EB worksearch requirements included the following: (1) registration with a referral union was to be considered as only partially meeting the active worksearch requirement, with individual job-seeking efforts required in every case to demonstrate an active search for work; (2) a broadening of the types of work claimants must seek with prolonged unemployment;[28] and (3) more stringent disqualification penalties for not meeting the above criteria (including subsequent employment in at least four weeks and earnings not less than four times the claimant's weekly benefit amount in order to remove such a disqualification).[29] In each of six states involved in a special study of the impact of these new EB regulations,[30] a minimum number of worksearch contacts was required each week and, in two of these states, the same employer could not be listed as a worksearch contact more than once during the EB claim period.[31] Yet another change brought about by the more stringent EB eligibility criteria was the increased use of eligibility reviews for EB claimants.[32]

To assess the relative merits and the likely impact of implementing stricter worksearch requirements, it is useful to consider the intended effects of the worksearch criterion. Stevens has emphasized two administrative rationales for the worksearch requirement: (1) a conscious desire to increase the costs to claimants of maintaining benefit eligibility, in order to discourage some potential claimants from filing for benefits; and (2) a belief that such requirements, as administered through state employment security offices, actually enhance claimant prospects of reemployment.[33] Some other plausible justifications include a recognition that: (3) more stringent requirements may

---

28. U.S. Department of Labor (1981a: 8).
29. U.S. Department of Labor (1981a: 9).
30. Corson and Nicholson (1984).
31. Corson and Nicholson (1984: 77).
32. Corson and Nicholson (1984: 78).
33. Stevens (1977: 41).

provide needed clarification and specificity to relatively vague availability requirements, so that such criteria can be more effectively enforced; and (4) public support for the UC program may depend, to a great extent, on perceptions that claimants are active job seekers. Each of these rationales for the existence of the worksearch requirement (and implicitly for the imposition of stricter requirements) is discussed in more detail below. The importance of administrative commitment in terms of effectively enforcing either present or stricter worksearch requirements also is considered.

Impact on Volume of Claims Filed. There is little doubt that stricter worksearch requirements will, at some point, significantly reduce the volume of UC claims filed. Stevens has summarized this point succinctly as follows:

> The fundamental issue is this: the eligible claimant population can be adjusted to *any* desired size, by simply increasing or relaxing the burdensomeness of eligibility requirements. So, there really is no question whether a work test, or any other continuing eligibility requirement, can be performed. The only question is whether the requirement can be carried out consistent with other efficiency and equity considerations.[34]

Evidence to support this view is available from a recently completed study of the impact of the more stringent requirements imposed on EB claimants.[35] The findings indicated that the stricter EB provisions caused significant declines in: (1) the likelihood that claimants would participate in the EB program; (2) the number of weeks of EB benefits drawn; and (3) the likelihood that EB benefits would be exhausted.[36] Similarly, in another study, Burtless and Saks reported that:

> In our judgement, the legal and administrative reforms in UI provide an explanation for most of the decline in insured unemployment relative to total unemployment that has occurred

---

34. Stevens (1980: 53).
35. Corson and Nicholson (1984).
36. Corson and Nicholson (1984: 60–65).

since 1980. Without more careful study of the experiences in individual states it is, however, impossible to suggest the precise impact of each of the individual changes. Nonetheless, there is considerable evidence of a widespread and systematic trend toward restricting benefit payments and toughening administrative procedures, and this trend is evident at both the state and federal levels. This survey of recent UI changes suggests that the relative decline in insured unemployment is primarily the result of executive, legislative, and administrative decisions to restrict or reduce the scope of the UI program.[37]

It should be noted, however, that the decline in claim filing documented in the above studies most likely did *not* result from increased detection of UC overpayments to ineligible claimants, but rather from the screening effects discussed earlier in this chapter, which would directly reduce the volumes of claims filed and paid (probably for both ineligible and potentially eligible claimants). In fact, evidence from the B-K-S study with respect to enforcement of the stricter EB worksearch requirement supports this view. EB claims affected by the stiffer eligibility requirements initially were included in the Random Audit program pilot tests. Once the virtual impossibility of verifying a claimant's compliance with these stricter requirements became evident, EB claims were dropped by USDOL from the RA program pilot tests.[38] The irony of this decision is that, while federal policymakers attempted to tighten eligibility criteria, those responsible for administering them determined that compliance could not be effectively monitored even in the Random Audit program in which the time devoted to processing each case was at least 50 times that available in the routine operating system![39]

Additional evidence on the impact of enforcing a stricter work test for UC claimants is available from the Claimant Placement

---

37. Burtless and Saks (1984: 79). Also see Vroman (1985: 4–8).

38. Kingston and Burgess (1981a).

39. Information supplied by state agency personnel indicated that, in some of the Random Audit pilot-test states, the difficulties of (equitably) enforcing the stricter EB requirements also tended to reduce the efforts by some agency personnel to enforce regular state UC program worksearch requirements as well. However, we are aware of no other evidence on this point.

and Work Test Demonstration project conducted in Charleston, South Carolina in 1983.[40] The design of this experimental project provided for improved communications between the state's UC and Employment Service offices to facilitate a more intensive application of the weekly eligibility criteria. All claimants in each of three "treatment" groups were required to report to an Employment Service office once they had received their first UC payment, whereas control group claimants were not so required to report. Claimants in two of the three treatment groups were given enhanced employment services, including job referrals and job development support and, in one group, workshop training in job search. Failure to report to an Employment Service office by a treatment group claimant triggered both a call-in notice for the claimant to report to a local UC office, and an order to stop payment until any issues had been resolved through the formal nonmonetary determination process. A comprehensive evaluation of the results of these procedures revealed that the average duration of benefits drawn for the treatment groups was about six-tenths of a week less than for the control group, but no important differences in average duration were found *among* the treatment groups that received differing levels of employment services.[41] In assessing the likely causes of the observed reduction in UC benefit payments to the treatment groups, Corson, Long and Nicholson concluded that:

> The final explanation (i.e., that claimants responded to the demonstration by leaving the UI rolls without necessarily finding a job) was probably also an important factor in the outcome. The data on responses to the call-in notices showed that many claimants did not respond to the notices, and the data on UI benefit receipt showed that the treatments had a significant impact on the rate at which claimants stopped claiming UI benefits early in their benefit period. Yet, no strong evidence indicated that these claimants necessarily found jobs, although no information

---

40. Johnson, Pfiester, West and Dickinson (1984).
41. Corson, Long and Nicholson (1984: 68). The results also showed that the number of weeks of benefits drawn by treatment-group claimants, compared with the control group, averaged about one week less for men but were not significantly different for women.

was available on whether claimants who left the UI roles continued to search for work or whether they dropped out of the labor force.

In conclusion, it appears that the reporting requirements, coupled with the cessation of UI payments for failure to report, were probably the most important elements of the treatments. And a major way in which these components had an impact on benefits was to cause claimants to leave the UI rolls both because some were formally denied benefits and because some simply stopped claiming benefits.[42]

The evidence from the study also suggests that more rigorous enforcement of the work test does reduce UC benefit payments, partly by denying payments to ineligible claimants and partly by reducing filing by (probably both) ineligible and potentially eligible persons.

Impact on Job Search and Reemployment. Stricter job-seeking requirements (or more vigorous enforcement of existing requirements) might be expected to increase the likelihood that claimants would search more effectively and thus: (1) return to work more quickly; (2) obtain more stable reemployment; and/or (3) obtain higher wage rates or otherwise obtain jobs of higher quality. However, what little direct evidence is available on these positive effects seems to suggest that they either are small or perhaps nonexistent. For example, as one part of the Charleston Claimant Placement and Work Test Demonstration Project, an effort was made to compare the reemployment experiences of treatment group claimants with control group claimants. Corson, Long and Nicholson found that: (1) the proportion of claimants who had some employment in the quarter following the one during which they began to receive UC support was not significantly different between treatment groups and the control group; and (2) the ratio of reemployment wages to preunemployment wages was not significantly different between the treatment groups and the control group.[43] Furthermore, even though a recent study of the impact of the stricter EB eligibility criteria revealed that UC claimants made more frequent use of the

42. Corson, Long and Nicholson (1984: 107–108).
43. Corson, Long and Nicholson (1984: 60–67).

Employment Service because of those criteria, actual job placements apparently were unaffected by the increased use of the services provided.[44]

Other evidence bearing on the impact of stricter worksearch requirements or enforcement efforts is much more indirect in nature. If it were assumed that the effects of stricter requirements on the search activities of claimants would be similar to those resulting from the specialized job search assistance provided in several special studies, some additional insights may be obtained. Evaluations of the service-to-claimants (STC) projects conducted in five cities over a decade ago by Burgess and Kingston indicated that specialized reemployment assistance significantly reduced the duration of single spells of unemployment in some cities, but had no consistent impact on reducing either the number of subsequent unemployment spells or the total benefits received by claimants for an entire year.[45] Furthermore, the findings indicated that the specialized job search assistance had no significant impact on the subsequent earnings or employment experiences of the groups that received such assistance.[46] The findings by Austermann, Crosslin and Stevens for STC projects conducted in other areas were even less optimistic that positive results could be attributed to such specialized services.[47] This indirect evidence collectively suggests that more stringent worksearch requirements/ enforcement efforts and increased attempts to provide positive reemployment assistance may not positively affect either the job search or reemployment experiences of UC claimants.

Moreover, it is even possible that stricter worksearch requirements or enforcement procedures could produce some unintended and undesirable effects. For example, in assessing the

---

44. Corson and Nicholson (1984: v). As Nicholson emphasized a number of years ago, however, measurement of the effects of services provided by the Employment Service involves a number of complexities that merit careful consideration. For example, some studies have found that those who use the Employment Service ultimately receive lower wages than those who don't, but this could simply reflect the fact that employers tend to list only low-wage jobs with the Employment Service. For more discussion on this point, see Nicholson (1981: 172-175).

45. Burgess and Kingston (1973: 4).

46. Burgess and Kingston (1973: 4).

47. Austermann, Crosslin and Stevens (1975: 96–101).

likely impact of UC program provisions designed to encourage
additional worksearch activity, Stevens has concluded such
measures may cause both claimant job search costs and employer
recruitment costs to increase; furthermore, he has argued that
requiring UC claimants to register with the Employment Service
may cause some additional inefficiencies.[48] In yet another study,
Stevens concluded that the Employment Service was not influ-
ential in facilitating a return to work by UC claimants, and that
the blanket referral of virtually all UC claimants to an ES office
was "patently undesirable."[49] Support for this view has come
from a number of additional studies. In a study undertaken a
number of years ago, Reid emphasized the importance of
informal job-seeking methods and reached a qualified conclusion
that a public employment service should serve as a last resort for
those unable to obtain reemployment without such assistance.[50]
Some years later, Barron and Mellow reported that requiring UC
claimants to register with the Employment Service may tend to
decrease the use of the ES both by other unemployed workers
and by employers who have job openings.[51] Shulenburger,
Krider and Pichler also reported that the services provided by the
Employment Service had no measurable impact on the earnings
of reemployed workers,[52] although their approach has been
subjected to some methodological criticisms.[53] More recently,
Keeley and Robins concluded that UC program job search
requirements may tend to result in sub-optimal search strategies,
and are not likely to significantly reduce the duration of
unemployment spells.[54] Consequently, any assessment of the
impact of stricter worksearch requirements or enforcement procedures should be based on an evaluation of unintended and
negative side effects as well as on the positive results expected
from such policies.

USDOL has recognized that relatively little factual informa-

48. See Stevens (1977: 40, 61–62).
49. Stevens (1974: 97).
50. Reid (1972: 493–494).
51. Barron and Mellow (1982: 381, 386).
52. Shulenburger, Krider and Pichler (1979: 78).
53. See Dong et al. (1980) and Katz (1980).
54. Keeley and Robins (1985: 351–353).

tion is available on the impact of the worksearch requirement on the job search or reemployment experiences of UC claimants. A 1985 Request for Proposal distributed by USDOL noted that:

> Finally, neither the study of denial rates nor the random audit data reveal any information about the effects that variations in active search-for-work provisions have on actual claimant behavior and/or on the job finding success of claimants. Very specific and consistently enforced active search-for-work requirements may increase denial rates and may either increase or decrease payment error rates but not lead to any significant change in the rate of reemployment among claimants or even to a significant decrease in benefit payments. Claimants may simply alter their benefit duration. Even more importantly, some types of specific requirements may lead to increased job-finding while others do not.
>   . . . the research shall attempt an investigation of the relationship among the denial rate for nonseparation issues, payment error rates attributable to active search-for-work provisions of UI law, and the rate of job-finding success of the UI claimant population, abstracting from such factors as differences in claimant characteristics and local economic conditions.[55]

It is hoped that the study solicited in the above proposal request will provide insights into the impacts of worksearch requirements on the unemployment and reemployment experiences of UC claimants that will be of use in assessing whether this requirement should be eliminated or altered in particular ways.

Impact on Enforcement of Criteria. The utilization of more stringent and specific criteria could increase the extent to which state UC program personnel could effectively monitor claimant compliance with such provisions. For example, the EB program provisions that narrow the definition of ''suitable work'' and that require ''tangible evidence'' of a ''systematic and sustained'' job search could combine to facilitate a more efficient identification of those who do not actively seek work. A study of the

---

55. U.S. Department of Labor, (1985c: C-11). USDOL funded a research project on the worksearch requirement in response to this Request for Proposal. This study currently is being conducted in 10 UC jurisdictions, with results available in 1987.

administration of the nonmonetary eligibility criteria by Corson, Hershey and Kerachsky clearly suggests that: (1) the states with more comprehensive and specific policies detailing such requirements had UC staffs who better understood their laws/policies; and (2) in such states, less administrative discretion was exercised by UC personnel in considering eligibility issues, consequently increasing the consistency with which laws/policies were applied.[56] Corson, Hershey and Kerachsky also concluded that more specific program requirements and enforcement procedures need not force UC agency personnel into unreasonable enforcement activities, and that such requirements/procedures probably do provide for more equity in the treatment of claimants. They state:

> Not having clear written rules, in contrast, makes it more difficult for adjudicators to justify their decisions, and more difficult for claimants to understand the standards they must meet and to prepare arguments in their defense. Agency adjudicators then apply unwritten standards which may be quite differently understood and interpreted by different adjudicators, and leave claimants with no reasonable basis for predicting the relationship between their behavior and the adjudication outcome. In such circumstances, high standards of due process may be difficult to achieve. [57]

In addition to increasing the equity with which UC claims are processed, it also should be noted that the presence of clear, written rules would tend to reduce nondeliberate payment errors on the part of both UC claimants and state UC agency personnel. Given the complexity and the vagueness of UC eligibility criteria, especially those that must be satisfied on a weekly basis, the presence of clear, written guidelines for the administration of these requirements would be expected to reduce overpayments by reducing misinformation and uncertainty about these eligibility criteria.

Impact on Public Perceptions. The introduction of stricter worksearch and perhaps other eligibility criteria could have a

---

56. Corson, Hershey and Kerachsky (1986: 129–131).
57. Corson, Hershey and Kerachsky (1986: 130–131).

positive impact on public attitudes about the UC program and public perceptions of the needs of the clientele served by the program. The results of two different surveys discussed by Adams indicate that it is commonly believed that UC claimants could return to work more quickly if they so chose.[58] In a more recent study undertaken by Curtin and Ponza for the National Commission on Unemployment Compensation, it was reported that the majority of households surveyed supported the notion of jobsearch requirements, and that over three-fifths of those surveyed believed that UC claimants should be required to take any "fitting" job.[59] To the extent to which the imposition of more stringent worksearch requirements received widespread publicity, it could generate additional support for a program that might then be perceived by the public as serving "deserving" claimants. This conclusion also is consistent with the findings of a special study recently conducted by the Missouri UC agency and reported on at a February 1986 meeting of the Quality Unemployment Insurance Project states. The Missouri agency found very strong support for the worksearch requirement among employers, even though employers admitted that it was difficult to suggest concrete and administratively feasible procedures for actually enforcing such a requirement.[60]

Importance of Administrative Commitment. Another important issue in assessing the likely impact of stricter worksearch requirements, especially if no additional resources were made available for administering such criteria, is the extent to which substantive efforts would be made to monitor compliance with the new requirements. Effective enforcement of seemingly similar jobsearch requirements appears to vary considerably among state UC programs. Given the extent of administrative discretion that exists in enforcing such criteria, it is useful to consider whether stricter (stated) criteria actually would materially affect the manner in which UC claims would be evaluated and processed.

---

58. Adams (1971: 21,56).
59. Curtin and Ponza (1980: 770).
60. See Missouri Division of Employment Security (1986) for the views of claimants and state agency personnel as well as for employer views.

Relatively little evidence is available on the administrative commitment issue. However, some indications of at least a potential problem were evident in both the K-B and B-K-S overpayment studies. In the former study—conducted in six cities in 1979-1980—it was found that one of the state UC agencies consistently chose not to establish overpayments for violations of the availability/worksearch criteria detected after payments already had been made.[61] In the latter study—conducted in five states during 1981-1982—some administrative resistance to the more effective application of existing employment security laws and policies also surfaced.[62] In at least one B-K-S study state, providing formal warnings to claimants instead of establishing overpayments became increasingly frequent during the course of the study.[63] Inferences from these events for the present discussion may be appropriate to the extent that more complete and consistent enforcement of *existing* employment security law and policy—as implemented in the K-B and B-K-S studies—may be viewed as essentially equivalent to the establishment of stricter criteria. On the basis of this and similar evidence—much of which is indirect and somewhat speculative in nature—it does appear that a strong administrative commitment to enforce stricter eligibility requirements will be necessary if more than superficial changes are to be realized.

Stricter Requirements Summary. The above analysis indicates that the desirability of implementing stricter worksearch requirements (or more comprehensive enforcement procedures) depends on a number of considerations. Evidence suggests that the effects of stricter requirements would include the following: (1) the volumes of claims filed and benefits paid would decline, with perhaps much of the decrease coming from reduced claim filing rather than from increased disqualification of claimants for detected worksearch violations; (2) some impact on the job search and reemployment experiences of claimants might occur, but available evidence suggests that any positive effects would likely be very small and might even be accompanied by

61. Kingston and Burgess (1981b: 35).
62. Kingston, Burgess and St. Louis (1986: 326–327).
63. Kingston, Burgess and St. Louis (1986: 327).

potentially adverse side effects; (3) more precise and formal statements of worksearch requirements might result in more effective enforcement of both worksearch requirements and other eligibility criteria; (4) public support for the UC program might increase, because those served by the program might be perceived as more "deserving" claimants; and (5) the effects of introducing stricter requirements (or enforcement procedures) would largely depend on the extent to which administrative commitment to such changes tended to be substantive.

Improved Administration of Existing (or Altered) Worksearch Requirements

In addition to the elimination of worksearch requirements or the imposition of stricter worksearch requirements, states also could respond to the worksearch problem by implementing improved procedures for enforcing existing (or altered) requirements. Essentially, two relatively distinct (but not mutually exclusive) approaches have been undertaken by state UC agencies in their efforts to effectively monitor claimant compliance with the weekly eligibility criteria, given the constraints imposed by available funding levels. These approaches are (1) specific monitoring and verification of worksearch contacts reported by claimants on a weekly basis, and (2) evaluations over longer periods (e.g., 8-10 weeks) to determine if substantive and reasonable efforts are being made by claimants to find employment.[64] Either of these approaches, which are separately discussed in the next two sections, could involve the use of statistically based screening profiles to target the use of administrative resources on certain claims or claimants. Such profiles are discussed separately in the third section below. The possible role that computer-based expert systems could play in improving the administration of existing (or altered) eligibility criteria is considered in the fourth section.

Weekly Verification of Contacts. This approach to monitoring claimant compliance with worksearch requirements typically

---

64. Corson, Hershey and Kerachsky (1986: 124).

requires that a minimum number of job search contacts be made each week. As noted earlier, however, the B-K-S study findings provide strong evidence that claimant-reported job contacts are extremely difficult to verify, even with an extremely large resource commitment for such verifications. Accordingly, it appears that the weekly reporting of job search contacts would not be very effective as an operational strategy. Supporting evidence for this view was recently supplied by Corson, Hershey and Kerachsky, who concluded that:

> Without serious review of and consistent response to insufficient employer contacts, routine weekly reporting of contacts is open to serious abuse and may serve little detection purpose. In State 4, for example, employer contacts are regularly reported, but only the most apparent fabrications of employer names prompt determinations, and the frequency of determinations on availability issues is at the bottom of the state ranking.[65]

Although weekly reporting of job contacts may not be an effective monitoring strategy for most or all claimants, it still should be noted that comprehensive audits of carefully selected samples of claimants might be used to induce greater claimant compliance with UC eligibility criteria. Indeed, this approach is suggested as a viable possibility in a subsequent section of this chapter.

Evaluation of Search Strategies. An alternative approach— and one that appears to have been more commonly adopted (though with many variations)—focuses on the substance of claimant search strategies over a number of weeks. This search-strategy approach places less emphasis on a claimant's work-search activities during any specific week than on the pattern of those activities over a period of time. It emphasizes search techniques and efforts as they relate to the type of work sought. The geographic focus, occupational content, and claimant wage expectations all might be considered in evaluating overall search strategies under such an approach.

---

65. Corson, Hershey and Kerachsky (1986: 124–125).

To some extent, the search-strategy approach to administering the worksearch requirement may have grown out of the experiments designed to provide "employability services" to claimants, which were conducted in a number of state UC programs during the 1970s.[66] A basic element of the employability service approach was to allow job-ready claimants substantial freedom in determining how they would look for work during the early weeks of an unemployment spell, with increasing direction and control provided for individuals who had not returned to work after a month or two of unemployment. This orientation also is found in the very comprehensive Statewide Worksearch Activity Program recently implemented in the State of Washington; the program provides that:

So as not to lower the working standards of individuals out of work through no fault of their own, the Department will allow claimants an adequate and reasonable amount of time to find work in a comparable position to one previously held. After this period, it becomes the Department's responsibility to actively assist claimants in finding employment. The Department may require the claimant to intensify work search activity based on individual work skills, length of time unemployed, local labor market, and customary local hiring practices.

As the length of unemployment increases, work search activity will increase, and may include, but should not be limited to, an increased number of work search contacts each week; increased number of days seeking work; work search in a secondary occupation; assessment and referral for potential participation in training including OJT, and supportive service (agency and/or community based) and/or intensified worksearch planning.[67]

Other details of the program include the acquisition and use of more effective labor market information than that previously available to claimants, and the provision of different levels/types of service and monitoring for different claimant groups.

---

66. See Burgess and Kingston (1972: 1-2); Burgess and Kingston (1973); and Austermann, Crosslin and Stevens (1975).

67. Washington State Employment Security, Unemployment Insurance Division (1985: 1).

Little direct evidence is available on the extent to which the provision of job search assistance or increased monitoring of UC claimant worksearch activities affect either the unemployment or reemployment experiences of UC claimants. As previously noted, evidence from the Charleston Claimant Placement and Work Demonstration Project indicates limited success with respect to either the reemployment assistance or the eligibility review objectives of the experimental study.[68] With no increase in administrative resources to support the new program in Washington, it would seem as if the overall impact of the program would depend importantly on the extent to which available assistance/monitoring efforts could be effectively targeted on claimant groups most likely to be affected by such measures. If the Washington program attempts to provide more than a minimal level of service to most claimants—whether such services tend to emphasize reemployment assistance or eligibility verifications—available resources would probably be spread so thin that significant overall impacts would not be likely to occur. In any case, the Washington Statewide Worksearch Activity Program should be closely observed and carefully evaluated to determine the impact of such services on the labor market experiences of claimants and to assess the cost effectiveness of the program.

Beginning July 1986, Washington's new program was being tested as part of an experiment implemented in a local office in Tacoma, Washington.[69] In this experiment, with the assistance of the W.E. Upjohn Institute for Employment Research, claimants were being assigned to a control group and to various test groups that would provide for considerably different levels of pressure and assistance to claimants in terms of finding work. At one extreme, the claimant merely signs the back of the benefit payment check certifying continued eligibility for benefits. At the other extreme, claimants who don't find work after a few weeks are given substantial assistance in seeking work. This experiment, covering a one-year period, should provide useful

---

68. Corson, Long and Nicholson (1984: xvii, 107–108).

69. This description of the Washington project is based on information provided to the authors by the W.E. Upjohn Institute for Employment Research.

information on how altering existing worksearch requirements and procedures affects claimant unemployment and reemployment experiences.

Screening Profiles.[70] Another approach to dealing with the worksearch problem in the existing UC system would be to develop procedures to enforce greater compliance with existing requirements and/or to emphasize the reemployment assistance objective of such requirements. Screening profile approaches for these purposes have previously been used in both experimental and operational settings. The specialized employability services provided in the various services-to-claimants projects, for example, were available only to job-ready claimants.[71] As another example, the "model cross-match" programs developed for states to implement postaudit procedures to detect overpayments due to unreported earnings contain a number of local options that allow states to target certain types of claims or claimants.[72] Currently, the State of Utah is undertaking experimental work to assess the operational feasibility of using screening profiles to identify claimants with high overpayment probabilities.[73]

What are the prospects for using statistical profiles to target state UC agency resources on claimants who (1) have high probabilities of violating worksearch/availability requirements (the negative emphasis) and/or (2) are most in need of employability services (the positive emphasis)? In addressing this issue, Stevens contends:

> Administrative sanctions for failure to satisfy continuing eligibility requirements affect claimant decisions about whether, and how, to seek employment. Local-office involvement in claimant job search behavior serves two not necessarily complementary functions: Continuing UI benefit eligibility enforcement, and positive job search assistance. One purpose for allocating local-office staff resources to revealing claimant job search activity is to fulfill the administrative *enforcement* function. The objective of

---

70. The discussion in this section draws heavily on Kingston and Burgess (1986) and Burgess, Kingston, St. Louis and DePippo (1983).
71. Burgess and Kingston (1972: 1–2).
72. Porterfield, St. Louis, Burgess and Kingston (1980: 575–576).
73. See Utah Department of Employment Security (1986).

this enforcement activity is to assure that availability, active search, and willingness to accept available (suitable) employment conditions for continuing eligibility are satisfied. . . . This means that *attempts to accomplish both enforcement and assistance objectives with a single claimant selection procedure will create target inefficiencies in pursuing each goal.* (A target inefficiency occurs when program resources are not restricted to serving the intended target population.) Furthermore, the procedures required to elicit information appropriate to the enforcement activity may be counterproductive in determining the need for positive job search assistance.[74]

To the extent to which Stevens' assessment is correct, separate statistical profiles would be required to efficiently identify claimants for reemployment assistance v. eligibility enforcement. Given limited administrative resources, a fundamental policy issue may be whether the enforcement function is to take priority over the reemployment assistance function. Since available evidence does not provide much basis for optimism about the possibility of effectively emphasizing reemployment assistance, the remainder of this section focuses on eligibility enforcement.

The use of screening profiles to increase claimant compliance with UC eligibility criteria by increasing overpayment detection likelihoods already was discussed in chapter 6. Alternatively or in combination with that approach, such profiles also could be used to *prevent* overpayments by identifying benefit claims that should receive more intensive review prior to payment. Most claimants could be paid simply on the basis of their certification that they had met the eligibility criteria, while very detailed verifications could be conducted for claimants identified as high-risk claimants by computerized screening profiles. Obviously, the number of claimants subjected to detailed eligibility reviews would depend on the availability of administrative resources, as well as on target-efficiency insights gained during experimentation with this approach. Evidence to support the use of statistical profiles for preventing overpayments is extremely

74. Stevens (1977: 12–13).

limited. However, based on the experimental work undertaken to construct such profiles for each of the five B-K-S study states, it was found that:

The overall conclusion of the study is that much more work with the techniques explored in this report clearly appears to be justified. Although the results differ among the states, the potential of utilizing screening profiles to target administrative resources on "high-risk" claimants in order to prevent overpayments that otherwise would occur certainly is established by the findings of this study.[75]

Similarly, in a more recent analysis, Kingston and Burgess concluded that:

. . . the results discussed above, combined with the findings of St. Louis, Burgess and Kingston on reported v. actual job contacts for the five states combined, strongly suggest that worksearch/availability noncompliance is systematically related to the expected benefits and costs of noncompliance, rather than randomly distributed among the claimant population. Accordingly, it appears that statistical profiles could be used to effectively identify high-risk v. low-risk claimants for differential administrative scrutiny.[76]

As discussed in chapter 6, screening profiles have been criticized as being potentially discriminatory in nature; hence political and legal factors also will be relevant in determining whether such profiles could be used on an operational basis in the UC system.

Computer-Assisted Monitoring. Monitoring claimant compliance with worksearch requirements and other aspects of the weekly eligibility criteria using "expert (computer) systems" was discussed in chapter 3. A basic implication of that discussion was that state UC agencies could better adapt to any given level of program complexity if computerized screening could be utilized for most claims. Such procedures could provide for a

---

75. Burgess, Kingston, St. Louis and DePippo (1983: ix).
76. Kingston and Burgess (1986: 38).

less expensive and more comprehensive screening of claims and claimants than typically is possible under current procedures. This approach also would allow "human experts" in UC agencies to direct their attention to more difficult cases that could not be handled by computerized expert systems. Presumably, such an approach would make it possible for UC agencies to more effectively prevent overpayments for any given level of administrative funding and program complexity.

Although many state agencies use computerized monetary eligibility determinations, computerized monitoring of claimant compliance with weekly eligibility criteria is virtually nonexistent in the UC system.[77] Accordingly, substantial research and pilot tests would be required before the expert system approach could be operationally implemented. Since it could be inefficient to have numerous state UC agencies working simultaneously on essentially the same project, it would be useful to have several (coordinated) research and demonstration projects initiated in this area, either through federal leadership or through the cooperative efforts of state UC agencies. As noted in chapter 3, evidence to establish the feasibility of computer-assisted monitoring is quite limited, but the potential benefits are so great that it is an approach that merits serious consideration.

Direct Reemployment Incentives

Consistent with the focus of this study on affecting claimant behavior through economic incentives, another approach that could be taken to encourage availability for work or active job search by UC claimants would involve increasing the financial returns to such activities. Such an approach contrasts with the emphasis of other approaches on obtaining increased claimant self-compliance by increasing the costs of noncompliance. Particularly interesting in terms of inducing faster reemployment by claimants are some experimental studies that have been initiated

---

77. Some experimental work has been conducted in this area. We are aware of no state that has actually adopted this approach on an operational basis, although some states do utilize computer-generated eligibility determinations (once agency personnel have gathered the necessary facts and made a decision).

during the past three years to determine the impact of various incentive schemes on the job search and reemployment experiences of UC claimants. These experiments, conducted in Illinois and New Jersey, are briefly described below.

Illinois Project.[78] During 1984, the Illinois Department of Employment Security, with the assistance of the W.E. Upjohn Institute for Employment Research, conducted two experiments that involved the use of reemployment vouchers to encourage job search and reduce the duration of compensated unemployment. The first experiment provided for the payment of a cash bonus of $500 to any member of a randomly selected group of UC claimants who had obtained employment of 30 hours per week or more before the end of the eleventh week of unemployment following an initial claim for UC benefits; in order to qualify for the cash bonus, the claimant had to hold the new job for a minimum of four months. An analysis of this experiment by Spiegelman and Woodbury has indicated that the duration of insured unemployment for the test group that was eligible for the reemployment cash bonuses was significantly less than that recorded for an otherwise similar control group not eligible for such bonuses. The amount of benefits paid to test group members over their entire benefit years was about $200 per claimant less than the amount paid to otherwise similar control group members. Since only part of the test group received bonus payments, the bonus cost per test claimant was less than $100. No information is yet available, however, on the quality of the reemployment jobs obtained by test v. control group members, but such an analysis will be possible with the information being collected from the Illinois study.

The second experiment conducted in Illinois provided for the payment of a reemployment bonus to the UC claimant's new employer, rather than to the claimant. In this case as well, reemployment must have occurred by the end of the eleventh week following the filing of the initial claim, and it was necessary that the claimant hold the new job for at least four

---

78. See Spiegelman and Woodbury (1986) for details of the Illinois Unemployment Insurance Experiments.

months in order for the employer to be eligible for the cash bonus. A preliminary assessment by Spiegelman and Woodbury has indicated that there may have been some initial reduction in regular state UC benefits received by the group whose new employers were eligible for the cash bonus, compared with an otherwise similar control group of UC claimants whose new employers were not eligible for such a bonus. This reduction in state UC benefit payments, however, did not persist throughout the benefit year for the entire test group involved in the study, although the effect did persist for white, female claimants. Based on the information now available, it appears that, overall, the payment of $500 cash bonuses to UC claimants had a larger impact in reducing the duration of their compensated unemployment spells than did the payment of $500 bonuses to the new employers of claimants.

The New Jersey Project.[79] The New Jersey Department of Labor and the U.S. Department of Labor recently approved the final design of an experiment that provides for, among other services and assistance, the payment of cash reemployment bonuses to those likely to exhaust their UC benefits and to have difficulties returning to jobs that are similar to their previous ones. This group includes those who are laid off, not subject to recall, and who are predicted, on the basis of additional demographic and labor force data, to experience reemployment problems.

The demonstration project is being conducted in 10 UC local offices in New Jersey, with approximately 9,000 claimants to be randomly selected for the experiment; this number is expected to produce the approximately 3,000 individuals who will receive the full range of services (including eligibility for the reemployment cash bonus) provided by the special study. Those who reach the fifth week of UC-compensated unemployment will be screened to identify those predicted to experience reemployment problems, and this group then will be randomly divided into a test and control group. Specialized assistance, including eligi-

---

79. See U.S. Department of Labor (1986a) for details of the New Jersey Unemployment Demonstration Project.

bility for the reemployment cash bonus, then will be provided to the test group, and the impact of the specialized assistance provided will be assessed by comparing the experiences of test v. control group members.

The following factors were considered in developing the design for the reemployment bonus payments: (1) the payment should encourage claimants to return to work quickly (i.e., it should reduce the reemployment wage rate they are willing to accept); (2) the bonus should be structured so that it provides claimants with clear incentives for reemployment that they can fully comprehend; (3) the bonus should be structured so as to discourage reemployment in minimum wage jobs, jobs far below the earnings potential of claimants, or very short-term jobs; (4) the bonus should resemble a UC "cash-out program" in which claimants receive a part of their remaining entitlement in exchange for not exhausting all of it; and (5) the bonus should have the potential of saving the UC program money if implemented on a statewide basis.[80]

Consistent with these criteria, the reemployment bonus was structured so that it would provide claimants with offers of one-half of their remaining UC benefit entitlements in exchange for becoming reemployed (it is estimated that this amount will equal about $1,500 for the average participant). Of interest as well is the fact that the amount of the bonus will decline at a steady rate of 10 percent per week after the fifth week until it reaches zero, again providing a strong financial incentive for rapid reemployment. Claimants become eligible for the bonus after five to seven weeks of their current claims filing period. Job tenure requirements also were established for the bonus payments; the individual must be employed four weeks to qualify for 60 percent of the bonus, and an additional eight weeks to qualify for the remaining 40 percent. Participation in the bonus program, however, does not necessarily exhaust the claimant's entitlement to benefits for the entire benefit year. If, for example, the individual becomes unemployed through no fault of his or her

---

80. U.S. Department of Labor (1986a: 15).

own, the claimant once again becomes eligible for any remaining weekly benefits.

An interim report on the New Jersey experiment is planned for the summer of 1987. The final report on this New Jersey project is anticipated in September 1988.

Conclusions on Reemployment Incentives. Evidence on the impact of reemployment bonus or subsidy schemes is only now becoming available and will continue to accumulate over the next several years. Current findings indicate that claimants do respond to the availability of reemployment bonuses by returning to work more quickly than in the absence of such bonuses. We believe that these limited findings provide additional evidence that UC claimants do respond to variations in the benefits and costs associated with job search activities. In light of the difficulties involved in enforcing either current or perhaps even revised availability for work and active job search eligibility criteria, we believe that additional experimentation with the payment of reemployment bonuses or similar incentive-altering schemes is warranted and should be encouraged. Needless to say, further work on appropriately increasing the costs of claimant noncompliance provides a complementary approach to such reemployment incentive schemes.

Conclusions

There can be no doubt that state agency personnel confront substantial difficulties in attempting to monitor claimant compliance with weekly UC eligibility criteria. Although the specific difficulties of attempting to enforce active worksearch requirements are discussed in this chapter, similar but even more serious problems probably are involved in attempting to monitor claimant compliance with the broader availability requirements included in all state laws. In any case, available evidence certainly indicates that noncompliance with existing worksearch/availability requirements may be quite substantial. Accordingly, policymakers and UC program administrators should consider the possibility of adopting new policies for dealing with such noncompliance.

A number of different responses to relatively high levels of noncompliance with stated worksearch/availability requirements might be considered, including: (1) elimination of the worksearch requirement; (2) replacement of the worksearch requirement with criteria that can be more objectively defined and enforced; (3) imposition of stricter worksearch requirements; (4) improved administration of existing (or altered) worksearch requirements; and (5) use of direct and positive reemployment incentives. The desirability of any of these approaches or others that might be considered obviously will depend on subjective evaluations that will vary among the states. However, as indicated by the analysis in this chapter, certain impacts of each approach can be clearly identified.

In our view, the analysis in this chapter suggests that some combination of the following approaches could make a substantial contribution to improving both agency monitoring efforts and claimant self-compliance with stated eligibility criteria: (1) research and demonstration projects to determine the impacts on the unemployment and reemployment experiences of insured workers of existing or altered worksearch requirements (including the elimination of such requirements); (2) research and demonstration projects to determine the impact of imposing stricter monetary eligibility criteria that include weeks-of-work requirements as either replacements for or as supplements to existing worksearch requirements; (3) adopting more specific and objectively identifiable measures for determining compliance with availability for work and active search provisions; (4) improving the administration of existing or altered worksearch requirements through the use of computerized screening profiles to target administrative resources on high-risk claimants; (5) the use of computerized expert systems to further screen claimants for compliance with the weekly eligibility criteria prior to the payment of benefits; and (6) further experimentation with direct and positive reemployment incentive schemes. Given the difficulty of effectively administering the weekly eligibility criteria, it is probable that the most effective solution will involve some combination of these approaches.

8
Summary and Conclusions

The principal findings and recommendations of this study are summarized in this chapter. Brief summaries are included for the analyses of: payment errors (chapter 2); adverse effects of program complexity (chapter 3); adverse federal impacts of administrative funding procedures (chapter 4) and performance criteria (chapter 5); adverse incentives within state systems that affect claimants, employers and state agency personnel (chapter 6); and the difficulties involved in attempting to monitor claimant compliance with weekly UC eligibility criteria (chapter 7). Some overall study conclusions complete the chapter.

Principal Findings

1. The high overpayment rates documented for some states, combined with the analysis in this study, indicate that overpayments constitute a major problem for the UC system as a whole. Moreover, many actual overpayments are not detected by routine operational procedures.

2. High overpayment rates are symptomatic of more fundamental problems that appear to be relevant for all states. These problems include: (a) difficulties posed by system complexity; (b) adverse incentives for system participants; and (c) the extreme difficulties state agencies have in attempting to effectively monitor claimant compliance with weekly eligibility criteria.

3. Although all social payment systems must have some criteria to distinguish eligible from ineligible participants, costs and benefits determine the optimum detail of such criteria. By

235

this measure, the UC system appears to be excessively complex, particularly since existing complexity levels likely result in a large number of adverse impacts.

4. The federal administrative funding procedures utilized from the mid-1970s through at least FY 1987 contained numerous incentives that very likely have adversely affected state UC systems.

5. Federal performance criteria neglect many important aspects of state UC program quality and tend to create adverse incentives by overemphasizing the speed v. the quality of claim processing and payments.

6. Adverse incentives within state UC systems typically do not discourage and may even encourage ineligible claimants to file for benefits.

7. With limited exceptions, employer participation in the UC system is likely to focus primarily on macro efforts by groups of employers to constrain overall program costs, since the tax incentives for individual employers to engage in micro monitoring of individual claimant compliance with eligibility criteria are quite weak.

8. State agency personnel typically have very limited incentives to prevent either underpayments or overpayments, to detect or recover overpayments or to emphasize certain other aspects of overall UC program quality.

9. The interaction of excessive program complexity, limited administrative funding and adverse incentives makes it extremely difficult for state agencies to effectively monitor claimant compliance with many UC program requirements, especially those that must be met on a weekly basis.

Recommendations

The appropriate responses to the problems analyzed in this study obviously depend on value judgments that federal/state policymakers and UC program administrators ultimately must make. Also, the specific applicability of particular responses to individual states obviously varies with state-specific circumstances. Nonetheless, the analysis strongly suggests that certain policy responses generally should be given serious consideration for the UC system as a whole. In our opinion, the most important of these generally applicable responses—for which details were provided in the pertinent chapters of this study—include the following:

1. Comprehensive analyses of the data bases available from both the Random Audit program in 46 states and from the Quality Control program in all states should prove useful in developing appropriate corrective plans in particular states.

2. Federal and state efforts should be undertaken to reduce the complexity of UC eligibility criteria and the forms, procedures and policies utilized to administer such criteria. Legislative contributions could include a greater awareness of the feasibility of effectively administering current or proposed UC program provisions, especially given limited administrative funding allocations. Legislators also could eliminate, revise or replace UC provisions that are inconsistent or particularly difficult to administer. Administrative contributions could include the development of less complex forms and procedures for implementing federal and state laws.

3. Because political realities undoubtedly will significantly constrain attempts to reduce complexity, another major contribution to an improved UC system would be to develop better policies and procedures for administering existing (or reduced) levels of program complexity. Detailed, written guidelines for administering law/policy would represent such an improvement in states that do not have such guidelines. Computerized expert systems appear to have the potential for cost effectively improving the consistency with which UC eligibility criteria are applied. Similarly, computerized screening profiles may represent a cost-effective technique for better utilizing existing administrative resources by identifying high-risk claimants for special scrutiny. Further experimentation and operational pilot tests should be conducted in order to better assess the feasibility of implementing both expert systems and computerized screening profiles as operational techniques.

4. The U.S. Department of Labor (USDOL) should reduce the complexity of both its administrative funding and performance

evaluations required in carrying out its responsibilities under federal law.

5. Major changes should be made to correct the numerous adverse incentives/impacts of USDOL's administrative funding process, or an alternative funding system should be developed. The changes implemented by USDOL in making FY 1987 funding allocations represent an important step in reducing the complexity of its past funding process and in giving the states a needed increase in spending flexibility. Alternative funding systems could include a system of federal block grants to states or "devolution" of administrative funding responsibility from the federal government to the states. However, adoption of either alternative alone would not eliminate all of the current problems associated with the allocation of administrative funds.

6. Existing USDOL performance criteria should be improved by introducing an effective emphasis on payment accuracy to balance the existing emphasis on processing and payment promptness. Such a balanced emphasis now would be possible, given the Quality Control program for detecting payment errors in state programs. In addition, substantial revisions should be made in USDOL's Quality Appraisal system, including a revised system for measuring overall program quality.

7. Steps should be taken to greatly increase the incentives of state agency personnel to prevent both underpayments and overpayments, to detect and recover overpayments that occur and to emphasize other aspects of overall UC program quality.

8. Existing claimant incentives for deliberate noncompliance with stated UC eligibility criteria should be altered substantially to encourage self-compliance by increasing the claimant's currently very low costs of noncompliance. A potentially effective technique for raising claimant noncompliance costs may be the application of computerized screening profiles to target administrative resources on high-risk claimants who belong to groups with above average likelihoods of violating availability/work-search criteria; such profiles should be developed and tested.

9. Claimant self-compliance with UC eligibility criteria also could be increased by: (a) increasing the nominal penalties for detected instances of noncompliance; (b) applying any nominal

penalties assessed for detected overpayments much more effectively; and (c) shifting more of the burden of proof for establishing eligibility for benefits from state agencies to claimants. Another possibility for increasing claimant compliance incentives and possibly speeding claimant reemployment may be to offer reemployment bonuses, such as those included in some recent experimental studies; these studies should be carefully evaluated to determine the benefits and costs of such bonuses.

10. States should adopt more specific and more clearly understood weekly eligibility criteria; they should develop more objective ways to assess claimant compliance with these criteria.

11. Research and demonstration projects should be undertaken to determine the impacts on the unemployment and reemployment experiences of insured workers of existing or altered worksearch requirements, the elimination of such requirements, and the use of direct reemployment incentives.

12. Research and demonstration projects should be undertaken to determine the impact of imposing stricter monetary eligibility criteria that include weeks-of-work requirements as either replacements for or as supplements to existing worksearch requirements.

13. Interstate cooperation in the research, policy formulation and evaluation stages of developing reform proposals should be strongly encouraged because of the substantial benefits many state programs can derive from the testing and evaluation of particular changes in a small number of states. In this regard, the efforts of the states involved in the Quality Unemployment Insurance Project from August 1985 to the present are particularly encouraging.

14. USDOL should provide substantial funding for the research, demonstration projects and technical assistance required to evaluate alternative proposals for improving the existing UC system.

UC System Payment Errors

Prior to 1980, accurate and substantive evidence on the extent of overpayments in the UC system was not available. Although concerns about fraud and abuse often surfaced during the first 45 years of the program, the first valid estimates of UC system overpayments were produced by the Kingston-Burgess study conducted for the National Commission on Unemployment Compensation during 1979-80. Some principal findings of the study—conducted in six major metropolitan areas over a six-month interval—were that: (1) the average overpayment rate for dollars of benefits paid for the six cities was nearly 14 percent; and (2) the resource-intensive methods used to verify claimant eligibility for benefits in the special study produced estimated overpayment rates at least four times (and in one city 42 times) the comparable rates detected by the regular operational procedures in five of those six cities. Subsequently, the Burgess-Kingston-St. Louis analysis of the U.S. Department of Labor's Random Audit program pilot tests, which were conducted in five statewide UC programs during 1981-1982, disclosed similar findings: (1) the average overpayment rate for dollars of benefits paid in the five states was just over 13 percent (and the percentage of weeks overpaid was even higher); (2) the total dollar amount of overpayments estimated for these five states for a one-year period ($392 million) exceeded by 60 percent the total dollar amount of overpayments detected/ reported through regular operational procedures by all 53 UC jurisdictions combined for a comparable one-year period; and (3) violations of the worksearch requirement accounted for a substantial proportion of all UC dollars overpaid in these five states.

More recent evidence for the 46 states that participated in the Random Audit program during FY 1985 was released by USDOL in May 1987. The simple average overpayment rate for these states during FY 1985 was 15.6 percent. Given that approximately $14.3 billion in UC benefits were paid during FY 1985, USDOL estimated that overpayments could have amounted to as much as $2.2 billion during that one-year period. Furthermore, if UC program outlays average $16 billion per year over the next four years, as USDOL recently projected, a 15 percent overpayment rate would result in overpayments during this interval of about $9.6 billion.

Payment Error Conclusions

The evidence on UC payment errors presented in this study and summarized above strongly suggests the existence of a significant overpayment problem that is much more serious than indicated by the overpayments routinely detected and reported by state agencies to USDOL. However, a major theme of this study is that high overpayment rates per se are not necessarily the fundamental issue to be addressed by policymakers and UC program administrators. Overall UC program "quality" in a state clearly cannot be judged solely on the basis of that state's overpayment rate. It is hoped that policymakers and UC program administrators will recognize that high overpayment rates are symptomatic of more fundamental problems which very likely represent important issues for all states, whether their detected rates of overpayments are low or high. These more fundamental problems are: (1) UC system complexity; (2) adverse incentives in federal-state relationships; (3) adverse incentives within state UC systems; and (4) largely because of the first three problems, extreme difficulties in attempting to monitor claimant compliance with UC eligibility criteria.

Payment Error Responses

Because payment error problems are not basically distinct from the fundamental problems just noted, responses to high payment error rates should focus primarily on these underlying causal factors. Some useful information about both high overpayment rates and the more fundamental problems could be obtained through comprehensive analyses of the Random Audit program data bases that exist in 46 states and the Quality Control program data bases that now are available in all states. Such analyses could provide insight into issues such as: (1) What are the main operational sources or causes of payment errors? (2) How are quarterly changes in error rates to be interpreted? (3) Do error concentrations suggest certain types of corrective actions? and (4) Are payment errors more likely to occur among certain types of claims or claimants? Certainly, information related to these questions would be useful in formulating specific corrective action plans in particular states. Interstate cooperation in the research, policy formulation and evaluation stages also would be desirable because of the similarities among state programs. Although the above analyses would yield some useful insights, responses to the fundamental problems noted would be central to any major effort to substantially improve the existing UC system. Consequently, those fundamental issues are stressed in the remainder of this chapter.

Adverse Effects of UC Program Complexity

The complexity of the UC program, particularly in regard to eligibility rules, is described in some detail in chapter 3. Although a number of different examples of such complexity are presented, the most compelling evidence is provided by the time required to fully verify claimant eligibility for benefits, given the specified rules. It was found in both the Kingston-Burgess and Burgess-Kingston-St. Louis studies, for example, that an average of between 8 and 13 hours of direct case time was required to determine if an *individual* claimant was actually eligible for a *single* week of compensated unemployment that already had been paid! Furthermore, as noted in chapter 7, even these comprehensive investigations often were not sufficient to determine if claimants actually had made the job search contacts they reported to meet eligibility requirements.

Conclusions on Adverse Effects of Complexity

Although the issue of whether existing eligibility rules are too complex is a matter about which reasonable individuals may disagree, this study strongly suggests that the existing UC system is excessively complex in terms of the costs, relative to the benefits, of such complexity. If existing levels of complexity remain unchanged, the costs (relative to a less complex system) almost certainly would include some or all of the following: (1) considerable uncertainty by both claimants and state agency personnel as to whether particular circumstances make a claimant eligible or ineligible for support; (2) perceptions by many claimants that substantive eligibility verifications could not be routinely conducted, and reduced incentives for claimants to engage in self-compliance because of the costs of doing so in a complex system; (3) reduced incentives for employers to assist state UC agency personnel in monitoring claimant compliance with weekly eligibility criteria because UC system complexity greatly reduces the net monetary returns of monitoring activities by employers; (4) reduced incentives for state agency personnel to prevent or detect payment errors because UC eligibility criteria may be perceived as too complex for effective or equitable enforcement in any case; (5) substantial discretionary authority for individual claim processors to selectively enforce eligibility criteria; (6) frequent violations of horizontal equity for claimants and employers who interact with the UC system under similar circumstances; (7) frequent payment errors (whether routinely detected or not); (8) very high administrative costs from attempting to fully administer complex provisions; and (9) possibly some effects on the volume of claims filed, either because potentially eligible claimants are discouraged from filing by complexity or because ineligible claimants are encouraged to file because of confusion or the relatively limited ability of agency personnel to identify some types of ineligible claims.

Responses to Adverse Effects of Complexity

Responses to the effects of program complexity could include a substantial increase in administrative funding, a reduction in program complexity or improved methods of administering any given level of program complexity. Because a substantial increase in administrative funding seems neither likely nor even desirable, particularly in the absence of other changes discussed in this study, chapter 3 focuses on either reducing program complexity or improving law/policy/administrative procedures. Given the variety of viable responses that might be considered and the strong likelihood that many of them undoubtedly would result in unintended side effects, however, it is difficult to overemphasize the importance of pilot studies in correctly assessing possible approaches for program improvements.

Reducing complexity in eligibility requirements would require policymakers and UC program administrators to confront the controversial issue of which subtle distinctions they are willing to forego. This issue also should be evaluated in light of the costs and difficulties involved in attempting to administer relatively complex eligibility distinctions. A policy dilemma in this process is that simplifying complex rules would almost inevitably alter the mix of claimants somewhat, perhaps allowing some "undeserving" claimants to receive benefits or precluding some "deserving" claimants from the receipt of benefits. Regardless of one's views on the desirability of distinguishing among various eligibility circumstances, it must be recognized that administrative resources represent a major constraint in terms of how much complexity can be effectively and equitably administered.

Even if the benefits of less complex rules and procedures might be substantial, there can be little doubt that political realities are likely to substantially constrain overall system simplification. Accordingly, implementing better policies and procedures for administering any given level of program complexity could represent an important contribution to an improved UC system. It appears that, at least in some states, more clearly specifying legislative intent could represent an improvement in this context. Other changes emphasized in chapter 3 include the following: (1) the development of detailed, written guidelines for administering state law/policy (in states that do not currently have such guidelines); (2) the development of computerized expert systems to improve the administration of UC eligibility criteria (particularly because of the increased consistency and presumably reduced costs that would result from this approach); and (3) the development of computerized screening profiles to identify high-risk v. low-risk claimants, so that claimant compliance can be increased by targeting administrative resources more heavily on the former group.

Adverse Incentives in Federal-State Relationships

The two dimensions of federal-state UC program relationships emphasized in this study relate to USDOL's administrative funding procedures for state programs and the performance criteria by which USDOL evaluates state programs. The incentives confronted by state UC agencies in these areas exert a strong influence on the quality of state UC programs.

Administrative Funding

USDOL's administrative funding system, as explained in chapter 4, has adversely impacted on payment accuracy and overall UC program quality in a number of ways. Consensus or near-consensus views on such impacts, at least by informed observers outside of USDOL, include the following: (1) the administrative funding system has been excessively complex; (2) funding complexity has discouraged long-range planning and made it extremely difficult for state administrators to accurately estimate the funding impact of implementing innovative programs or procedures; (3) underestimation of national workloads, combined with a conscious policy of underfunding the unit time factors implied by those workloads, has adversely affected state programs because of the base-contingency funding procedures utilized to allocate funds to the states; (4) administrative funding procedures often have forced states to rely heavily on part-time and seasonal employees, and this reliance may have increased the frequency of payment errors and otherwise may have reduced program quality; (5) administrative funding shortages have been particularly acute for nonpersonal services, which include computer costs; (6) administrative funding procedures have contained strong disincentives for states to automate their claim processing and payment systems; (7) funding procedures have failed to reward cost efficiencies in state programs and even may have encouraged states to increase the complexity of their programs; (8) funding procedures have failed to provide direct incentives for states to emphasize payment accuracy, overpayment prevention or overpayment detection and recovery efforts; and (9) largely as a reflection of the above factors, the funding process has contained strong disincentives for emphasizing overall UC program quality. It should be noted that USDOL does *not* accept each of the above statements as valid characterizations of the administrative funding process. Details of the positions taken by various parties on these issues are discussed in chapter 4. Some potentially important changes in the administrative funding process were implemented by USDOL for FY 1987 state allocations.

Administrative Funding Conclusions. Most states contend they are seriously underfunded. The analysis in this study indicates that they actually are much more underfunded than even they contend, relative to the funding that would be required to attempt to fully verify claimant compliance with existing law/policy. In fact, the evidence from the Kingston-Burgess and Burgess-Kingston-St. Louis studies cited earlier strongly suggests that, in the absence of other changes, it would take perhaps 30-50 times existing funding levels for state agencies to attempt to *fully verify* the weekly benefit eligibility of each claimant paid. Such a large increase in administrative funding obviously is neither feasible nor desirable. Although specific underfunding of automation costs appears to be especially acute in the existing system, an increase in *overall* funding levels certainly does not appear to be the appropriate solution for the administrative funding problems analyzed in this study. Rather, the focus should be on either eliminating the adverse incentives/impacts of USDOL's past funding procedures or on replacing that funding process with an altogether different one. Also, it appears that states should be encouraged to consider program simplification and administrative improvements as more effective responses to perceived underfunding of state operations than substantially increased administrative funding levels.

Administrative Funding Responses. The following four approaches to revising the existing administrative funding process are considered in chapter 4: (1) maintaining but greatly improving USDOL's funding system; (2) federal funding for "model" state UC systems; (3) a system of federal block grants to the states; and (4) devolution of administrative funding from the federal government to the states.

The main features of maintaining but improving USDOL's past funding system would include: (1) a much less complex system that would allow states to determine how funding allocations would be affected by organizational/operational changes; (2) incentives for states to adopt less complex eligibility criteria, other things equal; (3) incentives for states to minimize administrative costs for any given set of eligibility criteria and any given level of overall program quality; (4) incentives to encourage all state UC system participants (claimants, covered employers and UC agency personnel) to emphasize compliance with state law/policy, including incentives for payment accuracy and the prevention of payment errors; (5) incentives for state agencies to detect/recover benefit overpayments; (6) incentives to encourage appropriate administrative innovations, particularly appropriate automation of state operations; (7) considerable flexibility in allowing states to determine how to most efficiently allocate any given total administrative funding level among various expenditure categories; (8) incentives for states to emphasize overall UC program quality; and (9) incentives for states to conduct the research/pilot tests necessary to evaluate various proposals for improving the existing UC system. Many of the above issues and incentives also would be directly relevant for the other three approaches to revising USDOL's funding process. Significantly, it appears that USDOL's changes in its administrative funding process for FY 1987 include some of the above changes, especially greater spending flexibility (item 7 above) and apparently a less complex funding system that may help states determine how possible changes could affect their funding levels (item 1 above). Thus, it appears that USDOL already has taken some steps that could contribute to a greatly improved administrative funding system.

The second and third approaches to revising the administrative funding process also would leave control over the allocation of administrative funding among the states with USDOL, as would be the case with the first approach discussed above. Under the second approach, USDOL would fund each state only for performing the tasks contained in a model UC system that included cost standards to reflect efficient administrative operations; under this approach, a consensus view of an ideal or acceptable UC system would have to be developed, with federal funding provided to (efficiently) administer just the provisions of such a model system in each state. Funding for the administration of additional program provisions beyond those included in the model system would not be provided by USDOL, but rather would have to be provided by individual states. However, obtaining a consensus among the parties involved as to the components of such a model system obviously would be very difficult.

Under the third approach to improving the administrative funding process, USDOL would provide block grants to the states for administering their UC systems. This approach would allow each state to determine how best to allocate its grant among various administrative expenditure categories. USDOL's FY 1987 changes, and particularly the emphasis on increasing state spending flexibility, may be a step towards a funding system that more nearly approaches such a block grant concept. If this proposed approach were combined with the other improvements in USDOL's past funding system suggested above, it could represent a very substantial improvement over that past funding system.

The fourth approach to revising the administrative funding process would completely alter the existing responsibility and authority for determining administrative funding levels for state programs by shifting it from USDOL to the states themselves. One rationale for the devolution of administrative funding authority and responsibility to the states would be to correct several of the adverse incentives in USDOL's funding process noted above. In particular, making each state responsible for its own administrative funding might result in less complex state programs and greater incentives for administrative efficiency, automation and innovations than have existed in the past. In addition, such a change would effectively eliminate the inflexibility of USDOL in recognizing state diversity which has been a common complaint among the states. Another rationale for devolvement proposals is simply to make administrative funding (the smaller part of total UC program costs) comparable to benefit payment funding (the larger part of total UC program costs). Under devolution, the dollars spent for all UC program costs within a state—whether for benefit payments or for program administration—would be funded by employment security taxes collected from the covered employers of that state (and, in a few states, also from covered employees). Decisions about the most appropriate responses to the funding problems confronted by the UC system obviously depend on value judgments which policymakers will have to make. Despite the difficulty of dealing with the issues raised, it probably is the case that fundamental improvements in the existing UC system would, at the very least, be quite difficult to achieve without either substantial revisions in or replacement of USDOL's past administrative funding process. USDOL's FY 1987 changes in its funding process appear to be an important start toward potentially significant improvements.

Performance Criteria

The analysis in chapter 5 indicates that federal performance criteria also impact significantly on the operation of state UC systems. For nearly a decade, USDOL has utilized the Quality Appraisal system (or its predecessor) as a major source of information about the overall quality of state UC program operations. Fundamental to the portion of this system that deals with benefit and claim operations is the measurement of state compliance with a number of Desired Levels of Achievement (DLAs) related to both the quality and speed of claim processing and benefit payments. It is quite clear that these DLAs created adverse incentives for payment accuracy, the control of overpayments and overall program quality. In previous years, these performance criteria have reflected an overemphasis on the promptness with which claims were processed and paid, quite possibly at the expense of a reduced emphasis on payment accuracy. It should be noted, however, that a number of USDOL performance criteria—including those for prompt payments—have been introduced as a result of judicial decisions outside of USDOL control. Despite some encouraging steps to begin correcting this imbalance in very recent years, an *effective* emphasis on payment accuracy still appears to be lacking.

Performance Criteria Conclusions. The benefit and claim portion of the UI Quality Appraisal program contains a number of characteristics that limit its usefulness for evaluating the overall quality of state UC programs. These features include, but are not limited to, the following: (1) no DLA for payment accuracy, and no statistically valid quality measurement system for statewide UC programs; (2) an overemphasis on the speed v. the quality of claim processing and benefit payments; (3) inappropriate statistical design and sampling procedures to obtain valid, statewide estimates for the quality (but not for the promptness) measures included in the system; and (4) a relatively limited set of criteria for evaluating overall program quality. Other limitations are discussed in chapter 5.

Performance Criteria Responses. A major improvement in existing USDOL performance criteria would be to introduce an effective emphasis on payment accuracy to offset the existing emphasis on processing and payment promptness. The Quality Control program provides a statistically valid basis for estimating statewide *payment* errors for both overpayments and underpayments, though not erroneous denials of benefits. Thus, measures of payment accuracy could be added to existing performance criteria by utilizing results from this recently implemented program. In addition to payment accuracy criteria, it also would be important to recognize other dimensions of program quality, and to develop reasonable measures of those dimensions as part of an overall system for measuring state performance. Formulation of these additional criteria would be an extremely difficult task which would require both the expertise of federal/ state UC program personnel and technical research assistance. However, assuming USDOL continues to have a major role in state UC programs, the development of a better system for measuring program quality is important. Clearly, the costs as well as the benefits of developing/implementing additional criteria must be carefully identified and evaluated to determine appropriate responses. In many cases, this would require extensive research and pilot tests to evaluate the intended, as well as any unintended, effects of proposed performance criteria. Furthermore, the diversity of state UC systems should be recognized in the above process, but such diversity does not appear to justify arguments against implementing additional measures of program quality (including payment accuracy criteria).

Adverse Incentives Within State UC Systems

The incentives confronted by covered employers, state UC agency personnel and claimants also contribute to payment errors and other program quality problems. These issues are analyzed in chapter 6. Incentives for each of these UC system participants are briefly summarized below.

In considering employer incentives, it is useful to distinguish between macro and micro employer interests in the UC system. From a macro viewpoint, employers as a group have strong incentives to seek relatively strict benefit eligibility criteria for all claimants and to encourage effective administrative operations and strict eligibility interpretations by UC agency personnel. These macro interests are motivated by employer incentives to constrain UC program costs and therefore employer tax costs. In contrast, the incentives of individual employers to engage in micro monitoring to control charges to their own individual reserve accounts are quite different. In particular, holding aside job separation issues and the monetary eligibility of former employees who apply for benefits, the micro incentives for typical employers to attempt to monitor the compliance of their former employees with the weekly eligibility criteria (e.g., active job search) are quite low. The associated monitoring costs would be very high in most cases. Moreover, relatively weak experience rating of UC program costs further erodes the micro incentives of individual employers for such monitoring.

The incentives of state UC agency personnel to prevent underpayments or overpayments, to detect overpayments or to recover overpayments also are quite limited. Excessive program complexity, limited funds for administering UC eligibility criteria, performance criteria that place relatively greater emphasis on speed v. quality and typical state pay/promotion systems contribute to an environment in which the prevention, detection and recovery of payment errors typically have not been emphasized.

UC claimants also are confronted with a set of incentives that fail to discourage, and actually may encourage, payment errors and low levels of self-compliance. Payment errors may occur accidentally (particularly given UC program complexity), but

UC claimants also may knowingly accept UC benefits to which they are not entitled if the expected benefits of such actions exceed the expected costs. The costs of receiving UC benefits as an ineligible claimant are dependent on claimant estimates of: (1) the likelihood that noncompliance with UC eligibility criteria will be detected; (2) the likelihood that an overpayment will be established in instances of detected noncompliance; (3) the nominal penalties associated with established overpayments; and (4) the extent to which nominal penalties will be effectively enforced. It appears that the costs of noncompliance typically are quite low in the UC system, so that substantial (and deliberate) noncompliance with eligibility criteria would be expected.

Conclusions on Incentives Within State UC Systems

Employer participation in the UC system is likely to focus primarily on group efforts to constrain UC program costs. With the exception of monitoring separation issues and the monetary eligibility of former employees, employer incentives for attempting to independently monitor claimant compliance are likely to remain fairly weak.

It also appears that the incentives for state agency personnel to emphasize payment accuracy (and overpayment detection/ recovery efforts) and to consistently apply employment security law/policy are very limited. These limited incentives for state employees appear to be closely related to the adverse USDOL funding procedures and performance criteria that state systems as a whole confront. Nonetheless, careful reviews of the training, evaluation, pay and promotion systems in individual states undoubtedly would suggest many specific improvements, even in the absence of changes by USDOL.

The most effective approaches to reducing payment errors and increasing other dimensions of program quality—for any given degree of program complexity, administrative funding levels and performance criteria—are likely to be those designed to increase claimant self-compliance with UC eligibility criteria. These responses are discussed below.

Responses to Increase Claimant Self-Compliance

A number of measures could be introduced to increase claimant self-compliance with UC eligibility criteria. The use of computerized screening profiles to target administrative resources on high-risk claimants may be an especially effective response. The advantages of using such techniques, however, have not yet been demonstrated because experimentation with this approach has only recently begun. Even though the limited available evidence suggests that the construction of screening profiles is technically feasible, some state agencies have expressed reservations about the development of such techniques because of legal or political concerns. These concerns obviously would have to be resolved before screening profiles could be utilized on an operational basis. Use of screening profiles, however, would induce claimants to increase self-compliance with UC eligibility criteria. Altering "burden of proof" requirements so that claimants had additional responsibilities to demonstrate their eligibility for benefits also might increase both claimant incentives for self-compliance and the effectiveness of state agencies in monitoring claimant compliance with UC eligibility criteria. Other measures that would increase claimant self-compliance include: (1) increasing the rate at which overpayments actually are established for detected instances of noncompliance; (2) increasing the nominal penalties for established overpayments; (3) more effectively applying any nominal penalties assessed for established overpayments; and (4) increasing the financial benefits associated with successful job search, including direct reemployment incentive schemes.

Administering the Weekly Eligibility Criteria

The difficulties confronted by state agency personnel in monitoring claimant compliance with weekly UC eligibility criteria—especially worksearch and availability-for-work requirements—are analyzed in chapter 7. Evidence of the difficulties involved is quite compelling. The most frequent cause of the overpayments detected in both the Kingston-Burgess and Burgess-Kingston-St. Louis studies was noncompliance with worksearch/availability requirements. In three of the five Burgess-Kingston-St. Louis study states, nearly half or more of all worksearch contacts listed by claimants could not be verified as either acceptable or unacceptable (even though an average of between 8 and 13 hours of direct case time was devoted to each case). Despite the inability to verify a substantial proportion of all reported job contacts in these states, it still was possible to document that an estimated one-fifth of those who certified that they had made one or more job contacts definitely had made none.

Monitoring Conclusions

Effective monitoring of any substantive worksearch requirement for all claimants simply is not feasible within the UC system as it currently operates. Furthermore, because the worksearch requirement actually can be more objectively defined and more easily monitored than the general availability-for-work criteria (or certain other aspects of the weekly eligibility criteria), it appears that the monitoring problems for these other criteria almost certainly are more serious than those specifically documented above for worksearch/ availability requirements. Despite any monitoring problems, however, it must be recognized that worksearch requirements also may serve a screening function in preventing payments to at least some ineligible claimants who actually are *not* available for or seeking work. However, so little evidence presently is available on this screening effect—and other effects of the worksearch requirement on job search and reemployment experiences—that additional evidence on this point would be very useful in evaluating the overall impact of the worksearch requirement.

Monitoring Responses

The monitoring problems summarized above suggest that policymakers and program administrators should consider the possibility of adopting new approaches to both the content and the administration of the weekly UC eligibility criteria. With respect to the worksearch requirement, a number of approaches might be considered, including: (1) elimination of the requirement, with or without compensating changes in other criteria; (2) imposition of stricter requirements; and (3) improved administration of existing (or altered) requirements. Some expected effects of adopting any of these approaches are briefly summarized below.

Elimination of worksearch requirements in states that currently have them clearly would reduce overpayment rates in those states, even without any other changes. However, elimination of the worksearch requirement (without any other changes) also would be expected to: (1) increase the overall volume of UC claims filed for any given level of aggregate demand; (2) reduce the ability of UC program personnel to effectively administer other aspects of the weekly eligibility criteria, particularly the general availability-for-work provisions; (3) increase the proportion of claims filed that would be paid; and (4) increase the overall volume of UC benefits paid and, consequently, increase employer tax rates. The research and demonstration projects required to evaluate the extent of such effects should be undertaken as a basis for determining whether existing worksearch requirements should be retained or eliminated.

Replacement of the worksearch requirement with more concrete criteria may appear to be a more viable option to many states than merely eliminating this requirement. Assuming that the UC system should emphasize the *insurance* of lost wages, a strong contender as a replacement for the worksearch requirement would be stricter monetary eligibility criteria that would include weeks-of-work requirements. Emphasizing such (objective) measures of past work attachment—rather than measures of current (and subjective) intentions to seek or accept work— would make it possible for UC program personnel to more objectively, consistently and inexpensively monitor claimant compliance with UC eligibility criteria. Consequently, the research and demonstration projects required to evaluate the impact of stricter monetary criteria (including weeks-of-work requirements) should be encouraged. In fact, these experiments should be designed to reveal the impact of the stricter requirements, both with and without current worksearch requirements. It may be the case that the difficulties of enforcing compliance with the worksearch requirement would be substantially reduced for the group of claimants who would continue to qualify for benefits once stricter monetary (and weeks-of-work) requirements had been imposed. Such insights, combined with those obtained from the studies designed to determine the impact of existing worksearch requirements, would facilitate more informed judgments about the impact of imposing stricter monetary (and weeks-of-work) requirements, as either a replacement for or as a supplement to existing worksearch requirements.

Another approach already utilized in some states and in the federal-state Extended Benefits program is to adopt stricter or more specific worksearch requirements. Among other effects, available evidence indicates that *stricter* requirements (other things equal): (1) would tend to decrease the volumes of claims filed and benefits paid; (2) might have some impact on the job search and reemployment experiences of claimants, but it appears that any positive effects likely would be very small; and (3) might result in potentially adverse side effects on claimant search strategies and employer recruitment costs. However, *more specific* worksearch requirements—as opposed to just *stricter* requirements—might result in more effective enforcement of both worksearch requirements and other eligibility criteria.

Another possible response to the worksearch problem in the existing UC system would be to improve the administration of existing (or even altered) worksearch criteria. One possibility that merits serious consideration would be to develop computerized screening profiles to identify high-risk claimants who belong to groups with above average overpayment rates. The high-risk group would receive special administrative scrutiny before payment, whereas most (low-risk) claimants would be paid simply on the basis of their certifications that they had complied with stated eligibility criteria. Although only limited experimental evidence is available, it appears that such an approach to preventing overpayments and inducing increased claimant self-compliance might be an operationally feasible one. As either a supplement to the above screening-profile approach or as a separate approach, it also might be possible to more effectively screen claimants for compliance with the weekly eligibility criteria by introducing computerized expert systems to screen claims for potential eligibility issues prior to payment.

The above considerations suggest that some combination of the following approaches could make a substantial contribution to improving both agency monitoring efforts and claimant self-compliance with UC eligibility criteria: (1) undertaking the research required to determine the impact of existing worksearch requirements on the unemployment, reemployment and UC-related experiences of insured workers; (2) conducting the research necessary to identify the impact of imposing stricter monetary (including weeks-of-work) requirements, either as a supplement to or as a replacement for existing worksearch requirements; (3) adopting more specific and objectively identifiable measures for assessing compliance with availability-for-work and worksearch requirements; (4) exploring the impact of using screening profiles to target administrative resources on high-risk claimants who are less likely than most claimants to comply with stated worksearch/availability requirements; and (5) utilizing computerized expert systems to further screen claimants for compliance with the weekly eligibility criteria prior to the payment of benefits.

Overall Study Conclusions

The analysis provided in this study strongly suggests that the existing UC system could be substantially improved by adopting a number of the within-system reforms summarized in this chapter. Although a number of responses are suggested for the particular problems identified in the individual chapters of this study, it is important to emphasize that a systems approach should be taken in devising any overall set of reform proposals, either for federal-state relationships or for individual states. Such an approach is needed because of the interactive nature of the various components of the UC system. Because of these inter-relationships, apparently plausible responses to specific problems might well generate unintended and undesirable side effects in terms of other program aspects. Consequently, it would be difficult to even evaluate the desirability of certain changes, except in the context of whatever overall changes might be considered for federal-state relationships and in particular state systems. Moreover, because of uncertainty about the exact impacts of many suggested changes, the importance of further research and experimental pilot studies to fully evaluate many of these changes must be reemphasized. In this context and given the existing administrative funding mechanism, USDOL has an important role to play in initiating, funding and providing technical assistance for such efforts. Interstate cooperation through the Interstate Conference of Employment Security Agencies or other organizations and through smaller groups of states interested in particular issues also would greatly facilitate UC system reform. In this latter regard, the recent efforts of some states in the Quality Unemployment Insurance Project appear to be important.

Although within-system reform is emphasized in this study, it very well could be that society's long-run interests might be better served by completely replacing the existing UC system with one that would be quite different from even a reformed version of the present system. However, a serious analysis of the many issues that would be involved in designing an optimal replacement for the existing system was completely beyond the scope of this study. Accordingly, such issues were not addressed.

Whether the within-system policy responses emphasized in this study, still other within-system responses, or a major restructuring of the entire UC system ultimately is selected by policymakers, the analysis in this study strongly suggests that certain guidelines would be important in evaluating whatever proposals might be advanced. These general features of a desirable UC system—some of which obviously entail tradeoffs with others—would include at least the following: (1) appropriate economic incentives for all system participants, including strong incentives for claimant self-compliance; (2) to the extent possible, simple rather than complex system features and eligibility criteria; (3) to the extent possible, little emphasis on intensive administrative scrutiny of claimant behavior and motives in the routine operational system, with emphasis instead placed on claimant self-compliance with relatively objective and easily measurable criteria; (4) minimizing the administrative discretion that makes selective application and enforcement of eligibility criteria possible; (5) horizontal equity for system participants; and (6) incentives for both administrative efficiency and smaller administrative bureaucracies.

Bibliography

Adams, Leonard P. *Public Attitudes Toward Unemployment Insurance.* Kalamazoo, Michigan: The W.E. Upjohn Institute for Employment Research (1971).

Alchian, Armen and Harold Demsetz. "Production, Information Costs and Economic Organization." *The American Economic Review*, 62 (December, 1972).

Anderson, Joseph P., Sheryl Greenberg, Donald Merwin, Paul L. Burgess, Jerry L. Kingston and Robert D. St. Louis. "Arizona's Unemployment Insurance System: An Overview from the Claimant's Perspective," Phoenix: Arizona Department of Economic Security (1977).

Arizona Department of Economic Security. *Benefit Policy Rules.* Phoenix: Arizona Department of Economic Security (n.d.).

_____. "Precedent Decision No. PD-144." Phoenix: Arizona Department of Economic Security (1982).

Arizona Unemployment Insurance Administration. "A Comparison of FY 1986 Administrative Funding Allocations Among the States." Phoenix: Arizona Department of Employment Security (1985).

Austermann, V. Christine, Robert L. Crosslin and David W. Stevens. *Can the Unemployment Insurance Service Improve the Employment Prospects of Claimants?* Columbia, Missouri: Human Resources Research Department (1975).

Balcer, Don A. "Transmittal of Revised FY 1987 UI Grants to States." San Francisco, California: U.S. Department of Labor, Employment and Training Administration, San Francisco Regional Office (November 18, 1986).

Barron, John M. and Wesley Mellow. "Labor Contract Information, Search Requirements, and Use of a Public Employment Service." *Economic Inquiry.* 20 (July, 1982).

_____. and Wesley Mellow. "Search Effort in the Labor Market." *Journal of Human Resources* 14 (Summer, 1979).

Becker, Joseph M. *Experience Rating in Unemployment Insurance.* Baltimore, Maryland: The Johns Hopkins University Press (1972).

261

_____. *The Problem of Abuse in Unemployment Benefits.* New York: Columbia University Press (1953).

_____. *Unemployment Insurance Financing: An Evaluation.* Washington: American Enterprise Institute for Public Policy Research (1981).

Black, Matthew and Timothy J. Carr. "An Analysis of Nonsearch." *Unemployment Compensation: Studies and Research.* 2 Washington: National Commission on Unemployment Compensation (1980).

Blaustein, Saul J. *Job and Income Security for Unemployed Workers.* Kalamazoo, Michigan: The W.E. Upjohn Institute for Employment Research (1981).

_____. "Letters to Jerry L. Kingston, dated March and April, 1986." Kalamazoo, Michigan: The W.E. Upjohn Institute for Employment Research (1986).

_____. and Isabel Craig. *An International Review of Unemployment Insurance Schemes.* Kalamazoo, Michigan: The W.E. Upjohn Institute for Employment Research (1977).

Blue, Warren G. "Letter to Jerry Kingston dated June 7, 1985." Columbus, Ohio: R.E. Harrington, Inc. (1985).

Brechling, Frank. "The Unemployment Insurance Tax and Labor Turnover: Further Empirical Results." Arlington, Virginia: The Public Research Institute (1979).

Broden, Thomas F. *Law of Social Security and Unemployment Insurance.* Mundelein, Illinois: Callaghan & Company (1962).

Brown, Harry B. "Memorandum of June 25, 1984 on FY 85 State Agency Resource Planning Targets—UI." Seattle, Washington: U.S. Department of Labor, Employment and Training Administration, Seattle Regional Office (1984).

Burgess, Paul L. and Jerry L. Kingston. "Estimating Overpayments and Improper Payments," *Unemployment Compensation: Studies and Research.* 2 Washington: National Commission on Unemployment Compensation (1980).

_____. *The Five Cities Service-to-Claimants Project: Intercity Comparisons.* Washington: U.S. Department of Labor, Manpower Administration, Unemployment Insurance Service (1973).

_____. "The Impact of Unemployment Insurance Benefits on Reemployment Success." *Industrial and Labor Relations Review.* 30 (October, 1976).

_____. *The Phoenix Service-to-Claimants Project: An Analysis of Short- and Long-Run Project Effectiveness.* Washington: U.S. Department of Labor, Manpower Administration, Unemployment Insurance Service (1972).

_____. "UI Benefit Effects on Compensated Unemployment." *Industrial Relations.* 20 (Fall, 1981).

_____. and Robert D. St. Louis. "A New System for Identifying Payment Errors in the Unemployment Insurance Program." *Monthly Labor Review.* 107 (December, 1984).

_____. *The Development of an Operational System for Detecting Unemployment Insurance Payment Errors Through Random Audits: The Results of Five Statewide Pilot Tests.* Washington: U.S. Department of Labor, Employment and Training Administration, Unemployment Insurance Service (1982).

_____. "Overpayments in the Unemployment Insurance Program in the United States." *International Social Security Review.* (1981).

_____. and Paul DePippo. *Predicting Worksearch Overpayments in Unemployment Insurance Programs.* Washington: U.S. Department of Labor, Employment and Training Administration, Unemployment Insurance Service (1983).

Burnett, Thurman D. and James Pendleton. "Letter to Paul Burgess dated June 17, 1985." Tallahassee: Florida Division of Unemployment Compensation (1985).

Burtless, Gary and Daniel H. Saks. *The Decline in Insured Unemployment During the 1980s.* Washington: The Brookings Institution (1984).

Cogan, John. "Unemployment Insurance-Employment Service Reform Proposal." Washington: Office of Management and Budget (1985).

Commerce Clearing House. "Unemployment Insurance Reports, Number 1253, Dated 3-26-85." Chicago, Illinois: Commerce Clearing House (1985).

Congress of the United States, Congressional Budget Office. *Unemployment Insurance: Financial Conditions and Options for Change.* Washington: U.S. Government Printing Office (1983).

Corson, Walter, Alan Hershey and Stuart Kerachsky. *Nonmonetary Eligibility in State Unemployment Insurance Programs: Law and Practice.* Kalamazoo, Michigan: The W.E. Upjohn Institute for Employment Research (1986).

_____. David Long and Walter Nicholson. *Evaluation of the Charleston Claimant Placement and Work Demonstration Project.* Princeton, New Jersey: Mathematica Policy Research, Inc. (1984).

_____. and Walter Nicholson. *Final Report: An Analysis of the 1981-1982 Changes in the Extended Benefit Program.* Princeton, New Jersey: Mathematica Policy Research, Inc. (1984).

Curtin, Richard T. and Michael Ponza. "Attitudes Toward and Experience with Unemployment Compensation Among American Households." *Unemployment Compensation: Studies and Research.* 3 Washington: National Commission on Unemployment Compensation (1980).

Dong, Fred B., Arden R. Hall, Terry R. Johnson, and Randall J. Pozdena. "The Impact on Earnings of the Employment Service." *Industrial Relations*. 19 (Winter, 1980).

Dunn, Gerald E. "Memorandum of May 15, 1985 to UI Committee of Interstate Conference of Employment Security Agencies on Allocation Nationally of BPC Monies." Albany: New York State Department of Labor (1985).

_____. and Kathleen Griffin. "Financing the Administration of the UI Program." In Michael R. Stone (ed.), *Perspective*. 1 Frankfort, Kentucky: International Association of Personnel in Employment Security (1985).

_____. "Financing the Administration of the Unemployment Insurance Program." Albany: New York State Department of Labor (1984).

Ehrenberg, Ronald and Ronald Oaxaca. "Unemployment Insurance, Duration of Unemployment and Subsequent Wage Gain." *American Economic Review*. 66 (December, 1976).

Evans, John, Victor Atyieh and Charles Robb. "Reforming the Employment Security System: A Comprehensive Proposal." Washington: Chambers Associates, Inc. (n.d.).

Federal Register. "Notices in Vol. 50, No. 151, dated August 6, 1985." Washington: Government Printing Office (1985).

Felder, Henry. *A Statistical Evaluation of the Impact of Disqualification Provisions of State Unemployment Insurance Laws*. Arlington, Virginia: SRI International (1979).

Feldstein, Martin. *Lowering the Rate of Unemployment*. Joint Economic Committee, Congress of the United States. Washington: U.S. Government Printing Office (1973).

Feldstein, Martin. "Unemployment Compensation: Adverse Incentives and Distributional Anomalies." *National Tax Journal*. 27 (June, 1974).

Ford, Ford B. "Remarks of February 4, 1985, U.S. Department of Labor Press Conference on the Fiscal Year 1986 Budget." Washington: U.S. Department of Labor, Employment and Training Administration, Unemployment Insurance Service (1985).

General Accounting Office. "A Comprehensive Approach Needed for Further Productivity Improvements in the Unemployment Insurance Program." Washington: The U.S. General Accounting Office (1984).

Golding, Carolyn M. "Letter to Jerry Kingston dated July 22, 1985." Washington: U.S. Department of Labor, Employment and Training Administration, Unemployment Insurance Service (1985).

Green, Polly, Joseph P. Anderson, Robert D. St. Louis, Paul L. Burgess and Jerry L. Kingston. *A Special Study of the Application of Arizona's*

Nonmonetary Criteria for Benefit Eligibility. Phoenix: Arizona Department of Economic Security (June, 1978).

Haber, William and Merrill G. Murray. *Unemployment Insurance in the American Economy.* Homewood, Illinois: Richard D. Irwin, Inc. (1966).

Hamermesh, Daniel S. "Entitlement Effects, Unemployment Insurance and Employment Decisions." *Economic Inquiry.* 17 (July, 1979).

_____. *Jobless Pay and the Economy.* Baltimore, Maryland: Johns Hopkins University Press (1977).

_____. "Unemployment Insurance and Labor Supply." *International Economic Review.* 21 (1980).

Hanna, James S. "Letter to Jerry Kingston dated June 6, 1985." Carson City, Nevada (1985).

Heartwell, William L., Jr. "Memorandum of May 24, 1985 Outlining Views of the UI Committee of the Interstate Conference of Employment Security Agencies on the Quality Control program." Washington: Interstate Conference of Employment Security Agencies, Inc. (1985).

Hills, Steven M. "Estimating the Relationship Between Unemployment Compensation and the Duration of Unemployment—the Problem of Eligible Nonfilers." *Journal of Human Resources* 17 (1982).

Holen, Arleen and Stanley A. Horwitz. "The Effect of Unemployment Insurance and Eligibility Enforcement on Unemployment." 12 *Journal of Law and Economics* (1976).

House Committee on Appropriations, Surveys and Investigations Staff. "March, 1985 Report on Nonpersonal Services Funding for Unemployment Insurance Activities of State Employment Security Agencies." Washington: The Committee on Appropriations, U.S. House of Representatives (1985).

International Association of Personnel in Employment Security Legislative Committee. "Information Memo dated August 2, 1985." Frankfort, Kentucky: International Association of Personnel in Employment Security (1985).

Interstate Conference of Employment Security Agencies and Macro Systems, Inc. "Description and Critique of Unemployment Insurance and Job Service Grants-to-States Funding." Washington: National Commission on Unemployment Compensation (1979).

_____. "Employment Security Administrative Financing: ICESA Recommendations Based on an Analysis of Recommendations by Macro Systems, Inc., With Comments by the Employment and Training Administration of the Department of Labor." In National Commission on Unemployment Compensation, *Unemployment Compensation: Studies and Research.* 2

Washington: National Commission on Unemployment Compensation
(1980).

Johnson, Robert E. "Memorandum on Quality Improvement Project, dated
November 6, 1985." Seattle, Washington: U.S. Department of Labor,
Employment and Training Administration (1985).

Johnson, Terry R., Jennifer M. Pfiester, Richard W. West and Katherine P.
Dickinson. *Design and Implementation of the Claimant Placement and
Work Test Demonstration*. Menlo Park, California: SRI International
(1984).

Jones, Robert T. "State Employment Security Agency Administrative Financing System, DOL Planned Changes." *Federal Register* 51 (May 16,
1986).

Kansas Department of Human Resources. *Kansas Non-Filers 1978*. Topeka:
Kansas Department of Human Resources, Research and Analysis Section
(1982).

Katz, Arnold. "The Impact on Earnings of the Employment Service."
Industrial Relations. 19 (Winter, 1980).

Keeley, Michael C. and Philip K. Robins. "Government Programs, Job
Search Requirements, and the Duration of Unemployment." *Journal of
Labor Economics*. 3 (July, 1985).

Kingston, Jerry L. and Paul L. Burgess. "How Do UI Benefits Affect the
Benefit Utilization Rate?" *Industrial Relations*. 16 (February, 1977).

_____. "Monitoring Claimant Compliance with Unemployment Compen-
sation Eligibility Criteria." Paper prepared for conference entitled, "Unemployment Insurance: The Second Half-Century," sponsored by the
University of Wisconsin-Madison in February, 1986. Tempe: Arizona State
University Department of Economics Working Paper (1986).

_____. "UI Random Audit Bulletin #12." Washington: U.S. Department of
Labor, Employment and Training Administration, Unemployment Insurance Service (1981a).

_____. *Unemployment Insurance Overpayments and Improper Payments in
Six Major Metropolitan Areas*. Washington: National Commission on
Unemployment Compensation (1981b).

_____. and Robert D. St. Louis. "Overpayments in the Unemployment
Insurance System in the United States," *International Social Security
Review*. 34 (1981).

_____. "Unemployment Insurance Overpayments: Evidence and Implica-
tions." *Industrial and Labor Relations Review* 39 (April 1986).

_____. "The Unemployment Insurance Random Audit Program: Some
Results and Implications." Washington: U.S. Department of Labor,

Employment and Training Administration, Unemployment Insurance Service (1983).

McLure, Charles E., Jr. "The Incidence of the Financing of Unemployment Insurance." *Industrial and Labor Relations Review.* 30 (July, 1977).

Michigan, State of. "Michigan Employment Security Act/February 1984." Ann Arbor: Michigan Department of Economic Security (1984).

Missouri Division of Employment Security: "Work Search Survey." Jefferson City: Missouri Department of Labor and Industrial Relations (1986).

Munts, Raymond C. "Previous Work Requirements and the Duration of Benefits." *Unemployment Compensation: Studies and Research.* 1 Washington: National Commission on Unemployment Compensation (1980).

Murrie, David E. "Memorandum to Paul Burgess on Quality Checklist and UI Worksearch Requirements, dated June 18, 1986." Oklahoma City: Oklahoma Employment Security Commission (1986).

Nagy, Thomas J., John DiSciullo Jr. and Robert Crosslin. "Reducing Costs and Improving Services in Unemployment Insurance Nonmonetary Determinations Using Expert Systems." *UI Research Exchange: UI Occasional Paper 83-4.* Washington: U.S. Department of Labor, Employment and Training Administration, Unemployment Insurance Service (1983).

National Commission on Unemployment Compensation. *Unemployment Compensation: Final Report.* Washington: National Commission on Unemployment Compensation (1980).

National Foundation for Unemployment Compensation & Workers' Compensation. "Administration Proposes Reform of U.C. Administrative Financing, dated May 13, 1985." Washington: National Foundation for Unemployment Compensation & Workers' Compensation (1985a).

_____. "Bulletin No. 143-U.C." Washington: National Foundation for Unemployment Compensation & Workers' Compensation (1985b).

_____. *Highlights of State Unemployment Compensation Laws.* Washington: National Foundation for Unemployment Compensation & Workers' Compensation (1985c).

_____. *Highlights of State Unemployment Compensation Laws.* Washington: National Foundation for Unemployment Compensation & Workers' Compensation (1986a).

_____. *Highlights of State Unemployment Compensation Laws.* Washington: National Foundation for Unemployment Compensation & Workers' Compensation (1987).

_____. "The Unemployed Outside the UC System." Washington: National Foundation for Unemployment Compensation and Workers' Compensation (1986b).

National Governors' Association. *A Study of the Federal Unemployment Tax Administrative Fund Allocation Methodology.* Washington: National Governors' Association (1983).

Nicholson, Walter. "Issues in Unemployment Insurance Research." *UI Research Exchange.* Washington: U.S. Department of Labor, Employment and Training Administration, Unemployment Insurance Service (1981).

Niskanen, W. A. *Bureaucracy and Representative Government.* Chicago: Aldine Press (1971).

O'Keefe, Patrick J. "Testimony Before the Subcommittee on Public Assistance and Unemployment Compensation, Committee on Ways and Means, U.S. House of Representatives, dated February 20, 1985." Washington: U.S. Department of Labor, Employment and Training Administration (1985).

Owen, Robert I. and Edward A. Wood. "Timeliness in Deciding Second-Level Appeals." *Unemployment Compensation: Studies and Research.* 3 Washington: National Commission on Unemployment Compensation (1980).

Packard, David R. "Unemployment Without Fault: Disqualification for Unemployment Insurance Benefits." *Villanova Law Review.* 17 (March, 1972).

Peterson, Gerald W. "Memorandum for Albert Angrisani, Assistant Secretary of Labor Dated May 16, 1983." (Letter of transmittal for Final Report on Audit of "Unemployment Benefit Payment Controls: Improvements Needed.") Washington: U.S. Department of Labor (1983).

Pleatsikas, Christopher, Lawrence Neil Bailis and Judith Dernburg, *A Study of Measures of Substantial Attachment to the Labor Force.* I Washington: U.S. Department of Labor, Employment and Training Administration, Unemployment Insurance Service (1978).

Porter, Richard and Amanda Bayer. "A Monetary Perspective on Underground Activity in the United States." *Federal Reserve Bulletin.* 70 (March, 1984).

Porterfield, Richard L., Robert D. St. Louis, Paul L. Burgess and Jerry L. Kingston. "Selecting Claimants for Audits of Unreported Earnings." *Unemployment Compensation: Studies and Research.* 2 Washington: National Commission on Unemployment Compensation (1980).

Quality Control Subcommittee, Interstate Conference of Employment Security Agencies. "Quality Control: A Briefing Paper." Washington: Interstate Conference of Employment Security Agencies (1985).

Reid, Graham L. "Job Search and the Effectiveness of Job Finding Methods." *Industrial and Labor Relations Review.* 25 (July, 1972).

Richey, Frank. "Letter to William E. Sager, Assistant Administrator for Programs Dated April 30, 1985." Salem: Oregon Employment Division (1985).

Roche, George S. *Entitlement to Unemployment Insurance Benefits.* Kalamazoo, Michigan: The W.E. Upjohn Institute for Employment Research (1973).

Rubin, Murray. "The Appeals System." *Unemployment Compensation: Studies and Research.* 3 Washington: National Commission on Unemployment Compensation (1980).

_____. *Federal-State Relations in Unemployment Insurance.* Kalamazoo: The W.E. Upjohn Institute for Employment Research (1983).

Scheaffer, Richard L., William Mendenhall and Lyman Ott. *Elementary Survey Sampling.* 2nd ed., North Scituate, Massachusetts: Duxbury Press (1979).

Semerad, Roger D. "Draft Memorandum on State Employment Security Agency Administrative Financing System: DOL Planned Changes, dated May, 1986." Washington: U.S. Department of Labor, Employment and Training Administration (1986).

Shulenburger, David E., Charles E. Krider and Joseph A. Pichler. "The Impact on Earnings of the Employment Service." *Industrial Relations.* 18 (Winter, 1979).

Spiegelman, Robert and Stephen Woodbury. "Summary of Preliminary Findings from the Illinois Unemployment Insurance Experiments." Paper prepared for conference entitled "Unemployment Insurance: The Second Half-Century," sponsored by the University of Wisconsin-Madison (February, 1986).

St. Louis, Robert D., Paul L. Burgess and Jerry L. Kingston. "Reported vs. Actual Job Search by Unemployment Insurance Claimants." *The Journal of Human Resources.* 21 (Winter, 1986).

Stevens, David W. *Assisted Job Search for the Insured Unemployed.* Kalamazoo, Michigan: The W.E. Upjohn Institute for Employment Research (1974).

_____. *Unemployment Insurance Beneficiary Job Search Behavior: What is Known and What Should be Known for Administrative Planning Purposes.* Washington: U.S. Department of Labor, Employment and Training Administration, Unemployment Insurance Service, (1977).

_____. "The 'Work Test:' Goals and Administrative Practices." *Unemployment Compensation: Studies and Research.* 1 Washington: National Commission on Unemployment Compensation (1980).

Study Committee on Unemployment Compensation and Employment Service. *Unemployment Compensation and Employment Service.* Washington: Report Submitted to the U.S. Commission on Intergovernmental Affairs dated June, 1955, Government Printing Office (1955).

Tanzi, Vito. "The Underground Economy in the United States: 1930-1980." *International Monetary Fund Staff Papers.* 30 (June, 1983).

Templeman, Cheryl. "Letter to Robert Knisely dated September 27, 1984." Washington: Interstate Conference of Employment Security Agencies, Inc. (1984).

Thorne, Raymond P. "Letter to Jerry Kingston dated June 10, 1985." Salem: Oregon Employment Division (1985a).

_____. "Letter to Paul Burgess dated March 8, 1985." Salem: Oregon Employment Division (1985b).

Topel, Robert H. "Experience Rating of Unemployment Insurance and the Incidence of Unemployment." *Journal of Law and Economics.* 27 (April, 1984).

_____. "Financing Unemployment Insurance." Paper prepared for conference entitled, "Unemployment Insurance: The Second Half-Century," sponsored by the University of Wisconsin-Madison (February, 1986).

_____. "On Layoffs and Unemployment Insurance," *American Economic Review.* 73 (September, 1983).

_____. and Finis Welch. "Unemployment Insurance: Survey and Extensions." *Economica.* 47 (August, 1980).

UBA, Inc. "Socialized Costs & Fund Solvency," Bulletin No. 124 U.C. Washington: UBA, Inc. (February, 1981).

U.S. Department of Labor. *A Briefing for the National Commission on Unemployment Compensation on Benefit Payment Control.* Washington: U.S. Department of Labor, Employment and Training Administration, Unemployment Insurance Service (1979).

_____. *Comparison of State Unemployment Insurance Laws.* Washington: U.S. Department of Labor, Employment and Training Administration, Unemployment Insurance Service (1985a).

_____. *ET Handbook 336, 2nd ed. FY 1985 State Agency UI Program and Budget Planning (PBP) Guidelines.* Washington: U.S. Department of Labor, Employment and Training Administration, Unemployment Insurance Service (1984a).

_____. *ET Handbook No. 336, 2nd Edition, Change 1. State Agency UI Program and Budget Planning (PBP) Guidelines.* Washington: U.S. Department of Labor, Employment and Training Administration, Unemployment Insurance Service (1985b).

_____. *ET Handbook No. 365. Unemployment Insurance Quality Appraisal.*

Washington: U.S. Department of Labor, Employment and Training Administration, Unemployment Insurance Service (n.d.).

_____. "ETA 207 Tables 57A and 57B." Washington: U.S. Department of Labor, Employment and Training Administration, Unemployment Insurance Service (1984b).

_____. "ETA 5159 Table 1A." Washington: U.S. Department of Labor, Employment and Training Administration, Unemployment Insurance Service (1984c).

_____. "First Payment Analysis—December 1982." Washington: U.S. Department of Labor, Employment and Training Administration, Unemployment Insurance Service (1983).

_____. *General Administration Letter 21-81.* Washington: U.S. Department of Labor, Employment and Training Administration, Unemployment Insurance Service (1981a).

_____. *Handbook for Interstate Claims Taking.* Washington: U.S. Department of Labor, Employment and Training Administration, Unemployment Insurance Service (n.d.).

_____. "Initial Claims and Weeks Claimed Under 'Regular' Unemployment Insurance Programs." Washington: U.S. Department of Labor, Employment and Training Administration, Unemployment Insurance Service (1984d).

_____. "The New Jersey Unemployment Insurance Reemployment Demonstration Project." Washington: U.S. Department of Labor, Employment and Training Administration, Unemployment Insurance Service (1986a).

_____. "Office of the Assistant Secretary for Administration and Management, Request for Proposal: RFP L/A 85-12." Washington: U.S. Department of Labor (1985c).

_____. "Office of Inspector General, Financing the Unemployment Insurance Program Has Shifted From a System Based on Individual Employer's Responsibility Towards a Socialized System (dated 3-22-85)." Washington: U.S. Department of Labor (1985d).

_____. "Request for Proposal OAA-85-14," Washington: U.S. Department of Labor, Office of Acquisition and Assistance, Employment and Training Administration (1985e).

_____. "Request for Proposal DDA-87-31," Washington: U.S. Department of Labor, Office of Acquisition and Assistance, Employment and Training Administration (1987).

_____. "Selected Administrative Data on Benefit Payment Control." Washington: U.S. Department of Labor, Employment and Training Administration, Unemployment Insurance Service (1982a).

_____. "Selected Administrative Data on Benefit Payment Control (State UI)." Washington: U.S. Department of Labor, Employment and Training Administration, Unemployment Insurance Service (1985f).

_____. "Unemployment Insurance Program Letter No. 1-83 dated November 8, 1982." Washington: U.S. Department of Labor, Employment and Training Administration, Unemployment Insurance Service (1982b).

_____. "Unemployment Insurance Program Letter No. 2-85," Washington: U.S. Department of Labor, Employment and Training Administration, Unemployment Insurance Service (1984f).

_____. "Unemployment Insurance Program Letter No. 3-85." Washington: U.S. Department of Labor, Employment and Training Administration, Unemployment Insurance Service (1984g).

_____. "Unemployment Insurance Program Letter No. 14-81." Washington: U.S. Department of Labor, Employment and Training Administration, Unemployment Insurance Service (1981b).

_____. "Unemployment Insurance Program Letter No. 19-84." Washington: U.S. Department of Labor, Employment and Training Administration, Unemployment Insurance Service (1984e).

_____. "Unemployment Insurance Program Letter No. 29-86 dated April 18, 1986." Washington: U.S. Department of Labor, Employment and Training Administration, Unemployment Insurance Service (1986b).

_____. Unemployment Insurance Quality Appraisal Results for FY 1980. Washington: U.S. Department of Labor, Employment and Training Administration, Unemployment Insurance Service (1980).

_____. Unemployment Insurance Quality Appraisal Results FY 1982. Washington: U.S. Department of Labor, Employment and Training Administration, Unemployment Insurance Service (1982c).

_____. Unemployment Insurance Quality Appraisal Results FY 1984. Washington: U.S. Department of Labor, Employment and Training Administration, Unemployment Insurance Service (1984g).

Utah Department of Employment Security. "Utah Unemployment Insurance Improper Payment and Worksearch Predictability Study." Salt Lake City: Utah Department of Employment Security, UI Research Memo No. 3–1986 (May, 1986).

Vaughn, Thomas L. "Letter to Paul Burgess and Jerry Kingston dated May 31, 1985." Phoenix: Arizona Department of Economic Security (1985).

Vroman, Wayne. The Funding Crisis in State Unemployment Insurance. Kalamazoo, Michigan: The W.E. Upjohn Institute for Employment Research (1986).

_____. "Unemployment Insurance Financing: Problems and Prospects." Washington: National Governors' Association (1985).

Wander, Stephen and Robert Crosslin. "Measuring Experience Rating." *Unemployment Compensation: Studies and Research.* 2 Washington: National Commission on Unemployment Compensation (1980).

Ward, Sally A. "Letter to Jerry Kingston dated July 20, 1985." Chicago: Illinois Department of Employment Security (1985).

Washington State Employment Security, Unemployment Insurance Division. "Statewide Work Search Activity Program." Olympia: Washington State Employment Security, Unemployment Insurance Division (1985).

W.E. Upjohn Institute Unemployment Insurance Research Advisory Committee. *Strengthening Unemployment Insurance.* Kalamazoo, Michigan: The W.E. Upjohn Institute for Employment Research (1975).

Winer, B.J. *Statistical Principles in Experimental Design*, 2nd ed. revised, New York: McGraw Hill Book Company (1971).